29.95
60B

PRECISIONS

Le Corbusier

translated by Edith Schreiber Aujame

The MIT Press
Cambridge, Massachusetts
London, England

PRECISIONS
ON THE PRESENT STATE
OF ARCHITECTURE
AND CITY PLANNING

WITH

AN AMERICAN PROLOGUE
A BRAZILIAN COROLLARY

FOLLOWED BY

THE TEMPERATURE OF PARIS
AND THE ATMOSPHERE OF MOSCOW

The publisher and the translator take sole responsibility for the English translation of this work. Every effort has been made to respect the style and format of the original French edition where technically possible. The illustrations on pages 39, 43, 59, 61, 69, 151, 156, and 243 appeared in color in the original edition.

This book was set in Bodoni book and Univers by Achorn Graphic Services and printed and bound by Halliday Lithograph in the United States of America.

Library of Congress Cataloging-in-Publication Data

Le Corbusier, 1887–1965.
    [Précisions sur un état présent de l'architecture et de l'urbanisme. English]
    Precisions on the present state of architecture and city planning : with an American prologue, a Brazilian corollary followed by the temperature of Paris and the atmosphere of Moscow / Le Corbusier.
       p.   cm.
    Translation of: Précisions sur un état présent de l'architecture et de l'urbanisme.
    ISBN 0-262-12149-2 (hc)
    1. Architecture, Modern—20th century. 2. City planning—History—20th century. I. Title.
    NA680.L3613   1991
    724'.6—dc20   90-6330
                                                  CIP

CONTENTS

PREFACE
to the Second French Printing of
PRECISIONS
on the Present State of Architecture
and City Planning

For a number of years I have been giving lectures all over the world. I have learned how much climates, peoples, cultures are different, and men everywhere extravagantly different also. Stop and think about this an instant: men, like women, have a head, two eyes, a nose, a mouth, two ears, etc. They are disseminated by billions all over the world. When two men or two women are perfectly identical, it is such a surprise that they are shown in circuses!

Our problem is this: men live on the earth. Why? How? Others will answer you. My task, my search, is to try to save these men of today from misfortune, from catastrophes, to establish them in conditions of happiness, of everyday happiness, of harmony. It concerns especially reestablishing or establishing harmony between men and their environment. A live organism (man) and nature (the environment), this immense vase containing the sun, the moon, the stars, indefinable unknowns, waves, the round earth with its axis inclined on the ecliptic producing the seasons, the temperature of the body, the circulation of blood, the nervous system, the respiratory system, the digestive system, the day, the night, the solar cycle of twenty-four hours, its implacable but varied and beneficent alternation, etc.

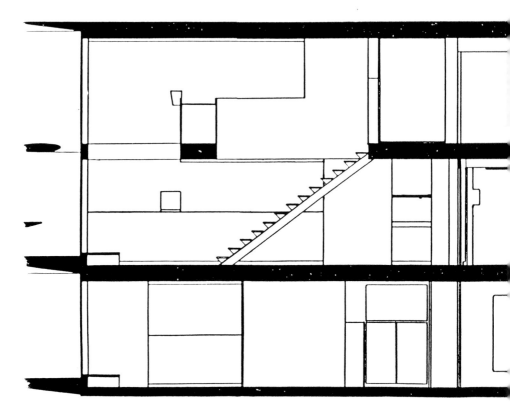

A machine age has established itself cunningly, secretly, under our noses without our realizing it. It has precipitated us into and maintains us today in a debatable existence. Symptoms of disorder appear in the health of individuals, in economic, social, religious transformations. A machine age has begun. Some do not notice it; others submit to it.

But where are the snows of yesteryear? What difference does Rome make to us in this enterprise? What are the seven orders of architecture to us? What are the titles, the diplomas, so many milestones along the way of our profession?

Gold and silver circulate in our activities, at the same time as honors, pride, and vanities.

The earth is round and its surface uninterrupted. Nuclear power upsets strategies. For twenty years planes have literally been transporting men. Briefcase in hand, they embark on a plane; in ten

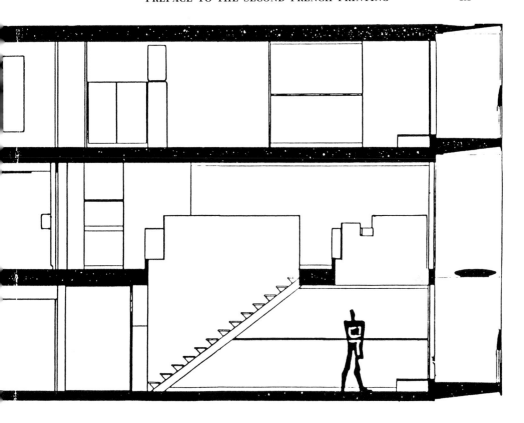

*hours, in twenty, they will be in the antipodes. As soon as they arrive
they will meet the person who is waiting for them, who is informed,
who can discuss, who is really empowered to decide. Aggressiveness
will always be here with the spirit of competition, the spirit of chal-
lenges, of victory, the choice of being between an atomic war or
rivalry on the plane of ideas, of techniques, of trade.*

*But today, we are conscious of the problem: the earth is poorly
occupied by mankind, it is even mostly unoccupied. Monsters have
appeared, they are the spread cities, the cancer of our agglomerations. Who is in charge, who is concerned, who can see clearly?
There is not yet an accepted method; there are no properly educated
specialists. Contemporary problems are so dense, so interdependent,
so overlapping one on another, so solidary that to analyze them, to
treat them separately, is impossible; the solutions are also dependent
on each other, are linked together, are indissociable. . . .*

But electricity has been domesticated, mankind has adopted it. Already there are miracles and prodigies. Electronics is born, that is to say, the possibility of letting robots study and establish files, prepare discussions, propose solutions. Electronics is used to make films, to make sound recordings, television, radio, etc. Electronics will offer us a new brain of incomparable capacity that will give persons charged with responsibilities access to facts, allow them to explain their solutions, to repeat their demonstrations tirelessly, their calls to action, their propositions, their solutions, today, tomorrow, in a month, in a year, at home or abroad. And this again in a perceptible time.[1]

The South American lectures improvised in 1929, often before different audiences, are reprinted here thirty years after their first edition. They concern man and his environment. They raise problems common to the work of engineers and architects. They have, I can say modestly, opened doors and windows. They are illustrated by sketches made right before the eyes of the public. They have allowed the author to see clearly within himself, to be naive once again, to limit himself to raising problems and to giving them the most natural answers. One sketch, for instance, shows how to sit in a house; another how to place a city in a site; another compares an ocean liner,

---

1. *The "Electronic Poem" of the Philips Pavilion at the Brussels World's Fair of 1958 fascinates one million two hundred fifty thousand spectators, five hundred at a time, entering them for ten minutes each into a torrent, a mass, a depth of sensations, showing, demonstrating, and perhaps proving something.*

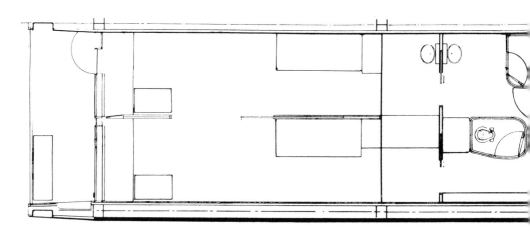

*a modern public building, and a modern business skyscraper (the
public building was our project for the headquarters of the League
of Nations in Geneva, designed in 1927; the skyscraper, later called
"Cartesian," was to become the Secretariat of the United Nations in
New York in 1947); another drawing shows the architectural consequences of acoustical science as demonstrated by Gustave Lyon.*

This reprint of Precisions *(the legal declaration is "The Lainé
and Tantet Printers, Chartres, 12-8-1930") reproduces the original
book in offset, page by page photographically; not a punctuation
mark or word has been changed.*

*The first lecture at Buenos Aires was entitled: "To Free Oneself
Entirely of Academic Thinking" (October 3, 1929). "The declaration
of academic faith is no more than a mirage; it is the peril of our
time. . . ." Today the believers in Rome announce in the press that
they are the elite of the architectural profession, and after having
evolved slowly and wisely, they have decided in favor of the most
modern ideas. They are even good enough to mention your servant,
whom they characterize as an "individualist."[2] "As to the influence
of Le Corbusier, it is, evidently, fundamental. What is perhaps special to France is that it is the influence of his city planning theories
rather than of the purely aesthetic aspect of his architecture. But it
seems that today there is a tendency to avoid the somewhat baroque
character of his works in order to return to better balanced designs.
This tendency seems reasonable to me: if it is good to follow this*

---

2. To assert that he is unfit to participate in a joint task: "Please move over."

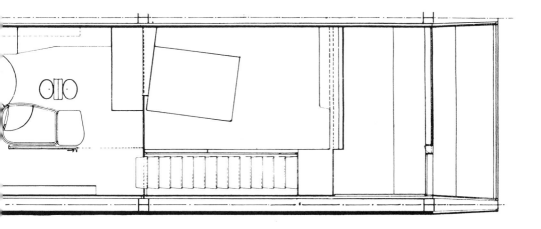

great theorist in his ideas, it is no doubt dangerous to want to imitate an architecture marked by such a strong, and if I may say so, so individualistic a personality. . . ." It is Mr. Zehrfuss who thus warns his fellow architects.

Such an "information" only cost him the effort of writing it down.

A drawing meant for "builders" ends this introduction. A new stage that from now on puts in permanent, brotherly, equalitarian contact two professions whose destiny is to equip the machine age, to lead it to an entirely new splendor. These two professions are those of the engineer and the architect. One was advancing, the other sleeping. They were rivals. The tasks of the "builders" link one to the other, from the dam, the factory, the office, the home, the public building, all the way to the cathedral, all the way. The symbol of this association appears on the bottom of the drawing: two hands with fingers crossed, two hands placed horizontally, two hands at the same level.

Paris, June 4, 1960   *LE CORBUSIER*

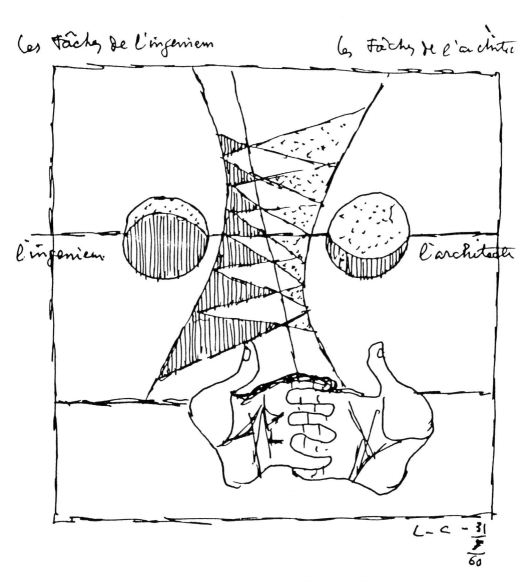

les tâches de l'ingénieur/the tasks of the engineer // les tâches de l'architecte/the tasks of the architect // l'ingénieur/the engineer // l'architecte/the architect

NOTICE

This book consists of ten lectures on architecture and planning given at Buenos Aires, and a prologue on America.

The prologue has nothing to do with American architecture, but expresses the state of mind of an architect in America.

One doesn't come this far to give lectures on architecture and planning if one doesn't feel capable of contributing some adequate realities. These ten lectures were given with the unceasing desire to offer certitudes. That is why this book is entitled *Precisions*.

It ends with a "Brazilian Corollary" (Sao Paulo and Rio de Janeiro), which is also Uruguayan (Montevideo); this corollary is a comment on the state of rising tension in these places of headlong growth: cities.

December 10, 1929
aboard the *Lutetia*
off Bahia

AMERICAN PROLOGUE

The South Atlantic Company has kindly offered me a luxury apartment and I can therefore, far from the noise of the engines and at the quietest point of the ship, undertake the writing down of the ten lectures of Buenos Aires that were improvised, spoken, and drawn; the drawings are here and I shall unroll them presently; it is they that will restore the meaning and the sequence of my lectures.

It is full midsummer, the sun is magnificent; together, the week before, they had created before my eyes the unforgettable magic of Rio de Janeiro that fired me with enthusiasm. My head is still full of America and till this morning (I embarked yesterday) there was no European infiltration into that powerful mass of American sensations and sights that, because of my itinerary and the passage of seasons (first the Argentine spring and then the tropical summer of Rio), succeeded, staged, were superimposed, as in a pyramid of which Rio was the summit, and this summit was crowned as with fireworks. Argentina is green and flat, and its destiny is violent; Sao Paulo is at 800 meters, a varied plateau whose soil is red like embers, and the city still seems to undergo with its site the spiritual autocratic weight of the coffee planters who formerly gave orders to slaves, and who today are like severe and insufficiently busy rulers. And Rio is red and pink from its soil, green with its vegetation, blue from the sea; waves break with a little foam on numerous beaches; everything rises; islands piercing the water, peaks falling into it, high hills and great mountains; its wharves are the most beautiful in the world; the sand of the ocean comes to the edge of houses and palaces; an immense light puts its motor in your heart. How powerful, beautiful, and stirring is my pyramid of American trophies!

. . . At home, in Paris, when I get there in twelve days, it will be the Place de la Madeleine and its Christmas trees, its asphalt streaming with rain, the sun rising at ten o'clock and setting at four; the shades of winter, the landscape of purgatory. And everything that makes it Paris, the soot and the dirt, and the decaying buildings. And also that strange precipitation of all the elements of the universe that makes Paris the City of Light. Admittedly so intellectually, but travel shows that in other places, light . . .

This intellectual reputation of Paris empowered me to say what I had to say "in the name of . . ." at Buenos Aires, at Montevideo, at Sao Paulo, at Rio. This voyage became a mission. At moments I was treated officially, without warning (for God knows that I withdraw like the horns of a snail as soon as it is a question of "pull," of "friends of my friends"). At Buenos Aires I am the guest of the Amigos del Arte (Friends of the Arts) and of the Faculty of Exact Sciences. Nevertheless, now and then, autos come to fetch me, journalists and flashbulbs, and, in the name of a certain committee, I make visits and listen to speeches preceded by lunches. I had a long conversation with Mr. Luis Cantilo, the city manager of Buenos Aires, at a moment of my stay when that gigantic city, one of the most inhuman imaginable, had crushed, compressed me enough that I reacted and imagined (quite humbly) something like a remedy. At that site on the Rio de la Plata, one of the essential points of the globe is being developed. In Brazil I was invited by the state legislature of Sao Paulo, and the generous orator who addressed his speech to me goes on at length (I am very moved by this) about the impression that was made there, in 1920, by *L'Esprit Nouveau*, our magazine on contemporary activities. The future president of Brazil, Mr. Julio Prestes, knows the chronology of all our efforts; before coming into office, he is already concerned by the important works of city planning he will have to undertake; he will try through architecture to show how he envisions the new times. In every big city of South America, enthusiastic groups are cultivating new ideas. Fermentation is general. At Buenos Aires, the South American Aviation Company had invited me to join the inaugural passenger flight to Asuncion in Paraguay in its ten-seater. The imperturbably smiling captain Almonacid (how Arabic that sounds), descendant on one hand of the northern Indians and on the other of the Guiraldès, a *campo* family from which the poet Ricardo Guiraldès and his major work *Dom Segunda Sombra* have come, runs the company and sends planes every day, at 180 kilometers an hour, toward Chile over the Andes, toward Rio, Natal, Dakar, and Paris over the pampa, the rain forest, and the ocean. This American country is dimensioned for the plane. It seems to me that airline networks will become its efficient nervous system. Look at the map! Everything is gigantic, and from time to time a town, a city. We know the boastings of Ulysses in all their details. But I saw, in the home of my friend Alfredo Gonzalès Garraño in Buenos Aires, the history of the settlers of Argentina, told by those admirable draftsmen of the lithographs of the mid-nineteenth century. That odyssey on the pampa is less than a hundred years old. There are still witnesses in the depths of the grasslands. There are still in Argentine families the sons of those who lived it. There are still fabulous people, settled far away in some magnificent *estancia* (pampa dwelling), reigning over a ranch or all alone, whose greatness is measured by the daring they had, by the perseverance, by their isolation. From the Latecoere plane at 1,200 meters altitude, I saw the cities of the pioneers, rectilinear villages, or farms laid out in a regular checkerboard pattern, and even outposts. An outpost is a house surrounded by orange trees planted regularly, then some trails going to a water hole, then to a field, then to pastures. The plain all around. Where is the neighbor? Where can one shop? Where is the doctor? Where is the girl one would want to love? Where is the postman who brings the letters? Nothing, no hope, except in oneself alone. I saw the odyssey of the settlers in the lithographs of 1830–40. The paddleboat is on the Rio. No pier: special wagons went into the water to meet the landing boats. The emigrant is there with all his gear. He has definitively left everything, everything. He has sailed on the ocean, how many days? We, we took fourteen days between sky and sea, with nothing in sight; they, probably five times more. And finally, the flat shore of the Rio and Buenos Aires on a hitherto unexplored plain. The completely hostile Indians are everywhere, at the gates of the town. They left with a few horses, some arms, and those enormous wagons evoking the Huns invading Europe. Roads? But since they themselves were the first settlers! The sky of Argentina? Yes, the only great consolation. For I have seen it, this sky, on the endless plain of grasslands punctuated occasionally by a few weeping willows; it is unlimited, as sparkling by day as by night with a transparent blue light or with myriads of stars; it spreads to all four horizons; to tell the truth, all this landscape is one single and same straight line: the horizon. Leafing through the albums of Gonzalès Garraño, I said to my friend, "I'd like to write a book with you who know this story in all its details, whose father and grandfathers took part in the adventure, illustrated with your detailed documents: *The magnificent history of the Argentine settlers.*"

From the plane I saw sights that one may call cosmic. What an invitation to meditation, what a reminder of the fundamental truths of our earth! From Buenos Aires we flew over the delta of the Parana, one of the major rivers of the world; this delta swarms with canals, it is cultivated intensely; they raise fruit here, and to protect the fruit from the violent drafts of the Rio, they plant endless rows of poplars to fence in very small fields. It takes eight years for a poplar to grow, the silt there is so prodigiously rich; it is then worth eight pesos, which it seems is a fortune. From the plane, this delta reminds me on a bigger scale of French or Italian Renaissance engravings in books on the art of gardens. Then we flew over the Uruguay; we were over it for hours. Then, finally, the Paraguay River, which is at its end here, at the confluence with the Parana that continues indefinitely to the north, into the tropical rain forest of Brazil until very near the Amazon. The course of these rivers, in these endless flat plains, demonstrates peacefully the inevitable consequences of the laws of physics; it is the law of the steepest gradient, and then, if everything becomes really flat, the affecting theorem of the meander. I say theorem, because the meander resulting from erosion is a phenomenon of cyclical development absolutely similar to creative thinking, to human invention. Following the outlines of a meander from above, I understood the difficulties met in human affairs, the dead ends in which they get stuck and the apparently miraculous solutions that suddenly resolve apparently inextricable situations. For my personal use, I have baptized this phenomenon *the law of the meander*, and in the course of my lectures, at Sao Paulo and at Rio, I used this miraculous symbol to introduce my propositions for reforms in city planning or architecture, to base them on nature in a situation where I felt the public might accuse me of charlatanism.

From a plane, one understands still many other things:

The earth is like a poached egg, it is a liquid spherical mass contained in a wrinkled skin. The Cordillera of the Andes or the Himalayas are nothing but wrinkles; some of the folds of the wrinkles are broken, that is the reason for those daring outlines of rock that give us an idea of the sublime. Like the poached egg, the earth is saturated with water on its surface; this is constantly in the process of evaporating and condensing. From a plane you can see on the plains of Uruguay the clouds that will sadden a home, or assure abundant crops, or rot grapevines; or that encounter of clouds which results in lightning and thunder, feared as if gods. At this extreme hour, just before sunrise, the cold is at its worst; it is the longest moment since sunset; the sleeper pulls his woolen blanket closer, and the tramp sleeping outdoors curls up like a fetus. The water vapor in suspension in the atmosphere is precipitated and suddenly the whole earth is covered with water: dew. And at this moment, like a cannonball, the sun bursts up at the very edge of the horizon. See how it is advancing fast; it is dizzying; one has the impression that it took a leap to come up! But no, that impressive speed, which one can measure on the line of the horizon, is its usual one, but seeing the vault of the sky, one thinks: "The distance is enough for the whole day." To observe that extreme speed of the sun is to realize the speed, the transience of our lives and the irreparable loss of time. How severe that is: the irreparable loss of time! The sky was clear, orange at the eastern end, full of a blue light everywhere, without a stain, and our plane in full joy. Now it is ten o'clock: blue everywhere, above and below, except in front of us. We are in a line of clouds, a heavy line, facing us, *all around us*. This line of clouds is not completely opaque; looking down through it is a marvelous sight: the plain of Uruguay is an immense panther skin, green and yellow from its lit-up pastures spotted by an infinite number of circles of seemingly black shadows. How black and thick the shadows of clouds are on the earth and on cities. These innumerable circles are all the same size. The dew has begun a new metamorphosis and a magic has taken over, militarized it, formed it into squadrons. This putting in order is striking. Here is therefore a clear expression of a uniform repartition (dew), then a first state of grouping: equality, concentration around a center, creation of different centers, an original form of government made up of administrative units. Events don't stop there; great uncontrollable phenomena follow: the sun bursts through, gnaws, churns the atmosphere, density operates, the masses of unequally dense air glide over each other. There are even some steep dizzying slides. The peaceful administration of small clouds was subjugated by an irresistible power, there are meetings, adhesions, annexations, coalitions. Now in the afternoon, the colossal masses of mobilized clouds, an army of combat. And here are the storm, the encounter, the shock, the noise, the fire of lightning.

Events that sharpen the curiosity of a planner on a lecture tour!

Here, the poached egg inclines us to melancholy, even to despair; I believe the "poached egg" is neurasthenic. Let your poached egg rot, or, if you are short of time, remember the appearance of your mother's jams; formerly, pots of jam were covered with a paper soaked in alcohol or in milk. And a few months later, a frightful mold had grown on the paper. The rain forest, the exuberant vegetation of the meanders, are the molds on our earth. There are the palm trees! The American palm tree grows naturally in accordance with a law I do not understand, on plains, widely and regularly spaced in the midst of arid stretches of meager pastures. There are estuaries, junctions, and also, at regular intervals, reeds in great concentric closed circles, absolutely round, like atolls of coral in Polynesia. There are the plains: the shades of grass indicate the degree of humidity in the soil. All biology, all fundamental organic life is evident from above: beautiful fields or weeds: it is always the law of the steepest gradient on or under the ground. The earth is not a uniform green; it has all the veinings of rotting bodies. Elegant palm trees, flowering fields, majestic rivers or charming streams, rain forests, forms that, below and close up, give sensations of nobility, exuberance, the opulence of life—*you, trees,* all of you, seen from the sky, seem nothing but mold. And you Earth, Earth so desperately damp; you are nothing but mold! And your water, in vapor or in liquid, manipulated by such a faraway star, brings you, all at the same time, joy or melancholy, abundance or misery.

The indifferent plane also shows us for hours the great floods of the Parana and the Uruguay. This limitless earth belongs to the daring settler who enters it on foot with his eye on the level of the reeds. The settler stops; here, he says, is fertile soil. Water is not far off, etc., etc. If you had seen the anguishing rise of water in these immense plains! This one is lucky; the layer of liquid stopped a hundred meters from him. But that one? The ridge of his roof rises above a yellow flood, as do the green tops of his orderly plantation of orange trees. He must have fled the encirclement in a hurry. His cattle are drowned. From the plane, I saw a roof in the middle of an immense lake. No other farms at enormous distances. He was a daring settler. At Montevideo, capital of Uruguay, where there is no census, do they know what was probably the epic of this pioneer who had spent his life building houses, raising cattle, planting trees? City novelists, with your adulteries and academic virgins, there are subjects for epics when one sees the world from above.

At 500 to 1,000 meters altitude, and at 180 to 200 kilometers an hour, the view from a plane is not rushed but slow, unbroken, the most precise one can wish: one can recognize the red or black spots on a cowskin. Everything takes on the precision of a tracing; the spectacle is not rushed but very slow, unbroken; along with the plane, it is only the steamer on sea or the feet of the pedestrian on a road that can give what may be called sight at human scale: one sees, the eye transmits calmly. Whereas what I call inhuman and hellish are the sights offered from trains and automobiles, even bicycles. I exist in life only if I can *see.*

Thus leaving all vehicles behind and depending only on my legs, I left for Asuncion to see the homes of the Indians. In this country the Indian ancestry seems to be predominant. Asuncion!

It is there that I came suddenly on the red earth. At Sao Paulo also I later made exact watercolors of that earth. Looking at them now, against the blue of the ocean, they seem crazy to me.

Asuncion! One generation earlier, and the invasion of ready-made standard international clothing had not yet been achieved. A small town set in an admirable vegetation: 50 percent grass of an understandable rawness next to the 50 percent of red earth; immense trees entirely lavender, yellow, or shrimp pink. Women in white tunics with scarves on their heads, and those Indian houses in the suburbs of the town that are the most total act of devotion of a sensitive soul: the ground around them tamped earth, extraordinarily clean, and always well maintained—a red carpet, "reception at the Elysée" style, a small house in wood siding or in bamboo, the joints filled with earth mortar. And, of course, whitewash under the portico of bamboo or twisted beams supporting a vine (as wherever people want to live well); but, rising exceptionally out of the red soil, long-stemmed flowers (lilies or bright-colored daisies, to simplify their names) arranged in an order giving the greatest impression of distinction, an extraordinary idea of distinction. The women are Indians with yellow skins, high cheekbones, and they are very beautiful.

Gaiety is all over the town, thanks to the Italians who, as the result of a tradition created by the Spanish Jesuits, at every step present the silhouettes of Palladian balusters against the sky.

Oh, South American balusters! Italian macaroni! What profusion, what exaggeration! Tragic Buenos Aires tries to laugh with its Italian balusters; that only succeeds outside the central business district. There is obviously exaggeration. I was tempted to curse the baluster. But by it is affirmed the Latinness that likes to smile, and the balusters bring a cardboard richness and a Latin smile. Nevertheless, the USA exercises an enormous pressure, by its ships, its capital, and its engineers. And one sees the suburbs of Buenos Aires covered with houses in corrugated sheet metal, without a heart or a soul, and which nevertheless have one or the other, but different, new, unknown. And I saw a workman's hut entirely in sheet metal, perfectly neat, with a pink rose bush decorating the door. It was a complete poem of modern times.

I look with real greediness for houses that are "houses of people" and not of architects. The question is serious. One may say that a man's home is *love*. Allow me to explain by the following, which concerns the cinema: watch one day, not in a luxury restaurant where the arbitrary interference of waiters and wine-waiters destroys my poem, but in an ordinary small restaurant, two or three customers who are having coffee and talking. The table is still covered with glasses, with bottles, with plates, with the bottle of oil, the saltshaker, pepper mill, napkins, napkin rings, etc. Look at the inevitable order that relates these objects to each other; they have all been used, they have been grasped in the hand of one or the other of the diners; the distances that separate them are the measure of life. It is an organized mathematical composition; there isn't a false point, a hiatus, a deceit. If there were a moviemaker there not hallucinated by Hollywood, filming this still life, in a "close-up," we should have a *testimonial to pure harmony*. No joking? No, and those are unfortunate who search for false harmonies, fakes, dodges, the academic harmonies of Vignola whether of 1925 or off the last boat. I find again in what I call the *houses of men* these inevitable arrangements. I have already explained these ideas in *A House, a Palace*.[1] But important Brazilian personages are furious to learn that in Rio I had climbed the hills inhabited by the blacks: "It is a shame for us, civilized persons." I explained serenely that, first of all, I found these blacks basically *good:* good-hearted. Then, beautiful, magnificent. Then, their carelessness, the limits they had learned to impose on their needs, their capacity for dreaming, their candidness resulted in their houses being always admirably sited, the windows opening astonishingly on magnificent spaces, the smallness of their rooms largely adequate. I thought of the low-cost housing in our Europe poisoned by the princes of the Renaissance, the popes, or by Mr. Nénot, and my eternal conclusion, after so many countries visited in over twenty years, becomes more certain every day: it is the concept of life that we must change; it is the concept of happiness that must be made clear. That is the reform, the rest is only a consequence: "The blacks will kill you in those awful neighborhoods; they are extremely dangerous, they are savages; there are two or three murders every week!" I answered, "They only kill

---

1. *Une Maison—Un Palais, à la recherche d'une unité architecturale* (Collection de l'Esprit Nouveau, Crès et Cie., Paris).

the thief of love, he who wounded them profoundly in their flesh. Why do you want them to kill me, who look at them with perfect understanding? My eyes, my smile protect me, don't worry."

And I remembered that back in 1910 the people of Pera said to me of the Turks of Stamboul: "You're crazy to go there at night; they'll kill you, they're toughs." But the houses of Pera, their banks, their trades, their customs houses, their European protectorates, the ambiguous nature of their architecture showed me the real site of evil thoughts.

If I think of architecture as the "houses of man," I become Rousseauist: "Man is good." And if I think of architecture as "houses of architects" I become skeptical, pessimistic, Voltairian, and I say: "All is for the worst in the most hateful of worlds" (Candide). This is what the analysis of architecture leads to, architecture being the result of the state of mind of a period. We have come to a dead end, the social and psychological gears are disorganized. We are thirsty to be Montaigne or Rousseau undertaking a voyage to question the "naked man." The reform to be undertaken is profound; hypocrisy reigns over love, marriage, society, death; we are entirely and totally falsified, we are *false!*

We are at the saturation of Brillat-Savarin: cooking for diplomatic lunches and dinners, wearing dinner jackets or tails (in the style of the generals of the Grande Armée). We take leeks, asparagus, potatoes, beef, butter, spices, fruit; and using a science that has filled whole books, we denature everything and reduce everything to the same taste. The only result is that with the wine and the smelly cheeses, one has filled stomachs enough so they lose some intellectual control. And then they talk business: war, alliances, customs, taxes, innumerable speculations are treated. Like snakes they digest the uncountable dangerous schemes of a world that really no longer exists.

That's where architecture is at. The academic palaces of Geneva were the most inconceivable baldachins of red plush and golden ribbons imaginable. There was a purpose to that palace: to work for the welfare of the world, in the same way that there is a purpose to a meal: to nourish. Imagine! To do clear, exact work, to go fast? And diplomacy, what do you make of that? And the culinary art of architecture?

For instance, an expression that escaped me at the Sao Paulo

Automobile Club when I was shown with insistence the album of the sculptures of a famous Indian who had accomplished miracles for the Spanish priests: one could think oneself at Bern, at Basel, at Prague, at Cracow, etc. This Jesuit style (Brillat-Savarin), which mixed Hellenic clarity with the torments of the Inquisition: "What the f....... hell did the Greeks and the curés come here for; we are on the violent red earth of the Indians, and these people had a soul. From my catechism I still remember this saying of Jesus Christ: 'If someone offends one of these little ones who believes in me, it were better to attach a stone to his neck and throw him into the sea.' "

Tell me if the taste of the cooking of the big international hotels, cooking with that Brillat-Savarin sauce and the indigestion due to the goose liver paste with truffles, doesn't throw up in you when facing these jaundices of the Salon des Artists Français.

Tell me if you find Brillat-Savarin in the porches of Chartres or Vézelay? They are from before the academies, are they not? And in the Indian masks of the museum of Rio?

Tell me if it is still reasonable to adorn cities with embroidered flower beds, when contemporary man is so sensitive to spreading lawns, to a tree whose living scrollwork speaks to his heart? One evening in Rio I saw a miserable little park with beds of shaved lawn, cut up into squares with rounded corners like "Louis XVI woodwork" and efforts at 1925-style embroideries. "It was a sports ground in the middle of this charming neighborhood, but it was turned into a pompous garden." I felt strongly then what the academic mummy was.

For twenty-five years I have heard profound musics in the people under all the skies of the world. I declare: "I like Bach, Beethoven, Mozart, Satie, Debussy, Stravinsky." That is classical music, which is made in the head of a man who has tried everything, measured everything, and who has chosen and created. Architecture and music are instinctive manifestations of human dignity. Through them, mankind affirms "I exist, I am a mathematician, a geometer, and I am religious. That means that I believe in some gigantic ideal that dominates me and that I can achieve. . . ." Architecture and music are intimate sisters; matter and spirit; there is architecture in music, music in architecture. In both of them, a heart that tends to rise above itself.

To rise above oneself is a profoundly individual act. One doesn't do so with second-hand clothing—the costume of a general of the Grande Armée—but with this which is nothing but is everything: *with proportions*. Proportions are a series of interacting relationships. They need neither marble, nor gold, nor a Stradivarius, nor to be Caruso.

When Josephine Baker on November 27, 1929, in Sao Paulo, in an idiotic music hall show, sings "Baby," she brings to it such an intense and dramatic sensitivity that tears rush to my eyes.

In her steamship cabin, she picks up a little guitar—a child's toy—that someone gave her and sings all the blacks' songs: "I'm a little blackbird looking for a white bird; I want a little nest for the two of us . . ." or "You're the wings of the angel who came, you're the sails of my boat, I can't do without you; you're, etc., etc.; you're the weave of the cloth and I put all you are in the cloth, I roll it up and take it away; I can't do without you. . . ."

She lives all over the world. She moves immense crowds. So there is a real heart in crowds? Music finds its way there. Man is a magnificent animal. But he has to be raised above himself, he has to be torn away from the abominable lies that make a hell of his life, without his understanding the reasons and denouncing them.

That is what I was thinking in the rain forest of San Martino, twelve hours by express train toward the center of Brazil. "One must always be *ready to judge*, always. You are in the Brazilian tropics, in the Argentine pampa, in Asuncion of the Indians, etc. Know how to overcome the encroaching tiredness and to judge by a *standard*, by oneself, whatever is in harmony with all the contacts surrounding it and consequently *does not shock at all*. Except for the red soil and the palm trees, one is in the eternal landscape of anywhere: steppe or pampa, it is only a stretch of ground, rain forest or French woods, they are only branches. To understand! To see the blacks, the mulattos, the Indians, in the San Paulo crowds! To measure the *style* of Buenos Aires!

Let me explain: Everything corresponds to the books, to the stories of our childhood: the rain forest, the pampa. But in summer, the earth is green everywhere. The rain forest is like the others; but there are lianas, one must not forget to see them. There are jaguars: our companion shot at one eight days ago, but we

don't see any! We go to a stalking shelter built in bamboo and
branches in the heart of the forest; after fifteen minutes: nothing.
Why would the animals come here just where we are waiting with
a gun? At night we hear the parrots calling wildly; they are green
like the leaves; one doesn't see them. There are enormous snakes;
here are some photos of them; last month, a man on the plantation
was killed; we don't see any. The pond is full of crocodiles; they're
at the bottom. Here on the trail are the tracks of the deer, the
boar. Here on the trail a tatou was run over. The forest is silent,
motionless, thick, impenetrable, perhaps menacing.

But on French beaches, when we amateur fishermen go out
with our nets, do the fish come to us?

Everything is here in the American forests, but one sees
nothing.

Stand still, watch, listen for one or two days, and the forest
will speak. One never has the time!

And so goes life!

To know how to be ready to judge!

In the North American music invented by the blacks, there
is an invincible stock of "contemporary" poetry. You search for its
bases: the tom-tom of Chad shaking the folk music of the Bavarian
mountains or of Scotland, Basque songs, etc. Clergymen visiting
Uncle Tom's cabin. Thus today in the extraordinary melting pot
of the USA where everything is of the new twentieth century, and
where the timidity of big clumsy boys has till now paralyzed the
expression of a contemporary poetry, you have the simple naive
black who has made this music that pours all over the world.
Sound films invade like Attila. One cannot resist such a violent
assault and so much truth. I see in this music the basis of a style
capable of being the expression of the feelings of a new time. We
must realize that it contains the most profound human traditions:
Africa, Europe, America. I feel in it an energy capable of wearing
away the methods of the academic conservatories of Brillat-Savarin, as the architectural techniques dating from the Neolithic
through Haussmann and broken off cleanly by Eiffel or Considère
are now being worn away. A page is turned. New explorations.
Pure music. Scholastic forms, codified by music institutes, make
their little noise in the concert halls and on the radio (a shameful
abuse of confidence!). Sonora addresses the modern crowds; and

on the steamship, to the sailor and the beautiful passenger, in high-class Rio and in the favellas of the blacks, in Buenos Aires in the tragic streets without hope, the melody of "L'Angelo Peccador" cradles innumerable and different hearts.

The emotions of the machine age are different from heavy and "sophisticated" cooking. Quite different! Much closer to the heart, and tears have come back to the edge of eyelids.

To know how to judge, always; to realize; to judge by oneself; to understand relationships; to have one's own feelings; to tend to be *entirely disinterested*; to force one's material self into the background—is to conquer *reasoned conclusions* from life. Rather than submit to the constraints of a declining age, one may as well sacrifice oneself, as well rush into adventures, take risks, be sensitive to everything, and open one's heart more and more to others.

The very history of America seems to me a powerful lever of stimulation, despite its horrors, its pitiless massacres, its destructions ordered in the name of God. The study of a history demonstrated so diversely and so usefully by written documents, so honestly by its architectures, so finely by the visual arts and music, seems to me the solid basis of an intelligent education, granting that contemporary scientific realities represent its useful application. Besides, scientific truths in their constant mobility sometimes lead to thinking, to a "what use is it" and, by a really personal conclusion, to wisdom. . . .

My two close American friends, Gonzalès Garraño of Buenos Aires and Paulo Prado of Sao Paulo, happen both to be descendants of very old American families. Both are enthusiastic about their past, their sense of history, the feeling for what has been accomplished. That history? The conquistadors of the crown of Castile, the *banderios* of the state of Sao Paulo. They searched for gold, a nasty trade; but what courage, what initiative, what perseverance! If one looks at the map of America and imagines that army of three hundred men going down to the feet of the Andes, from Mexico to the Rio de la Plata; these "Sao Paulo gangs" entering the rain forest in groups of fifty up to the source of the Amazon; if one imagines that they were a handful, and that they imposed their will on the peoples they met, that they fought or went astray, one sees them like gods; isn't that so, Homer? It is a question of moral force, and that is what I retain of it. I should like someday to find the time to study that history, which is not made up of legends but is documented in European libraries.

European progress invades these countries and distills its rationalism and its cupidity. Yet how their hearts are wide open to things of the spirit! One Sunday morning at eleven Gonzalès Garraño said to me, "I want you to know the private intimate side of Buenos Aires." We went to the big Colon theater. Beethoven's Missa Solemnis was sung to a frozen audience. After the last note, the crowd exits without applause, without a gesture. The Argentines are reserved. They say they are timid. They think about a lot of things, but don't talk about them. Around the Friends of the Arts in Buenos Aires there are many people who are very concerned by things of the spirit: music, painting, architecture, in which there are activities every day. On Tucuman Street there is a little bookshop, in very good modern style, run by two little Frenchwomen, which is a real intellectual embassy. Everybody who is anybody goes there, reads, buys; there aren't any academic works, but only what is best in Paris. Paris! It is a mirage for the Argentines. The Argentine who isn't obliged to "make America" (make money) shares his life and his thoughts between his country and France. Oh, France, that offered to this new country for its centenary, this country full of well-informed knowledge of what constitutes the intellectual strength of Paris, this enormous ice cream cake sculptured in white marble under the auspices of the Institute, you insult yourself in insulting the beautiful promenade of Alvear and Palermo!

Buenos Aires has been usefully active in favor of art for only ten years. That can be seen in architecture, which has passed into entirely new hands. It is the big cattlemen, the big landowners, the big tradesmen who started the movement. Till now Madame Victoria Ocampo was alone in making a decisive gesture in architecture by building a house considered scandalous. Well, Buenos Aires is like that, with its two million inhabitants, emigrants with the worst tenderness for junk, colliding with the *willpower* of one woman. There are Picassos and Légers in her house, in a pure background such as I have rarely met.

In Brazil, Paulo Prado, coffee grower, financier, and philosopher, introduced Cendrars. Sao Paulo, on a high plateau at

800 meters altitude, a city hard to understand it appears so old-
fashioned despite its skyscrapers and even though its fashionable
neighborhoods are so recent, Sao Paulo is moving. In Brazil (as
well as in Argentina) *L'Esprit Nouveau*, our magazine of 1920,
aroused desires. These countries, Argentina—old Castile, Brazil—old Portugal, have come to the moment when they want to
create their history themselves. The history of a people is never
anything but the expression of a contemporary ideal, a spiritual
fabrication that is like a doctrine, a description of oneself, a self-
definition. History doesn't exist, it is made up. Thus one sees
arising the fiction of "race." Travelers, you laugh at Buenos Aires
or at Sao Paulo when an overconfident patriot sings you that song.
You're wrong. For one becomes an American in America even
though one is an immigrant from anywhere. The youth of Sao
Paulo have explained their thesis to me: we are "cannibals."
Cannibalism is not a gluttony; it is an esoteric rite, a communion
with the best forces. The meal was very light; we were a hundred
or five hundred eating the flesh of one captured warrior. This
warrior was brave, we assimilated his qualities; and more so, this
warrior had in turn eaten of the flesh of one's tribe. Thus, in eating
him one assimilated the very flesh of one's ancestors.

The youth of Sao Paulo, calling themselves cannibals, wanted
to express in this way their opposition to an international dissolute-
ness, by proclaiming heroic principles whose memory is still
present.

Such a burst of courage is not useless there. I often told them:
"You are timid and fearful, you are afraid. We, the Paris team,
are more daring than you, and I shall explain that to you: for you
the problems are so numerous, so immense, the frontier to be
settled so big, that your energies are immediately diluted by the
dimensions, the size, the quantities, and the distances. Whereas
we in Paris have nothing to do. There is no frontier. The country
is saturated. If you are one person for ten jobs, we are ten for one.
Thus our energies concentrate themselves on themselves, they are
not worn out, they bend, go down deep and spring up high, and
we are the daring ones of the world. Paris is without mercy; a
pitiless battlefield. It is a place of championships or of gladiators.
We face and kill each other. Paris is paved with cadavers. Paris

is a synod of cannibals, who establish the dogma of the moment. Paris selects.

Such may be the impressions of a traveler.

When you have the pleasure of crossing the ocean on a big liner, of flying over estuaries by plane, over gigantic rivers, unlimited plains, of seeing cargoes piling up in harbors, of recognizing on a wall map the uncolonized size of an immense country, when you feel the notion of frontiers, of countries waver under the pressure of progress, when you realize that habits tend to become the same, but that only a remaking of morality would break the incoherent loops of the meanders of an outworn civilization; that France, because it was artistic and Cartesian, is a guiding lighthouse everywhere (this lighthouse that seeks vainly to put out part of its own official institutions), that the USA is the great motor of the modern world, that Moscow is the glittering mirror; that the youth of Montevideo play basketball with convincing ardor, that they talk with a cigarette in their lips, hands in pockets, and that with them, respect is in the eyes, and the hat stays on the head; when one realizes that Buenos Aires is the potential New York of the coming episode where a sublime order will be the result of assimilations and where greatness will be a lever for yet unknown poetry—that the cities of the world, and in particular the cities of the countries known as "old," could become not the museums of a beauty that had been revolutionary in its time, but irresistible generators of mass enthusiasms, of collective actions, of common joy, of pride, and consequently of widespread individual happiness; and that it would be enough if a policy maker—a man—sufficiently poetic started the machine, edicted a law, a regulation, a doctrine; and then the modern world would come out of the blackening of the face and hands of hard labor, and would smile, powerful, content, full of faith—when one sees the world from up high, most high, stretched out wide—and everything gives one this possibility—one realizes then that architecture is something new, at its beginnings, that it will be immense and coherent, under a single sign on seas and continents. The wave of architecture like a wave of electricity surrounds the earth and there are antennas everywhere.

How old we still are in a new world! How squalid!

Sport—of the heart too—will save us. Let us try the adventure. The adventure: the Rio de la Plata five hundred meters below is red from its silt; it is unlimited on all four horizons. We are twelve in the cabin; the Argentine sky all around us. The plane of the wing is parallel to that of the water, the edge of the wing touches the horizon. Everything is in new materials: pearl, the aluminum of the wing, the pink water, the transparent sky; lines are straight, planes horizontal. The overall feeling is of smoothness. The flight is uniform, continuous, undisturbed.

Architecture? But it is in this that one sees and feels, in this is all the ethic of architecture: truth, purity, order, organs . . . and adventure.

*
* *

I attempted the conquest of America by implacable reasoning and by the great tenderness I devoted to things and people; I understood in these brothers separated from us by the silence of an ocean the scruples, the doubts, the hesitations, and the reasons that explain the present state of their activities, and I put my trust in the future.

Under such light, architecture will be born.

*
* *

It was at the home of the charming and so intelligent duchess of Dato, in Paris, that I had met Gonzalès Garraño. He urged me to go to Buenos Aires, to express the realities and the approaching destiny of modern architecture in that city in gigantic birth pangs. Besides, since 1925, Paulo Prado had been writing to me from Sao Paulo and Blaise Cendrars, in Paris, pushed me forward with arguments, geography maps, and photographs.

One doesn't undertake such a long voyage lightly. One will certainly not present approximate ideas of baseless hypotheses there.

Until now, in European capitals, I had tried to limit my lectures to two subjects: one, architecture, the other, city planning, and I had been able to keep a public interested for two, three, or four hours, who followed, at the tip of my charcoals and chalks, the frightening steps of logic. For a technique of lecturing had come to me. I set up my stage: a block of a dozen big sheets of paper on which I draw in black or in color; a rope stretched across the stage behind me, on which I have the sheets hung one after the other as they are filled with drawings. Thus the audience has the complete development of my ideas facing it. Finally a screen for the hundreds of projections that materialize the preceding reasonings. Each city I visit appears to me under its own light, I feel

certain needs, I set myself an appropriate line of conduct for my public; besides, during the lecture, that line may sometimes be modified. And I improvise, for the public likes to feel that one creates for it. Thus it doesn't fall asleep.

At Buenos Aires, we agreed to divide the subject into ten lectures. The initiative was taken by the Friends of the Arts, directed masterfully by Ms. Helena Sansinéa de Elizalde. The Faculty of Exact Sciences with its dean (younger than I am), Mr. Butti, took responsibility for four of the lectures, and finally the Amigos del Ciudad (Friends of the City) organized one.

The following is the list of the lectures in Argentina:[2]

Thursday, October 3, 1929		Friends of the Arts: "To free oneself entirely of academic thinking"
Saturday	5	Friends of the Arts: "Techniques are the very basis of poetry"
Tuesday	8	Faculty of Exact Sciences: "Architecture in everything, city planning in everything"
Thursday	10	Faculty of Exact Sciences: "A dwelling at human scale"
Friday	11	Friends of the Arts: "The plan of the modern house"
Monday	14	Friends of the City: "A man = a dwelling; dwellings = a city"
Tuesday	15	Faculty of Exact Sciences: "A house, a palace"
Thursday	17	Faculty of Exact Sciences: "The world city"
Friday	18	Friends of the Arts: "The Voisin Plan for Paris and the plan of Buenos Aires"
Saturday	19	Friends of the Arts: "The undertaking of furniture"

The series ended, I was asked to leave a useful trace of it. I had never before had the opportunity to express myself so fully. I was happy to be able to present precise facts, but nevertheless, at every lecture, time was at my heels; I could have given a hundred lectures!

I ended by finding a powerful consolation to the profession of itinerant improvising lecturer; here it is: I experienced moments of sharp lucidity, of crystallization of my own thoughts. You are

2. For reasons of convenience, these lectures were not given in the order of the program I had submitted to those who invited me to Buenos Aires. The distribution of the chapters in this book reestablishes the logical line of my program.

facing a numerous and hostile audience. By hostile I mean to say that it is in the position of a diner whom one wants to make eat chicken without chewing it. New ideas after new ideas are thrown at him; his means of absorption are overwhelmed. So you have to give him food he can swallow, that is, to show him clear, indisputable, even crushing systems. When you are at your daily work, you are not forced to make such instantaneous crystallizations. When you are facing an audience whom you have little by little attracted into the imaginary regions outlined by your charcoal, you must *express, enlighten, formulate*. And there it is, the tiring but fertile gymnastic of the improvising lecturer. He has discerned clear means. And he has even retained their benefits for himself!

At the end of the series, in which I had wandered over the paths of architecture, the idea of setting down the web of my ideas for an unknown reader appealed to me. The drawings had been put aside for me. It is around these drawings, reproduced here,[3] that I shall recompose my Buenos Aires song.

---

3. In order to reestablish as well as possible the relationship between the present text and the drawings, which then corresponded closely to the spoken word, these have been numbered and the numbers cited in the text.

First lecture
Thursday, October 3, 1929
Friends of the Arts

TO FREE ONESELF
ENTIRELY OF
ACADEMIC THINKING

I have walked a considerable number of streets in Buenos Aires and that represents an impressive number of kilometers, doesn't it? I have looked, seen, and understood. . . .

I am to speak to you of a *New Spirit*, you who are of the New World. Well, I wonder if I shall make an impression on you.

For Buenos Aires is a monolithic phenomenon. There is a formidable unity here: a single block, homogeneous, compact. No fault in this heavy cast iron. Yes, the interior of the house of Ms. Ocampo.

How, then, dare to say to you that Buenos Aires, southern capital of the New World, a gigantic agglomeration of insatiable energies, is a city of mistakes, of paradoxes, a city that has neither the new spirit nor an old one, but is simply a city of between 1870 and 1929, whose present form is temporary, whose structure is indefensible, excusable but unsustainable, as indefensible as are the enormous neighborhoods of European cities built hastily at the time of industrial expansion at the end of the nineteenth century,

in the most lamentable confusion of ends and means. The history
of the busy cities born under stress, Berlin, Chemnitz, Prague,
Vienna, Budapest, etc., or under the pressure of the gigantic push
of the industrial revolution: Paris.

Nevertheless there are fundamental elements here at the beginning of the estuary of the Rio de la Plata. These are the three
chief bases of city planning and architecture:

> the sea and the immense harbor,
> the magnificent vegetation of the Park of Palermo,
> the sky of Argentina. . . .

But it can be said that one does not see one or the other from
inside the city. The city is lacking in sea, in trees, in sky.

Then one discovers this other reality that counts for a big city
and that forecasts a prodigious destiny:

the *estuary of the Rio*, an enormous door through which things
enter from all over the world,

the plain that ends at the sea and on which a city trembling with the sublimity of human creation can be built without
problems,

and this *immense back country* of the pampas, of tablelands
and of mountains, with enormous rivers, land for cultivation and
for pastures, sites of ore and mineral deposits. All that is needed
for industry to be born and for agriculture to produce.

There are few countries possessing such a topography and
geography from which can arise a city destined to be a *command
post*.

*What has been produced all over the world at the beginning
of the industrial revolution is only the result of mental confusion
and of misunderstanding. I believe coldly that all this must
disappear.*

The force from which these monsters have risen, our so-called
"modern" cities, this force multiplied by its own impetus will soon
get rid of this incoherence, destroy these first worn-out tools,
and, replacing them with order, getting rid of waste, enforcing
efficency, it will produce beauty!

* *
*

The subject I am going to undertake, architecture and planning, is so vast, so changing; it has its roots in so many events; it rushes itself toward such distant perspectives, that the ten lectures I have taken on could be a hundred; I should not at all run out of material.

When for twenty-five years one has carried on research step by step, when this research seems at last to lead to a clear, simple, and complete system, it is a relief as well as a risky test to come to justify onself before X by precise demonstrations, allowing—as they will allow you—to question me, to correct me, to contradict me; in a word it is useful to submit to a general verdict this series of related facts which make up a *doctrine*. The word doctrine does not frighten me at all. I have often been called dogmatic. A doctrine means a set of concepts leading closely from one to another in accordance with the laws of logic. Even so, this doctrine needs an impulsion, logical reasons, and a motive to be persuasive. Even so, urgent events are necessary to force us to quit the old pillow of ancient habits and to go into the unknown to forge a new attitude for our thoughts, to assign fertile ends to our gestures, and to shake, brutally even, a calm so long assured by the ruling and omnipotent mechanism of academies responsible for the edition of the reassuring acts of faith of peoples.

The declaration of faith of academism is no more than a mirage; it is a lie; it is the danger of our time.

The world is in a complete state of disturbance.

A new event has occurred: *mechanization.*

A formidable century of scientific conquest, the nineteenth century, has operated the molecular transformation of the world; we are no longer related to yesterday, we are in a different social body: *an age of mechanization* is born, it succeeds the preindustrial age that goes far back into history. A page is turned.

Mechanization has overwhelmed everything.

Communications: in the past, men organized their undertakings at the scale of their legs: time had a different duration. The idea of the world was its great size, without limits. The flowers of mankind (I mean by that the cultural flowers created by the mind) were varied, multiple: customs, habits, the manner of acting and thinking, of dressing were ordered by innumerable administrative centers similar to the little clouds of this morning, centers that express the primitive form of aggregation, of administration: one rules what one sees, what one can reach, what one can control.

Interpenetration: one day Stephenson invented the locomotive. They laughed. And as businessmen—the first captains of industry, who will be the new conquistadors—take it seriously, ask for rights-of-way, Mr. Thiers, the statesman who was leading France, intervenes immediately in Parlement, begging the deputies to keep to serious things. "A railroad" (interpret the phrase literally: a road made of iron) "could never connect two cities. . . ."

Came the telegraph, the telephone, steamships, airplanes, the radio, and now television. A word said in Paris is with you in a fraction of a second! The long intercontinental transfers that were based on an annual rhythm now obey hourly schedules. Crowds of emigrants cross the seas, new states are born, made of a mixture of all races and peoples: the USA or your country. One generation is enough for this lightning alchemy. Airplanes go everywhere; their eagle eyes have searched the deserts and penetrated the rain forest. Hastening interpenetration, the railway, the telephone unceasingly run the country into the city, the city into the country. . . .

The destruction of regional cultures: what was held most sacred has fallen: tradition, the legacy of ancestors, local thinking, the honest expression of that first administrative unit; all is destroyed, annihilated. The printing press is really only generalized in the nineteenth century. Everything is seen and known with frightening speed. Newspapers date from the nineteenth century. Photography is nineteenth-century, cinema also. And sound films are recent. So you read everything that happens. At noon every day, you have known the palpitations of the whole world. Here in your movie houses, you hear the sound of the North American sea, the waves breaking against the rocks; you hear the cries of the crowd at the boxing match at the other end of the world. You hear and see on the screens of all the movie houses of Buenos Aires the voice of Mr. Hoover addressing his citizens, and you will learn English. You hear the melodious and fascinating songs of Hawaii, and you see the fishermen dive to the bottom of the sea, seize the oyster that gives them their daily bread, you even see in a flash the frightful shark passing. You see how the Chinese, the Yankees, the Germans, the French practice seduction. All landscapes are familiar to you. An extraordinary knowledge of the world has developed. The earth is small; you know how it is made: it has no more mystery, you have seen the blocks of ice of the North Pole close up.

And the locomotive has brought you the suits of London and the fashions of Paris. You are wearing bowlers!

A phenomenal blending together, more hurried every day, soon to be complete. Only events beyond the power of mechanization seem to resist: the blacks stay black and the Indians red. And even then! Everywhere black blood creeps into white, and red into black or white.

Whiners curse the disturbing machine. Intelligent active persons think: Let us record while there is still time, in photos, films, or tapes, in books, magazines, the sublime evidence of age-old cultures. It is in studying them that we shall find tomorrow's lessons; these are the yardsticks of human greatness. We must forge a new greatness for the machine age, the new face of the new soul of modern times. And in the course of this rushing interpenetration, pollution invades everything, brutalizing, devastating, annihilating. A sort of death dance grimacing at all that is pure and noble. A thirst for gold had seized these migrating populations. Who will explain some day why ugliness, horror, falseness were the delicate nurture of our fathers? South or North America, and you, all those European cities of the robber barons, and that famous culture that we have brought to the Chinese, the Hindus, the Arabs, the Japanese, all under the wiggling sign of swagger, of showing off, of appearance, of brazen pretension, of the most notable abdication of dignity. I think that going after gold debases the soul and that one has no reason to live unless animated by a high purpose. Without a high purpose, base powers dominate, produce, pollute, and they have ravaged the world. Nevertheless, I say that the nineteenth century, destructive of all civilizations, was sublime. . . .

A sudden, intense mobility in families and cities: work is not dealt out as before: the father of a family is no longer the key of a hierarchical system. The family was annihilated. The sons and daughters, father and mother, each went every morning to a different workshop or factory. They made all sorts of contacts, good or bad. They rubbed against those new social tendencies that day after day transformed the molecular state of the world. The ancestral home has lost its soul; the home remains, it is overwhelmed with disorder; each member brings to it his parcel of belief, of ideals, of fetishism. These different fetishes in the old home create a terrible noise and everywhere the family has split up.

The city? It is the sum of these local cataclysms. It is the addition of inappropriate things; it is equivocal. Sadness weighs it down. And what an admirable machine man is who, among so many ruins, in so much precariousness, obstinately seeks a new equilibrium. The city suddenly has become gigantic: trolleys, suburban trains, buses, the metro create a frenzied daily mixture. What an expense of energy, what waste, what nonsense! And because the restaurant business is as powerful as the transports, at noon this cruel misadventure is repeated; except in a few countries the working day of the industrial revolution has not yet been created. And because I called for it once in writing,[1] a senator attacked me violently: "What are you interfering with? Stick to city planning!"

A brutal, rapid break

> with age-old usages,
> with habits of thinking.
> Everything is false,
> no longer resounds,
> needs to be adjusted:
> *the moral concepts,*
> *the social concepts.*

What I affirm here is implied in what I have already said. But I pause to go into this adjustment of moral and social concepts. I have the right to, for I am concerned by individual man and by that man living in society; and that is the very foundation of architecture and planning.

The *Cahiers de l'Etoile* insist on my answering the following:

A) Is there an anxiety peculiar to our time?

B 1) Do you notice it in your circles; what form does it take?

---

1. In *Vers le Paris de l'époque machiniste* (Redressement Français, 28, rue de Madrid, Paris).

*2) How does that anxiety express itself in and facing social
life?*

3) and in sex life?

4) and in religious belief?

5) What are its consequences for creative work?

*C) Is anxiety not the suffering of humanity trying to find its
unity in freeing itself from its prisons (time, space, and individual isolation)?*

*In that case, does a period of great anxiety not indicate
the awakening of a new conscience? And if we are in such a
period, can we not already define this new conscience and its
characteristics?*

Here are architecture and planning!

I believe we are living in profound ambiguity and in a depressing hypocrisy. The present "social contract" is only refuse. Its
morality is cruel, treacherous, lying; it is immoral. The biblical
dogma that begins by defining as sin the fundamental law of nature, the act of making love, has rotted our hearts, has finished
by ending in this twentieth century in notions of honor and honesty
that are facades sometimes hiding lies and crimes. The weight of
this social contract on our most legitimate, most normal acts en-
slaves entire populations—slavery measured in the secret of
hearts, suffered in privacy in hidden pain. The charity of priests
begins its work with an ambiguity that makes a foundation for
unhappiness, an ambiguity used to define that charity's Satan. It
is easy to say, easy to do; today, it is to judge without even looking:
well-known examples to point out from the height of a pulpit!
And, in effect, punishment is dealt out to sinners! Punishment by
whom? Quite simply, the cruel and unconscious "honesty" of
those who apparently follow the code. It is judged as well as the
fate of troops launched under the artillery fire of life: those who
have received the shells are the sinners! Is it not an anguishing
sight to see the daily papers describing this "scandalous
drama"—an offense to human dignity—of a poor girl who has had
an abortion? Do you want to know why she had an abortion?
Search: architecture and planning. For architecture expresses the
way of thinking of a period and today we are suffocating under
constraint.

Faith? Go up in a plane above the great plains of *nature*, the nature that has made us and whose forces appear here. There will be a debate in your soul and you will have immense anxieties (not those of Hell but of destiny). And your act of faith, you will base it on yourself, saying "Never mind, I will."

The effect of anxiety on your creative activity? You have said "I will." I want to act freely, by myself, to look, to see, to understand, to judge, and to decide. And I shall think that it is more agreeable to give than to receive, considering at the same time that there is always someone on hand to whom one can give. I shall think that happiness, that my happiness is in the power to create that is in each of us, a power we can cultivate, from which we can extract useful judgments for our line of conduct. I could participate in life by affirming my own point of view. I would be in conflict with the "social contract"? That will be painful! But abdication is also painful. And if we are a thousand, ten thousand, a hundred thousand, we shall blow up the "social contract."

We are facing a decision, our happiness depends on our loyalty. Our loyalty is unsinkable. I repeat: the evils that our attitude will result in will be less cruel than those of submitting like slaves. To be precise: men are haunted by liberty, that is the whole of history. Let us draw facts from this word, for ourselves, for our own use.

And here I am in the heart of my subject: architecture and planning. I feel free to act. I shall be able to denounce *academism*, in the name of all that is deepest in our hearts: to act animated by the spirit of truth.

The machine age has upset everything:

> communications,
> interpenetration,
> destruction of local cultures,
> sudden mobility,
> a break with age-old customs,
> and ways of thinking.

Three important bases of city planning have come into play:

> sociological,
> economic,
> political.

We are adopting new customs,
we are aspiring to a new ethic,
we are looking for a new aesthetic,
and for all these, what form of government?

One thing remains *constant: man*, with his reason and his
passions—his spirit and his heart—and, in this business of
architecture, man *with his dimensions*.

*
 * *

Who disturbed?
Who introduced the machine age?
The engineer. His work covers the world, it has put it in
motion. You will think it is unnecessary for me to insist. All right.
But I beg of you to try to realize the importance, the breadth of
the event, by going back a few hundred years. I want you to feel
taken up by that immense wave which like a cosmic happening
seized men by force, without their being able to react, to read, to
feel, or to realize it. A cosmic event without a dike or dam. . . .
Who is the visionary, the reader of the event, the prophet who
projects himself forward before events take place?
The poet.
What is a prophet? He who, in the heart of the whirlwind,
can see events, can read them. He who perceives relationships,
who denounces relationships, who points out relationships, who
classifies them, who foresees them.
The poet is he who shows a new truth.
The appearance of the present time? The brutality of figures,
of weights, of quantities, of profits, of punches (would they be
moral?).
Is it then no more than a black hole, decadence, despair?
Everything is dying for those who cannot judge but who
submit, who are *standing with their feet on yesterday*. They are
stretched out, torn apart. For them, everything is irreparable ca-
tastrophe, the death of happy days. . . .
The appearance of the present time? The most prodigious
epic, unknown heroisms, overwhelming discoveries, sensational
encounters. Oh, poet, it is useless to concentrate on graceful min-

uets; the whole world is bursting with life, with rebirth, with positive acts! It is enough to see, to realize: "A great period *has
begun.*"[2]

Turning its back on charnel houses, a violent dawn.

*
* *

Why evoke charnel houses? Because the emanations of innumerable dead things assail our nostrils. The modern machine is still
caught in the excrements of lazy participants. They are the sensu-
alists, the profiteers, those who happened to be there and don't
want to move aside. They are at all the faucets where the energy
of the nation is flowing. In biology, it is a dreadful disease, cancer,
which kills by strangling.

It is academism that is thus clutching the vital parts of the
social body.

*
* *

What is academism?
Definition of the academician:

        one who does not judge by himself,
        who accepts results without verifying their causes,
        who believes in absolute truths,
        who does not involve his own self in every question.

As for what interests us here—architecture and planning—
academism means accepting forms, methods, concepts because
they exist, without asking why.

In the grind of daily life, the crowd thinks academically. It
obeys, that is easier. But at this precise moment in which we
are living, its obedience places it in a state of disagreement, of
disharmony, for it does not react to relationships but to codes, to
labels, sold by merchants or religious leaders, stamped "good for"
by the Institutes (and there are all sorts of Institutes).

---

2. *L'Esprit Nouveau. Revue internationale d'activité contemporaine*, no. 1 (1920).

That state of slavery does not bring it great satisfactions; on the contrary. Its existence is passed in a junkyard of illegitimate objects. Conventions, customs are words of surrender! Among the objects that surround it, in the houses it builds, in the cities it inhabits, in its social life, in the moral code it submits to, everything is inexact, inappropriate, unsuitable, worthless. And the minutes of life flow on without real joy. And it is the heavy extinguisher laid on natural aspirations. It is acting in accordance with slogans and not by oneself. It is constraint, and that constraint is at the instigation of Academies! The Academy of Fine Arts determines the standards of what is beautiful, and other literary academies, through the theater, the cinema, or books, intoxicate these credulous hearts with the most artificial plots on love.

In an unquiet life, a life of incessant anxieties, I have experimented with the violent joys of *how* and *why*.

"How," "why"?

Today I am considered a revolutionary. I shall confess to you that I have had only one teacher: the past; only one education: the study of the past.

Everything,

for a long time,

and still today: the museums, travels, folk art. Useless to go on, isn't it? You have understood me, I have been everywhere where there were pure works—those of peasants or geniuses—with my question "How? Why?"

It is in the past that I found my lessons of history, of the reasons for being of things. Every event and every object is "in relationship to. . . ."

That is why I have no position concerning schools and till now have refused the teaching jobs I have been offered.

And in the face of contemporary events, it was again simply (but with what stubbornness, what insistence, what anguishing expectation): "How? Why?"

One cannot measure enough how much this "how" and "why," presented *simply* but also courageously, propounded with even a naive, indiscreet, or insolent artlessness, bring forth a *daring response*, unusual, staggering, revolutionary. For the facts of the problem, the reasons for the "how" and the "why" are much more upsetting today than one may think.

*
* *

Engineers were the disturbers, the bringers of facts, the persons predestined for the "how" and the "why." Nevertheless they are rapidly breathless on the slippery ground of the answers!

I hoisted engineers up the flagpole. *Toward an Architecture* (my first book, 1920–21, l'Esprit Nouveau) was mainly dedicated to them. It was somewhat by anticipation. I would soon foresee "the builder," the new man of the new times.

To be an engineer is to analyze and to apply calculations; a builder makes a synthesis and creates.

Notice this: engineers, admirable in painstaking tasks, bent over their slide rules, are generally in revolt against the children they create. They believe in them only as operative mechanisms. They do not recognize thinking entities in them. They don't *know* their works, they submit to them. They will even apologize for them, wishing to correct an attitude one might criticize. Only economy, lack of money, obliges them to abandon their work at this pure stage of functional brutality and in that state of purity. If money becomes available, they immediately destroy their work. I am not talking of course of the admirable Eiffel or Freyssinet or still others whose names slip my mind.

A passing evil, a crisis of growth, a link in evolution, a transfer of powers. We must admit that the machine age is new and that we need a little "wait and see" before everything is organized.

When the concept of new times will be relevant, when contemporary harmony will be grasped, exalted by a new mentality, conquered by the decision to move *forward* and not *backward*, when we shall be turned *toward life* and not congealed in death, builders will be born, and the enormous production of modern times will be oriented unanimously toward clarity, toward joy, toward limpidity. The hour is near, believe it. It sounds simultaneously in all countries, in Argentina as in France, as in Japan.

But it is necessary, first and everywhere, that the specter of academism be laid.

One must no longer think academically.

TECHNIQUES ARE THE VERY BASIS OF POETRY THEY OPEN A NEW CYCLE IN ARCHITECTURE

Ladies and gentlemen, I begin by drawing a line that can separate, in the process of our perceptions, the domain of material things, daily events, reasonable tendencies, from that specially reserved to spiritual ones. Below the line, what exists; above, what one feels.

Continuing my drawing from the bottom, I draw one, two, three plates. I put something in each plate. In the first: *technique*, a general word lacking precision, but which I qualify rapidly by these terms that bring us back to our subject: *resistance of materials, physics, chemistry* (1).

In the second plate, I write: *sociology*, and I qualify by: *a new plan for the dwelling, the town, for a new time*. My knowledge of the question makes me perceive in the distance a disquieting rumble. I hurry to add: *social peace*.

In the third plate: *economics*. And I evoke these fatalities of the present time that have not yet made the heart of architecture beat, and are why architecture is very sick, and the country sick of architecture: *standardization, mass production, efficiency:* three connected phenomena that rule contemporary activity pitilessly, that are neither cruel nor atrocious but, on the contrary, lead to order, to perfection, to purity, to liberty.

I step over the line and enter the domain of emotions. I draw a pipe and the smoke of a pipe. And then a little bird who flies off, and, in a pretty pink cloud, I write: *poetry*. And I affirm: *poetry = individual creation*. I explain what *drama* is, what *pathos* is, and I add: *these are eternal values* that in all times will relight the flame in the hearts of men.

Our trajectory has attained its aim: starting with material elements that are commonplace, that are consequently mobile, short-lived, but are no less the springboard of its momentum, it has traversed the human dream to touch eternal values: a work of art is immortal and will move us forever.

There you are!

I shall no longer speak to you of poetry, of lyricism. I shall draw precise reasonable things. My schemes, in their indisputable truth, will allow minds to advance easily. With them we shall abandon traditional practices. More exactly, we shall become conscious of the state of today; we shall see that our architecture of today is covered by the rotting dung of yesterday or the day before yesterday. And if you will, you'll do this: while I draw, you will pinch the strings of your lute, you will give free rein to your poetry. You yourselves will create, by yourselves, the true poetic vision of today that I shall show you. I shall talk "technique" and you, you will react "poetry." And I promise you a dazzling poem: the poem of the architecture of modern times.

1

les techniques sont l'assiette même du lyrisme/techniques are the very basis of poetry //
lyrisme = création individuelle/poetry = individual creation // drame, pathétique = valeur
éternelle/drama, pathos = eternal values // économique/economics // standardisation, in-
dustrialisation, taylorisation/standardization, mass production, efficiency // tâche urgente/
urgent task // sociologique/sociology // un plan nouveau de maison, de ville, pour l époque
nouvelle/a new plan for the home, the city, for a new period // équilibre social/social peace //
techniques/technique // résistance des matériaux, chimie, physique/strength of materials,
chemistry, physics // moyens libérants/means of liberation

I shall draw the decisive symbol of all that I came to talk to you about in Buenos Aires: on the one hand, masonry construction going back to distant centuries that is collapsing in the face of the steel and concrete of the nineteenth century. This masonry construction had its high points; its last expression was under Haussmann, where it reached its limits. It is on it that the Academies have sat down to lord it over us, to dogmatize, to exploit, to tyrannize, and to paralyze the life of new societies. In the two drawings I shall make—two sections—it is all there, everything is inscribed, the play is clear, the verdict definitive, and the outcome cannot be doubted.

A word in passing. I shall never speak of anything but the homes of mankind. It is a problem of homes for mankind, is it not? I have always refused to study houses for the noble inhabitants of Parnassus.

Before concrete and iron, to build a house in masonry, wide trenches were dug in the ground to find a firm soil for the foundations. As the earth along the trenches would slide down, it was easier to remove the earth between them. Thus were created cellars, mediocre spaces, dark or poorly lit, and generally damp (2).

Then the masonry walls were raised. A first floor was laid *on the walls*, then a second, then a third; windows were opened; finally above the last floor the attic was built. To open windows in a wall carrying floors is a *contradictory operation*, it means making the wall weaker. There was therefore an opposition between the function of carrying a floor and that of lighting its surface. One was restricted, one was hampered, *one was paralyzed*.

I am going to announce an outrageous fundamental principle: *architecture consists of lighted floors*. Why? You can easily guess: you do something in a house if there is light; if it is dark you are sleeping.

With reinforced concrete *you get rid of walls completely*. Floors are carried on thin columns spaced far apart. To found them, a small well is dug out for each one down to good soil. Then the column is raised above ground. And, at this moment, one takes advantage of the situation. I don't need to take away this inevitable mass of earth in the heart of the house. My ground is intact, *unbroken*. I shall make a good investment: columns in concrete (or iron) cost almost nothing. I shall raise them three meters above

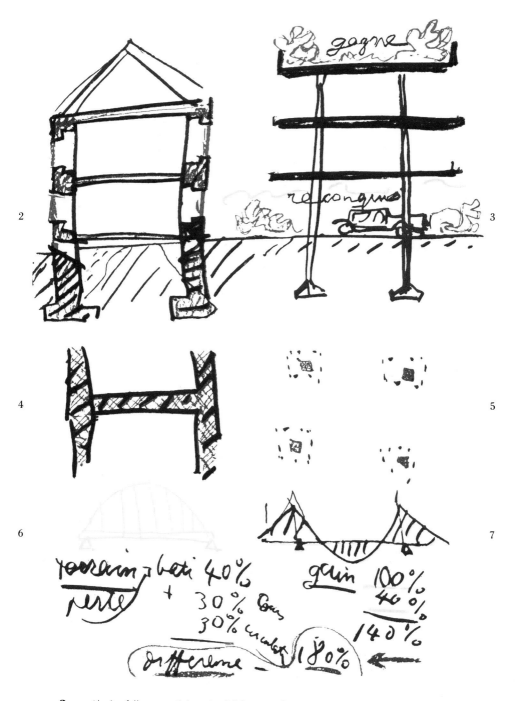

2

3

4

5

6

7

3 gagné/gained // reconquis/regained // **6** terrain bâti, perte/built-up ground, loss // gain/ gain // cours/courtyards // circulation/circulation // différence/difference

the intact ground and attach my floor up there. *Thus all the ground under my house is available* (3).

I draw an automobile on this regained ground, and I let air and vegetation go through.

I continue my floors, second, third. And the roof? I don't build one. For the study (and practice) of constructions with central heating in countries of heavy snowfall have shown me that it is better to evacuate melted snow *inside a house, where it is warm.* (I shall explain later.) My roof will therefore be flat with a slope toward the center of one centimeter per meter, which is imperceptible. But the study of roof terraces in hot countries shows us that the effects of expansion can be disastrous, and provoke cracks through which water will infiltrate. Therefore the roof terrace should be protected from the effect of strong sunshine. For this I create a garden on the roof of my house. These gardens—I have thirteen years of experience in them—in favorable conditions are real hothouses, and trees and plants grow there admirably.

Now I draw the plan, below the two sections; at ground level, the walls of stone of all the centuries before our days (4) and the columns of concrete or iron of the modern house with the ground entirely free (5).

But I draw the attention of technicians to the way in which the floor beams of the masonry house and those of the concrete floor work. Calculations show that the beams of the first (6) are subject to twice as much stress as the cantilevered (7) ones of concrete. That counts!

I have other things to point out to you: Where, in our reinforced concrete houses, are the walls carrying the floors and painfully pierced with windows? *There are no walls.* But, on the contrary, if I want to I can have windows on the entire surface of a facade—windows or other things I shall explain to you. If by chance I need an opaque surface on an elevation instead of a transparent one, it is no more than a screen, *it is the floors that will carry it,* a complete reversal of traditional practice.

"Architecture (more exactly, the whole building) consists of *lighted* floors." What a complete answer this is!

And furthermore, these columns of concrete or iron that you see on the inside of the house and that bother you, we shall see how useful they will be.

I therefore remember that *the ground is free under the house*, that *the roof is recovered*, that *the facade is completely free*, and that thus *I am no longer paralyzed*.

This much being propounded, let us do some reading:

A traditional masonry house:

ground built on, covered, lost: about 40% of urban surface
$$= \text{LOSS } 40\%$$
used for inside courtyards, about 30%
used for street circulation, about 30%

Concrete or steel frame house:

ground free for traffic and house .... = 100%
ground recovered on the roof .... = 40%
total gain .... = 140%
DIFFERENCE: 180%
acquired for free movement.

When we find ourselves facing difficult problems of circulation or hygiene in big cities, we shall remember this little text.

I begin the diagnosis of the traditional masonry house and the concrete or steel one again, in plan this time, starting from the bottom.

The masonry house: in the basement, thick foundation walls, poor light, limited use of space, high cost of construction (8).

On the ground floor: the same walls as below, at the same place; therefore the same size of rooms. Window openings limited as shown before: I place the kitchen, the dining room, the living room, the entrance, etc. there (9).

Second floor, same walls as below, in the same place (10).

Third floor, fourth floor: the same. The bedrooms go there, their shapes and dimensions will be the same as those of the dining room or living room or kitchen. Is that reasonable? Not at all.

Attic: maids' rooms. In general hot in summer, cold in winter. A poor policy for keeping maids. Besides, the question of service is in full crisis. That history is at its twilight. We shall see that later.

If I review my graphics, I see a miserable poverty in these architectural combinations. Why should a bathroom be as big as a kitchen, and the parents' bedroom as big as the living room?

What are the common factors in shape, arrangement, lighting, surface between a dining room and a bedroom? We are in the arbitrary, in the approximate, in the waste of building volume. To each question, the architect answers: "But I am forced to, my windows, my bearing walls, etc."

I write on this drawing with conviction: *waste, inefficiency, paralysis.*

Steel or concrete frame house:

Basement: nothing. Nevertheless, by digging in accordance with old formulas, we can provide a coal bunk, a heater room (admitting that individual heating may soon disappear; water, gas, electricity are distributed by industrial firms; and on the question of heating we shall be able to envisage new and agreeable solutions), eventually a wine cellar (11).

Ground floor: under the ceiling, which is three, four, or five meters above the ground, in this space that for more convenience I shall call "the pilotis" I place the entrance door, a staircase (eventually an elevator), a cloak room. And then the garage; so arranged that in front of the garage there is enough room to park the car sheltered from sun or rain, to wash it, and to go over the motor agreeably and in good light. The entrance door sheltered under the pilotis opens onto this big space, *dry*, covered, which will become the ideal playground for children.

Light, air flow under the house. What a conquest! The front and rear gardens are united; what a gain of space, and what a sensation of well-being! And the house will be seen off the ground. What pure architecture! We shall come back to this (12).

Second floor: now we have facing us only a few round or square columns, 20 to 25 centimeters in diameter; light is available *all around.* What liberty to arrange the organs of a private life, a real machine for living: bedrooms, cloakrooms, toilets, bathrooms, dressing rooms, etc. And all the desirable contiguities or separations. For we shall not build walls but partitions—in cork, in cinderblock, in straw, in wood chips, in anything you like. These partitions have no weight; they can be built on the reinforced concrete slab of the floor. They can stop halfway up. They needn't lean on the columns. They can be straight or curved at will. For every function, an exactly proportioned surface (13).

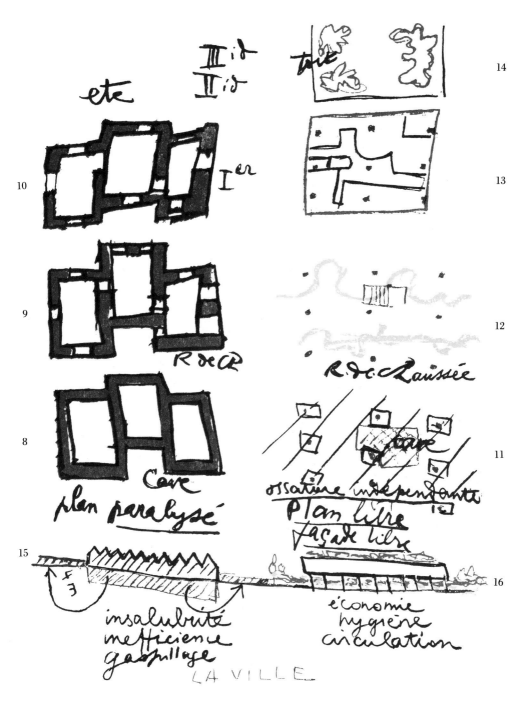

8 cave/cellar // plan paralysé/paralyzed plan // **9** R de Ch/ground floor // **10** etc // III id/fourth floor the same // II id/third floor the same // Ier/second floor // **11** cave/cellar // ossature indépendante/skeleton frame // plan libre/free plan // façade libre/free facade // **12** R de chaussée/ground floor // **14** toit/roof // **15** insalubrité, inefficience, gaspillage/ slums, inefficiency, waste // **16** économie, hygiène, circulation/economy, hygiene, circulation // LA VILLE/the city

Third floor: having moved away from the street, we have here, in the calm, the living areas, the dining room. The kitchen, high up, will send fewer odors into the house, it will be ventilated from above. By a subtlety of composition I shall make the reception areas communicate agreeably with the roof garden, full of flowers, of ivy, of arbor vitae, of Chinese laurels, of okubas, of spindle-trees, of lilacs, of fruit trees. Cement paving with grass joints (for a reason) or attractive gravels make a perfect surface. Covered shelters allow a siesta in hammocks. A solarium brings health. In the evening, we dance to a gramophone. The air is clean, noise is smothered, views are distant, the street is far away. If there are trees nearby, you are above the tops. The sky sparkles with stars; you see them all.

Until now, all these things were useful only to sparrows and for alley cat dating! (14)

Under this drawing I write: *Free plan, free facade.*

And for architecture they mean an immense liberation, a gigantic step forward from the masonry house. It is a contribution of modern times!

But before going on to something else, I *read* again:

I draw schematically the ground of existing cities (15).

I dig up four meters of city ground, I carry it away on mule carts, on trucks, on barges, out of town, and spread it over the suburbs of the city.

The soil of the city has gone to cover suburban lots! What crazy extravagance, what a waste of money and effort.

Then I build up the houses of the city with their roofs. I remember the figures:

built-up surface (ground lost) 40%
reserved for courtyards 30%
reserved for circulation .... 30% approximately

But now I draw the ground of the modern city.

One line: it is all of the ground available (almost 100%) in the thin forest of pilotis (16).

Raised on these pilotis, up in the air, the city.

On top of the city buildings, the roof gardens.

100 percent for the circulation of pedestrians, for light and heavy vehicles, 40 percent for gardens and walks, or for rest,

acquired for free. Such is the modern city, we shall remember that.

These "pilotis" of which I speak are a really great conquest of modern techniques. Please admit in passing that "naked man," what I call pure man, has used this resource in all times and places. Yet what resistances, what invectives today, in the name of academic standards, of course. The president of the Geneva government told me that because of my pilotis, I was kicked out of the League of Nations competition; it is a miraculously simple explanation (frank but characteristic) for infinitely less clear events. The pilotis of our Centrosoyuz in Moscow were violently discussed in the city soviet, but the president concluded dryly: "We shall build our palaces on pilotis, in order to inaugurate with them the works of Greater Moscow." Planning at last. We are getting there.

Let us stick to architecture. Here I draw the ground floor of a little private house in Boulogne-sur-Seine to which the preceding explanations apply (17).

Here is our small house model under the Loucheur low-cost housing law (18). A party wall in brick, in stone, etc., which I call diplomatic because they seal the alliance with the doubtful local shopkeepers (experiments I shall explain another time have led us to a diplomatic alliance with these). On either side of this wall, a few meters away, two steel columns carry the floors and the roof of the house. Thus, under the house henceforth healthy, there is a magnificent sheltered space for working, resting, setting up a small workshop, washing clothes outdoors, putting up a garden lean-to.

Here you see the building of the Centrosoyuz in Moscow: the offices of the food cooperatives administration, 2,500 employees (19). It is necessary to regulate the crowds entering and leaving all at the same time. A sort of forum is needed at those hours for people whose galoshes and furs are full of snow in winter; an efficient set of cloakrooms and the circulation around them are needed. And finally, Miasnitzkaia Street is too narrow for official cars to park. A set of pilotis covers the site entirely, or almost. These pilotis carry the office building, which starts only at the second floor. Under it one circulates freely, outdoors or in rooms

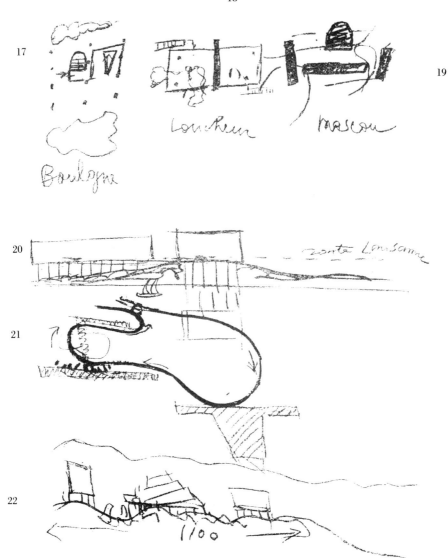

17 Boulogne // **18** Loucheur // **19** Moscou/Moscow // **20** route Lausanne/Lausanne road

opening onto a big space, fed by the two entrances and creating the "forum" suggested above. The elevators leave from this forum, as do the "paternosters" (cabins on a continuous cable) and immense helicoidal ramps, instead of staircases, allowing a more rapid flow. Doors are opened where useful, under the buildings, in front of them, far from them. Light is captured at will. The analysis is quite clear; such a building has two aspects. The first, an arrival in disorder, on a vast horizontal plane on ground level: it is a lake. The second aspect that of stable, motionless work, sheltered from noise and coming and going, everyone at his place and controllable: whereas it is rivers, means of communication, that lead to offices.

Circulation is a word I have applied unceasingly in Moscow to explain myself, so often that it finished by making some representatives to the Supreme Soviet nervous. I maintained my point of view. A second outrageous fundamental proposition: *architecture is circulation*. Think it over, it condemns academic methods and consecrates the principle of "pilotis."

Here is the project for the League of Nations international competition on the first site (20). Far back, the road to Lausanne, 300 or 400 meters from the lake. One enters that marvelous property of hundred-year-old trees, one goes through a magnificent stand of these and suddenly comes upon lawns sloping down to the lake. And Mont-Blanc and the Alps of Savoy, the Salève, are on the other side. A remarkable view! You will, you would say to me, take advantage of this level site near the Lausanne road, to avoid the hillside slopes and offer a horizontal circulation to your buildings. I am more Norman than that (isn't that so, Léger?), I want to eat my cake and have it too. I keep this flat natural esplanade to disengage my palace and to receive the crowds that will come there at certain hours.

And then, at the very edge of the grassy slopes, I set my zero level; I push the wings of the Secretariat and the library toward Geneva, at the +0 level; I push the floor of the big assembly hall toward the lake, those of the big committee rooms, and the pavilion of the President of the Assembly, all at the same +0 level. I get to the lake with the floor of the President high above it. Everywhere I have gotten clear of the woods, I have moved away from the noise of the Lausanne road, I am up in the air, up in the sky, in complete joy, in full light, everywhere.

And what carries these floors, so high above the uneven ground, above the lake, are the pilotis—the most economical means of construction.

Then someone will say to me in anguish, you have built walls around or between your pilotis in order not to give a sensation of fright with these gigantic elevated buildings?

Oh, not at all! I show these pilotis that do carry something with satisfaction, multiplied by their reflection in the water, pilotis that let light through under the buildings, destroying all notions of "front" and "back"—those "backs" depressed in opaque shadows, where melancholy mosses grow between paving stones and whose sad spaces we cross furtively. On the contrary, there is an abundance of sunlight, but even more, a dazzling view awaits me: under this magnificent portico I see reflections on the water, I see beautiful boats sail past, I see the Alps, framed as in a museum, panel by panel.

But I remember the colonnade of Saint Peter's in Rome, which carries nothing and nevertheless feeds our retinas with its adorable cylindrical forms. I also think, to defend myself, of the colonnade of my elder colleague Nénot, who was chosen to build the palace. His collonade carries nothing at all. But it projects a deadly shadow on the committee rooms whose small classical windows open behind it. So much so that the committee of ambassadors, in choosing his project to be built, addressed the following question to Mr. Nénot: "How do you plan to light the rooms behind the colonnade?"

Thus a colonnade that *really carries a building*, as my thighs carry my trunk, is a crime of lèse-architecture that earned us the guillotine.

It is under the pilotis that free immense sloping spaces, having assured the uninterrupted horizontal circulation of pedestrians throughout the palace, that I solved the complete one-way continuous circulation of automobiles and their parking, an open space under the pilotis of the Secretariat and a closed garage under the pilotis of the library (21). High up in the League of Nations hierarchy it was said, "No, the Secretariat, the committee members cannot work on top of automobiles."

Finally (22), here is the project for the World Center of Geneva (except for the League of Nations). The pilotis furnish such a powerful poetry that I feel incapable of making it felt in a few words to a new public. The site is a sort of acropolis, dominating the horizon in four marvelous directions, three of different mountain ranges, the fourth of the perspective of the upper lake. The plateau is in reality made up of softly rolling country, surrounded by immense sloping lawns, dotted with gigantic trees, the object of Genevan pride. Herds of cattle graze here and there. I do not want to disturb this moving rural sight that recalls the sentimental pages of Jean-Jacques Rousseau. Nevertheless, I choose the site of gigantic buildings: the World Museum, the World Library, the International University, the International Organizations; I even plan two skyscrapers for a business and financial center, an airport, and a big radio transmitter and receiver.

I have already begun, in referring to the Centrosoyuz of Moscow, to formulate one of my important convictions; that what happens on the ground concerns circulation, mobility, and what happens above, inside the building, is work, is motionless. This will presently become an important principle of city planning. I conserve the grass and the herds, the old trees, as well as the ravishing views of landscapes, and above them, at a certain level, on a horizontal slab of concrete, on top of the pilotis descending to their foundations, I raise the limpid and pure prisms of utilitarian buildings; I am moved by a high intention, I proportion the prisms and the spaces around them; I compose in the atmosphere. Everything counts: the herds, the grass, the flowers in the foreground on which one walks caressing them with one's eyes, the lake, the Alps, the sky . . . and the divine proportions.

And thanks to the pilotis, on this acropolis destined for meditation and for intellectual work, the natural ground remains, the poetry is intact.

Do you realize how much money is saved compared with the foundations of these fortresses of academic palaces?

One more word: the pilotis are the result of calculations, and their elegance of the modern tendency to economy (here taken in its noble sense). Pilotis: making predetermined points responsible for holding up exact loads in accordance with exact calculations, *without any waste.*

Examine the contractors' bills once a traditional house is finished.

For basements and foundations, you will find frightening amounts; and if your building is on a sloping site, a very steep one (as is the case for instance for most of the houses of Stuttgart where we have built on pilotis), their expense devours your budget; and your house is not even begun; it starts on the ground floor. I believe that the inhabitants of Stuttgart have buried enormous sums to provide the bases of their houses and the retaining walls, which are the walls of fortresses, walls that architects have finished by finding beautiful but that, for me, only displace the center of gravity of architectural design arbitrarily for their benefit; walls that, in addition, infringe on the site, whereas the pilotis, diving down the slopes, would sustain pure forms, create usable spaces at no cost, allow the planting of trees and lawns, replace the melancholy medieval stone landscape with uninterrupted stretches of vegetation from which would rise only the pure prisms of the houses. What grace, what well-being, and what economy! (23)

*
* *

Step by step, we carry out the contemporary revolution in architecture.

Here we are facing the astonishing adventure of the window.

I have allowed myself to de-Vignolize architecture by that prosaic affirmation: *architecture consists of lighted floors*. Mr. Vignola, who worked during the Renaissance, believed he had to fix for posterity the rules of the Greek art then honored so highly, though, by the way, he knew it only through heavy fake Roman copies. The Turks theoretically impaled on pointed stakes the pre-archaeologists of the time, who would have liked first to see, then to measure with their compasses the works of Phidias, of Ictinos, of Callicrates, on the Acropolis of Athens. Thus Mr. Vignola, full of daring, fixed for eternity the only rules of architecture capable of expressing the nobility of the human spirit (the academic profession of faith). These rules are false, but to an extent that you cannot imagine; it is something like a prodigious joke. I visited the Acropolis of Athens! I spent a month full of emotion there,

overwhelmed by so much precision, elevation, *superhuman invention*. You see that, with good reason, I respect Greek art. As to
understanding anything in the adventure that followed the preten-
tious initiative of Mr. Vignola, I give up. I know everyone will
think me wrong and that I am outnumbered with my isolated pro-
testations. Our Sââr Peladan, though he was a Hellenist as intelligent as passionate, used to say to me: "I should like to be king: I
would behead all those who dare to draw and to build a Greek
entablature today!" My protestation is purely theoretical, for Mr.
Vignola has become part of public, governmental, and international morality (the League of Nations). Everything is built in
Greek art, from American gaslights (Doric) to European (Corinthian) to the theaters, the parliaments, the palaces of the League
of Nations, the decoration of ocean liners, and more modestly the
furnishing of rooms for fast laying. One has often called this art
Louis XVI, to revarnish it. God, what a long life this king, legally
decapitated by due process, has had! Otherwise I do agree that
the Louis XVI style is beautiful, very distinguished, and shows
well the high degree of culture of the end of the eighteenth century. But I talk. Let me offer you another gem: in January I had
the visit of a professor from the Ecole des Beaux-Arts in Paris,
who came to see me about our common blackballing at Geneva
(his and mine . . . for very different reasons). He: "It is a real
pleasure to exchange a few words with you. Look here, we are
much closer to each other than it appears. I too apply a discipline:
at the Beaux-Arts I begin by teaching the 'orders' to beginners:
the 'Doric' to the first year, because the Doric is simple. Then,
when they know how to hold a pencil, the 'Ionic,' which is much
more difficult, because of the volutes. Finally, when they are
ready, the 'Corinthian,' for there are all the difficulties. I believe
in discipline!" Oh, Phidias, who stopped stupidly, like a beginner,
at the Doric of the Parthenon! From all this, one understands that
the students are well prepared to face the problems of the machine
age.

Mr. Vignola is not concerned with windows, but "between
windows" (pilasters and columns). I de-Vignolize with my "architecture is lighted floors."

I demonstrate it with a series of little sketches showing the
history of architecture by the history of windows throughout the
ages. As I said above, the object is to carry floors on walls that

one perforates with windows in order to light the interior. And this thankless contradictory obligation (*to carry floors on walls that one pierces*) marks the efforts of builders throughout history and gives architectures their character.

Here is the little classical window (24), then the big opening, unglazed, with nothing to close it, of Pompeii, the pretty Romanesque window, the gigantic Gothic effort toward the light that ends in the *pointed arch* with its abutments and its daring static system of piers, pinnacles, buttresses, flying buttresses, etc. But I note that when the Middle Ages built their little wooden houses overhanging the narrow streets, they *glazed all they could*, using all the resources of wood. And this was even so convincing that the skillful Flemish of Ghent, of Louvain, of the Grande Place of Brussels, on the basis of that tradition, made the miraculous glass facades with stone stiles that we still admire. Then here is the Renaissance with its stone mullions in a window that was made as big as possible to light up the domestic arts in full flourish. Then Louis XIV, who, Sun King, wants to let his patron the sun enter his home to reveal his ostentation. And now the architecture of stone is definitively formulated. Under Louis XV, under Louis XVI, the big grandiose gestures of the Great King are scaled down, humanized. One wants to live in comfort, in privacy. Architecture no longer evolves. The window is fixed, it is finished. Nevertheless, under Haussmann, at the dawn of the first ironmasters, rental housing becomes a business. One must exploit square meters of building. One must present a maximum of bedrooms on each elevation. One goes to the limit. Stop! no more holes, or the building will collapse. It is the final point. But I retain this ultimate solution of the vertical window that tends to touch its neighbor to allow the exploitation of floor space: *the problem is propounded.* The solution will come through new techniques.

Take a quick look at the appearance of the masonry facade of the Louis or of Haussmann, the appearance of the facade at which this architecture has stopped. It is a surface perforated regularly by holes as close together as possible. The design seems prosaic; *there it is, the architecture of masonry, the pure expression of a system of construction* (25).

Ladies and gentlemen, we shall now go ahead fast. Look at the section I started with, at the first plan: buildings in steel or reinforced concrete. I draw horizontal windows, *long continuous*

30 4 fois moins de pose (photo)/four times greater speed (photo)

windows. They have no limit, they have uninterrupted lengths of
10, 100, 1,000 meters. The columns are behind them at 1.25 or 2.5
or 3 meters behind the facade, inside. And behind the continuous
openings, which I shall close with window frames sliding horizontally one behind the other, it will be easy, by means of a childish
strategy, to bring a partition against them without its showing.
Such stops need not be superposed from floor to floor; I defy any
eye to be bothered by this (26).

And the ribbons of wall that separate the long windows from
floor to floor, that make up the sill and eventually the lintels, these
ribbons will be *carried on the floors!* I have already said that.

You must admit that this reform is impressive by its economy
and overwhelming on the plane of aesthetics. Nothing remains of
all the architectural sights to which we have been accustomed by
centuries of tradition. Should we then give up, by virtue of academic codes, the immense benefits of the ribbon windows that
give the best light to interiors, that allow all the subdivisions possible from floor to floor?

Now, launched in this direction, I have not finished.

The study of the first section, which I have called the *symbolic
section* of the contemporary architectural revolution, invites me to
new innovations. Related ideas assail my spirit. I have built many
of these "ribbon windows"; my attention has been drawn to the
sills that still do not seem frank to me, to these lintels that still
seem expensive to me. Houses are still too expensive, although
ours, for similar results, are infinitely cheaper than traditional
ones. I am obsessed by this law of economy to which I give a
meaning going beyond that of the wallet. My associate, Pierre
Jeanneret, is galvanized even more than myself by the problem of
economy. With the savings effected, he would like to offer comfort. He has read Ford, he is a Fordist! One day, this truth appears:
a window is made for lighting, *not for ventilation*. To ventilate let
us use ventilation devices; that is mechanics, physics. And further
still, the window is the most expensive organ of a house. In addition to its frame, there is the finish all around, very expensive.
Usually windows are in steel or wood, that is to say, something
extremely delicate, carefully built. And if one could with a single
gesture repudiate windows, while still lighting floors?

The examination of my symbolic section shows *facades* reduced to some ribbons 30 centimeters high. Well, let us go without them, *let us get in front of them.* By means of brackets we are going to hang vertical steel sections, well adjusted, really vertical, 25 centimeters in front of these ribbons of concrete. Then, across them, inside or outside, horizontal steel sections at distances determined by the glass or plate glass sizes available on the market. Here then in front of the facade is a "window wall." The facade is a window wall. But, as there is no need for all four sides of a building to be in glass, I shall build window walls (27), stone cladding (veneer, brick, artificial panels of cement or other materials; 28), and mixed walls (small windows or glass panes scattered like portholes in the stone cladding; 29).

This idea was originally developed at the Esprit Nouveau Pavilion in 1925. In 1926–27 we designed the Secretariat of the League of Nations with a double row of ribbon windows for the offices and a single one for the corridors. The walls of the main assembly hall were already window walls, in thick slabs of glass. In 1928, in Moscow, we are facing imperative problems of temperature: minus 42°C, 2,500 employees behind windows where the wind creeps in whistling. Windows are not necessary. We need window walls with airtight joints. For ventilation, we shall see.

It seems to me that I have come to the end of the road of this logic, that I have found the essence of truth: the architect disposes of new words; we shall see![1]

But I would not at any price leave you in a state of doubt. I affirmed that the horizontal window (which preceded the window wall) gives more light than the vertical window. Such is my observation in practice. Nevertheless I am contradicted vehemently. It has been thrown at me, for instance, that "a window is a man upright." All right, if one likes to play on words. But recently I found, in the exposure instructions of a photographer, these two explicit graphics; I am no longer swimming in the approximations of personal observations. I am facing sensitive photographic film that reacts to light.

The table says this: for an equal surface of glass, a room lit

---

1. Besides, these words had been applied in dazzling fashion by the nineteenth-century builders in steel in France, and in 1914 Walter Gropius at Cologne reapplied them in the language of modern architecture.

by a horizontal window, which touches both side walls (that is the whole point: the refraction of light waves) has two zones of lighting: zone 1 very well lit; zone 2 well lit (30). On the other hand, a room lit by two vertical windows with a pier between them has four zones of lighting: zone 1 very well lit (two very small sectors), zone 2 well lit (a small sector), zone 3 poorly lit (a big sector), zone 4 dim (big sector) (31). The table adds, *You should expose the photographic plate four times less in the first room.*

The sensitive film has spoken. Ergo!

Ladies and gentlemen, please let us read our situation on the map of architecture and city planning.

We have left the Vignolized shores of the Institutes. We are at sea; let us not separate this evening without having taken our bearings.

First, architecture:

The pilotis carry the measurable weight of the house above the ground, up in the air. The view of the house is delimited, without any connection with the ground. You can then understand the importance taken by the proportions, the dimensions given to this cube carried on pilotis. The center of gravity (32) of the architectural composition has been raised; it is no longer that of the old masonry architectures, which implied a certain optical relation to the ground (33).

The roof garden is a new tool for delightful use; the object of rooms inside a house can be inverted; new joys welcome the inhabitant. The horizontal window and finally the "window wall" have brought us to a point that has nothing in common with the past. With the window wall, *the scale of architecture is modified.* The means of composition are so new, to tell the truth *seem* so reduced, even to nothing, that, terrified, one says: *"But where is architecture going?"*

The new techniques have brought us new words and these new techiques, which we cannot resist, stimulate our imagination (33a).

Facing the problem of Moscow, what did architecture do? We were required to apply all the technical conquests of the time; we drew the quintessence of a building from them from the functional point of view. Here is what we did with the new words of architecture:

I draw (34) the first central wing of the building: the depth chosen for perfect day lighting; this wing contains big rooms for group work, it has a window wall on both sides. The end walls are opaque, made of a double layer of thin sheets of volcanic stone; later I shall explain how air will circulate in the intervening space.

I also sketch the two other office wings: a window wall on one side, a mixed wall (stone and glass) for the corridors; at the end, a wall clad entirely in stone.

The essence of the architectural composition is in the dimensions of the three prisms: they are laid out, in plan and section, in order to create two aspects, here steep, perpendicular, there a welcoming hollow. The central wing is lower by one floor than the two side wings, that was important.

The whole is elevated, on pilotis, detached.

You should realize this important completely new value in architecture: *the clean line of the underside of a building.* A building seen as in a showcase on a display support, *entirely* legible.

The pilotis bring a richness of cylinders, of light in shade or half shade, and also, for the spirit, an impression of striking tension. Underneath, the play of light has the most imaginative effects. Against the sky, there is the impeccable edge of a crystal prism, encircled by the volcanic stones of the roof terrace parapets. This clean profile is one of the most admirable conquests of modern techniques (suppression of roofs and cornices).

And to end this architectural symphony: coming forward from the buildings, all the way to the street, taking the familiar attitude of organs at our scale, are the porches of concrete and stone cladding used to shelter those getting in and out of vehicles. Here are a few objects arranged to create fine relationships in space and elevation: the mast of the Cooperatives and a few bases in steel or bronze meant, in my mind, for contemporary sculptures (the Lipschitzes, the Brancusis, the Laurenses) to play a dazzling role in the architectural symphonies. There are mathematical points that are like the center of gravity of a composition. These points command a space. It is no longer, as at the time of Mansart, "the engraver who will in this tympan carve some trophies." It is the visual artist who, with his works, similar to a fiery star or similar to a lighthouse, should hold in respect, at their proper distance, these great pure silent prisms of crystal or stone.

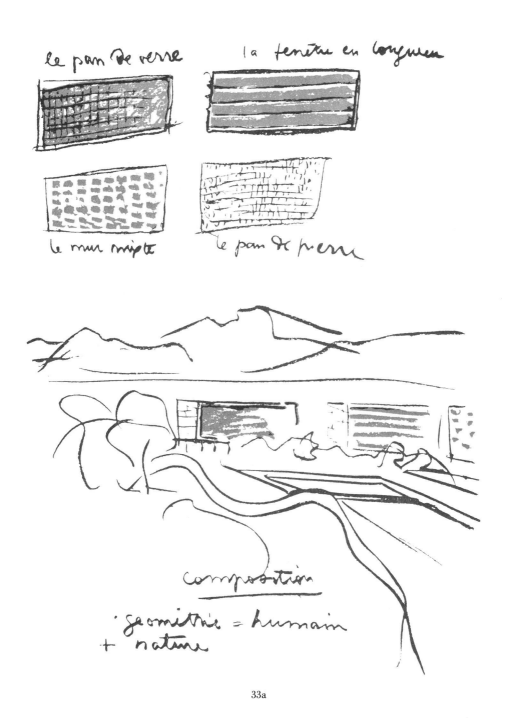

33a

le pan de verre/the window wall // le fenêtre en longueur/the ribbon window // le mur mixte/the mixed wall // le pan de pierre/nonbearing masonry or masonry cladding // composition: géometrie + nature = humain/composition: geometry + nature = humanity

To face the big limpid facades we shall transport some handsome trees here this winter whose arabesques will enrich the composition and whose presence, the more we study architecture and
planning, seems welcome to us. One of the most authentic titles
of the contemporary architecture of steel or cement to the grati-
tude of citizens will be to have introduced trees into the urban
landscapes. Trees, marvelous things beloved by mankind.

My eyes are again (they always are) turned to nature; to evoke
here the palace of Geneva, I draw this symphonic sketch: here is
the horizontal of the lake. Here are the undulations of the hills,
here is the line of the mountains engraved against the sky. And
then, here is our work, of men: geometry. Geometry animated a
little by the spirit of Pythagoras. Spiritual enjoyments, proportions. Here are thin verticals, here are unbroken surfaces: they
are reflected in the water; the basis of architectural sensations is
in these things (35).

For the love of God, what shall we do with the catalogues of
decorators? A great work of art uses simple means. But that is all
the game: with nothing, to prepare a miracle!

Now for city planning:

Here is a traditional street, the cowpath, and here are the
houses, anchored in the ground (36).

Imagine the problems of modern circulation: you are lost.

But here are modern buildings of steel or reinforced concrete,
on columns rising from below them. Five, ten, twenty, fifty floors
one on top of another. Above, gardens for strolling or for health.
But below, there are the pilotis. One hundred percent of the
ground is free, in every direction! Furthermore, in front of each
dwelling, above the pilotis, balconies project out. The front of the
balconies can meet and join up laterally with their neighbors; the
balconies become a second street: for pedestrians or light vehicles.
The trucks are down below. The circuits of the city are visible,
perceptible, within reach of eye or hand (37).

And here is something else. These are immense skyscrapers
200 meters high (38). At their base, open air, traffic. To be orderly
functionally and as architecture, the skyscrapers are laid out regularly 400 meters apart. They rise in moving dignity in an imposing
mass of space and light. The streets? They are no longer, to be
exact, streets, but rivers of circulation flowing wherever our stud-

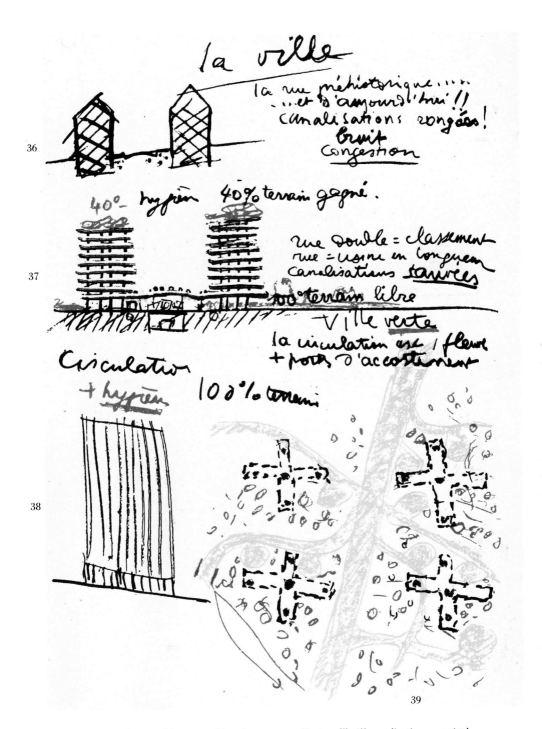

36 la ville/the city // la rue préhistorique . . . et d'aujourd'hui!! canalisations rongées!
bruit congestion/the prehistoric street and today's!! corroded drains! noise, congestion //
37 hygiène 40% terrain gagné/hygiene, 40% ground recovered // rue double-classement/
two-level street classification // rue = usine en longueur/street = factory alongside //
canalisations sauvées/drains conserved // 100% terrain libre/100% ground free // ville verte/
green city // la circulation est 1 fleuve + ports d'accostement/circulation is a river plus
harbors for docking // 38 circulation + hygiène/circulation + hygiene // 100% terrain/
100% ground

ies say they should; they branch out, they have their ports for parking cars under the skyscrapers. In addition, there are trees planted everywhere (39).

And I make this outrageous announcement on planning, which I shall soon explain to you in detail: *traffic, which is on a horizontal plane, has nothing to do with what is going on above. Streets are independent of buildings.* Streets are independent of buildings. Think it over.

I continue to develop my idea. It leads to imminent realities. Here is the section of an ocean liner shown between the two palaces of the Place de la Concorde (40).

I draw the liner in the opposite direction. Better still, I want to visit it from top to bottom. There are 2,000 to 2,500 persons on this liner. It is a big house. There is no confusion here, but perfect discipline. One eats, one sleeps, one dances here, one meditates, one strolls; everybody on earth without exception has a profound admiration for the ocean liner. *We are facing a new dimension in housing* (41).

I draw the floor of the League of Nations on pilotis: these are well-lit floors, and one gets around well on them (42).

I draw an American skyscraper. We are facing a new scale in buildings (43).

Therefore, we have decisions to take.

I spoke to you of sealing windows airtight. We shall speak of many other things still, for instance of organizing modern domestic life, to tear out of our flesh that frightful and stupid thorn that, flattening our purses, devouring our time, saddens us, I mean that our day of rest is not in proportion to our day of work as imposed by life under mechanization.

Our three plates filled with techniques (resistance of materials: we have come to a new stage of the new road. Physics and chemistry: I shall reveal immediate hopes to you. Sociology: we shall have to face an immense disturbance, an impending revolt. Economy: we must reduce costs) lead us, by the abundance of resources and solutions they propose, to a coming decision that will mark the profound transformation of the building industry. This change of scale means the beginning of *great works*. A house up till now had a facade 10, 20, or 30 meters long, it belonged to Mr. X. The coming house will be 1, 2, 5 kilometers long, and if it

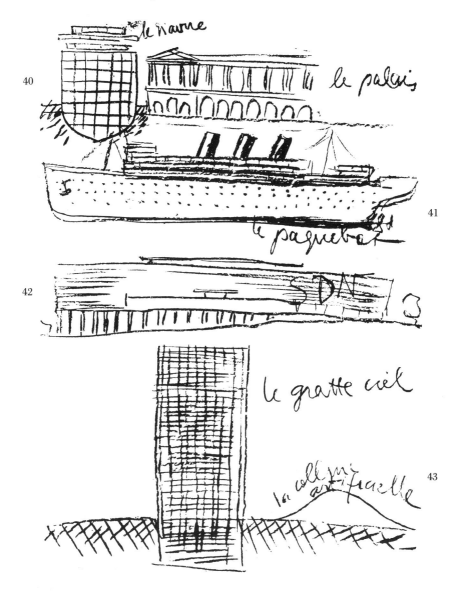

40 le navire/the ship // le palais/the palace // **41** le paquebot/the ocean liner // **42** SDN/ League of Nations // **43** le gratte ciel/the skyscraper // la colline artificielle/the artificial hill

is now foreseen so big, it is because the problems of city planning are urgent, dramatically urgent. We need plans corresponding to collective functions. Speeds are different, new. And all at the same time, everything will be resolved quietly, normally, when the great works have begun: circulation, a free home life, low costs, beauty and spiritual harmony.

To conceive these approaching realities, here is one of the answers to the "how" and "why" of which I have spoken.

A house: a lit-up floor.

What for? To live on.

What is the basis of life? *Breathing.*

Breathing what? Hot, cold, dry, damp?

Breathing pure air at a constant temperature and a regular degree of humidity.

But seasons are warm or cold, dry or damp. Countries are temperate, icy, or tropical; here the "naked man" (before London jackets) wore furs, and there he walked naked.

One more precision: the fundamental basis of Taylorism (a profoundly charitable work and not cruel) is to keep constant the factors concerning a task. The certitude given by experience is that men who suffer from heat or cold are less productive and that if they react against these, they tire and are quickly worn out.

Every country builds its houses in response to its climate.

At this moment of general diffusion, of international scientific techniques, I propose: only one house for all countries, the house of *exact breathing.*

I draw the floors, the cross section (44), and the longitudinal section (45) of the same, I set up the *factory for the production of exact air.* It is a small establishment, a few small spaces; I produce air at 18°C humidified according to seasonal needs. With a ventilator, I blow this air through carefully laid-out conduits. Means of expansion for this air have been invented to avoid drafts. Air comes out. This system at 18° will be our arterial system. I have laid out a system of veins. By means of a second ventilator I take in the same quantity of air. A circuit is established. Air that has been breathed in and out returns to the factory. There it passes over a bath of potassium where it loses its carbon. It goes through an ozonifier that regenerates it. It comes to compressors that cool it, if it has been heated too much in the lungs of the occupants.

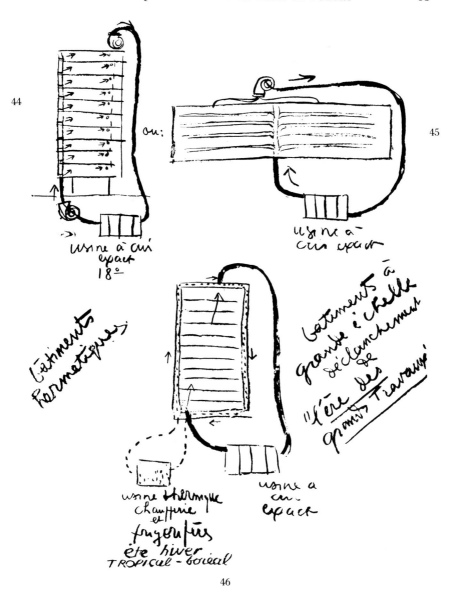

44 usine à air exact/air conditioning plant // **45** ou/or // usine à air exact/air conditioning plant // **46** bâtiments hermétiques/airtight buildings // bâtiments à grand échelle, déclanchement de "l'ère des grands travaux"/big-scale buildings, beginning of "the era of big works" // usine thermique, chaufferie et frigorifère, été, hiver, tropical, boréal/heating and cooling plant, summer, winter, tropical, northern // usine à air exact/air conditioning plant

I no longer heat my houses, nor even their air. But a continuous flow of pure air circulates regularly at the rate of 80 liters a minute per person.

And here is the second phase of the operation:

You ask how does your air, coming out at 18° from the factory, keep its temperature while spreading through rooms, if it is 40 below or 40 above outside?

Answer: it is the *neutralizing walls* (our invention) that will prevent this air at 18° from being influenced by anything whatsoever. We have seen that these neutralizing walls are in glass, in stone, or in both. They are made up of two membranes with a space of a few centimeters between them. On another sketch I draw this void that surrounds my houses, under the pilotis, on the facades, on the roof terrace (46).

Another little heating factory has been built, with heaters and compressors. Two ventilators, one blowing, the other pulling. A circuit in that narrow interval between the membranes, hot air is pushed if in Moscow, cold air if at Dakar. Result: one has regulated in such a way that the inside face, the inside membrane, stays at a temperature of 18°. There you are!

The Russian house, the Parisian, at Suez or in Buenos Aires, the luxury liner crossing the Equator will be hermetically sealed. In winter it is warm inside, in summer cool, which means that at all times there is *clean air* inside at *exactly* 18°.

The house is sealed fast! No dust can enter it. Neither flies nor mosquitos. No noise!

*
* *

Here, ladies and gentlemen, are what the new techniques bring us. Don't you think that my charcoal and crayon sketches encircle a fabulous poetry: the lyricism of modern times?

ARCHITECTURE IN EVERYTHING, CITY PLANNING IN EVERYTHING

There are many students of architecture in this audience.

I shall weigh my words exactly and choose the elements of discussion that are as the keystones of architectural perception. The other day we followed the growth of the structural organism. Today, the aesthetic organism; soon, the biological.

What I am going to say may strike young people who are floating violently and permanently in the midst of the hesitations of their age. Certain remarks heard at twenty have left an indelible impression on me.

Alas, would it be held against me, in a Faculty, to perhaps disturb a few youths profoundly?

Let us define precisely the subject of this lecture. I promised that after the generalizations of the first lecture, I should become pitilessly objective. The object of this objectivity is not exclusively mechanical, practical, or utilitarian. I have architecture in my heart, placed at the tensest point of my sensitivity. Finally, I believe only in beauty, which is the real source of happiness.

Art, product of the reason-passion equation, is for me the site of human happiness.

But what is art? I affirm that artificiality is around us, that it imprisons us. I cannot tolerate artificiality: it hides stupidity and laziness, and the spirit of lucre.

*
* *

I draw things known to everyone: this Renaissance window flanked by two pilasters and by an architrave under a hollowed-out pediment; this Greek temple, this Doric entablature; this one which is Ionic, this other Corinthian. And then this "composition," which as you see is "composite" and has been common, for a long time, to all countries and put to all uses (47).

I take a red chalk and I cross it all out. I take these things out of my tool kit. I don't use them, they don't clutter up my drawing board.

Firmly, I write: *This is not architecture. These are styles.*

So that my words should not be misused, so that I am not made to say what I don't think, I write again:

> *alive and magnificent originally,*
> *today they are only dead bodies,*
>   or women in wax!

*
* *

Architecture is an act of conscious willpower.

To create architecture *is to put in order.*

Put what in order? Functions and objects. To occupy space with buildings and with roads. To create containers to shelter people and useful transportation to get to them. To act on our minds

ceci n'est pas l'architecture
ce sont les styles

vivants et magnifiques à leur origine
ils ne sont plus que des cadavres

47

ceci n'est pas l'architecture/this is not architecture // ce sont les styles/these are styles //
vivants et magnifiques à leur origine, ce ne sont plus que des cadavres/alive and magnificent
originally, they are now only dead bodies

by the cleverness of the solutions, on our senses by the forms
proposed and by the distances we are obliged to walk. To move
by the play of perceptions to which we are sensitive, and which
we cannot avoid. Spaces, dimensions and forms, interior spaces
and interior forms, interior pathways and exterior forms, and exterior spaces—quantities, weights, distances, atmospheres, it is
with these that we act. Such are the events involved.

From there on, I consider architecture and city planning together as a single concept. Architecture in everything, city planning in everything.

*
* *

This act of willpower appears in the creation of cities. And, especially in America, where the decision was taken to *come* and,
having come, to *act*, cities were created geometrically, because
geometry characterizes man (48).

I shall show you how the sensation of architecture arises: in
reaction to geometric objects.

I draw a long prism (49),

another, cubic (50).

I affirm that there is the definition, the basis of architectural
sensation. The shock has been made. You have said, raising this
prism into space with its proportions, *"here is how I am."*

You feel it more clearly if the cubic prism gets thinner and
rises, if the drawn-out prism gets flatter and spreads out. You are
facing *characters*, you've created characters (51).

And no matter what you add to this work, in delicacy or sturdi-
ness, in complication or in clarity, everything here is already determined, you will no longer modify the first sensation.

You must admit it is worth the trouble to absorb such an
impressive truth. And before our pencil sketches anything that we
may love of the styles of past periods, let us repeat: *"I have determined my project."* Let us verify, meditate, measure, define, before going further.

And here is how the architectural sensation continues to act
on our spirit and our hearts:

I draw a door, a window, and still another window (52).

ba:bc = bc:ac

What has happened? I had to open doors and windows, it was my duty, my practical problem. But architecturally, what had happened? We have created geometrical places, we have propounded the terms of an equation. So watch out! What if our equation is false, insoluble, by which I mean if we have placed our windows and doors so badly that nothing *true*—nothing mathematically true—can any longer exist between these holes and the different surfaces of the walls determined by these holes?

Look at the Capitol of Michelangelo in Rome (53). A first sensation of a cube; then a second: the two pavilions of the wings, the center and the staircase. Realize then that *harmony reigns between these diverse elements.* Harmony, that is to say relationship—*unity.* Not uniformity, on the contrary, contrast. But a mathematical unity. That is why the Capitol is a masterpiece.

I have concentrated with real passion on playing with these fundamental elements of the architectural sensation. Look at the diagram defining the proportions of the townhouse at Garches (54). *The invention of proportions,* the choice of solids and voids, the determination of height in relationship to the width imposed by site regulations, result in a poetic creation: *such is the project sprung from one does not know what profound stock of acquired knowledge, of experience, and of powerful personal creativity.* Immediately, nevertheless, the mind, curious and eager, tries to read the heart of this raw project in which the destiny of the work is already definitively inscribed. Here is the result of this reading and of the corrections due to it: a setting in order (arithmetical or geometrical) based on the "Golden Section," on the play of perpendicular diagonals, on arithmetical relationships, 1, 2, 4, between the horizontals, etc. Thus this facade is made harmonious in all its parts. Precision has created something definitive, clear and true, unchangeable, permanent, which is the *architectural instant.* This architectural instant commands our attention, masters our spirits, dominates, imposes, subjugates. Such is the argumentation of architecture. To evoke attention, to occupy space powerfully, a surface of perfect form was necessary first, followed by the exaltation of the flatness of that surface by the addition of a few projections or holes creating a back and forth movement. Then, by the opening of windows (the holes made by windows are one of the essential elements of the reading of an architectural

work), by the opening of windows an important play of secondary
surfaces is begun, releasing rhythms, dimensions, tempos of
architecture.

Rhythms, dimensions, tempos of architecture, inside the
house and outside.

A motive of professional loyalty obliges us to devote all our
care to the interior of the house. One enters: one receives a shock,
first sensation. Here we are impressed by one dimension of a room
succeeding another dimension, by one form succeeding another
(55). That is architecture!

And depending on the way you enter a room, that is to say
depending on the place of the door in the wall of the room, the
feeling will be different. That is architecture!

But how do you receive an architectural sensation? By the
effect of the relationships that you perceive. These relationships
are provided by what? By the things, by the surfaces that you see
and that you see because they are in *light*. And even further,
the light of the sun acts on the human animal with an efficiency
profoundly rooted in the species (56).

Consider then the capital importance of the point where you
open a window; study the way in which that light is received by
the walls of the room (57). Here, in truth, an important game of
architecture is played, on this the decisive architectural impressions depend. You do see that it is no longer a matter of styles or
decoration. Think of those first days of spring when the sky is full
of clouds driven by gusts of wind; you are indoors; a cloud hides
the sky: how sad you are! The wind has driven the cloud away,
the sun enters by the window: how happy you are! New clouds
put you in the shade: how passionately you think of the coming
summer that will give you light all the time!

Light on forms, precise intensity of light, successive volumes,
acting on our sensitive being, provoking physical, physiological
sensations, which scientists have described, classified, detailed.
That horizontal or that vertical, this sawtooth line broken brutally
or that soft undulation, this closed concentric form of a circle or
a square, which acts profoundly on us, influences our designs,
and determines our feelings. Rhythm (58), diversity or monotony,
coherence or incoherence, marvelous or disappointing surprise,
the joyful shock of light or the chill of darkness, calm of a well-lit
bedroom or anguish of a room full of dark corners, enthusiasm or

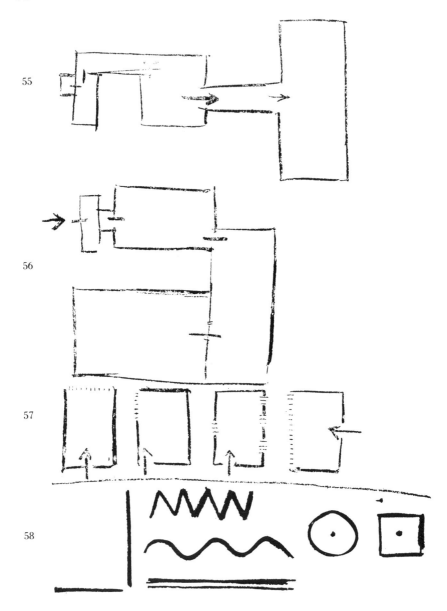

depression, these are the results of the things I have just drawn, which affect our sensitivity by a series of impressions no one can avoid.

I should so much like to make you appreciate the powerful eloquence of lines, so that from now on you may feel your minds free of small decorative events and above all that you may establish in the design of your future architectures the real chronology, the *hierarchy* that brings out the essential. And that you realize that this essence of architecture is in the quality of your choice, in the force of your spirit and not at all in rich materials, in marble or rare wood, nor in the ornaments whose role only exists as a last resort, when all is said, that is to say that these ornaments aren't much use.

I should like to lead you to feel something sublime by which mankind, at its best moments, has shown its mastery; I call it *the point of all dimensions*. Here it is:

I am in Brittany; this line is the limit between the ocean and the sky; a vast horizontal plane extends toward me (59). I appreciate the voluptuousness of this masterly restfulness. Here are a few rocks to the right. The sinuousness of the sandy beaches like a very soft undulation on the horizontal plane delights me. I was walking. Suddenly I stopped. Between my eyes and the horizon, a sensational event has occurred: a vertical rock, in granite, is there, upright, like a menhir; its vertical makes a right angle with the horizon. Crystallization, fixation of the site. This is a place to stop, because here is a complete symphony, magnificent relationships, nobility. The vertical gives the meaning of the horizontal. One is alive because of the other. Such are the powers of synthesis.

I wonder. Why am I so disturbed? Why has this emotion produced itself in my life in other circumstances and in other forms?

I evoke the Parthenon, its sublime entablature of such overwhelming power (60). I think, in contrast, in comparison, of those works full of sensitivity but as if aborted, unachieved: the Butter Tower of Rouen (61), the flamboyant Gothic vaults where so much "unused" genius was spent without achieving the brilliance of the brass trumpets of the Parthenon on the Acropolis (62).

So I draw with just two lines this *point of all dimensions* and

59

60

61–62

63

63 le lieu de toutes les mesures/the point of all dimensions

I say, having in my mind compared numbers of human works, I say: "Here it is, this suffices."

What poverty, what misery, what sublime limits! Everything is included in this, the key to architectural poems. Extent, height. And it is sufficient (63).

Have I made myself understood?

Extent, height! Here I am on the way to search for greater architectural truths. I perceive that the project we are designing is neither alone nor isolated; that the air around it constitutes other surfaces, other grounds, other ceilings, that the harmony that stops me dead in Brittany exists, can exist, everywhere else, always. A project is not made only of itself: its surroundings exist. The surroundings envelop me in their totality as in a room. Harmony takes its origins from afar, everywhere, in everything. How far we are from "styles" and from pretty drawings on paper!

You will see the same house—this simple rectangular prism:

We are on a plain, a flat plain. Can you see how the site designs with me (64)?

We are in the low wooded hills of Touraine. The same house is different (65).

Here it is, underlining the wild outlines of the Alps (66)!

How our sensitive hearts have perceived different treasures each time.

These inherent realities determine the atmosphere of architecture, they are always present for someone who knows how to see and wishes to extract a fertile profit from them.

This same house—the rectangular prism—here it is at a street crossing, influenced by surrounding constructions (67).

Here it is at the end of a line of poplars, in an attitude somewhat touched by solemnity (68).

There it is at the end of a naked road, lined with hedges to left and right (69).

And there it is at last, appearing suddenly, unexpectedly, at the end of a street. A man goes by, his gestures are outlined clearly like those of an actor on a stage, intimately related to the "human scale" that orders its facade (70).

*
* *

64 le dehors est toujours un dedans/the outside is always an inside

68

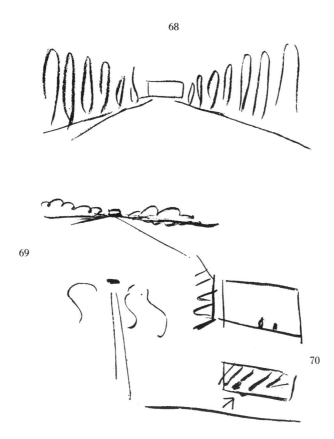

69

70

Having left *in search of architecture*, we have arrived in the domain of simplicity. Great art is made of simple means, let us repeat this tirelessly.

History shows us the tendency of the mind toward simplicity. Simplicity is the result of judgment, of choice, it is the sign of mastery. Tearing oneself away from complexities, one will invent means showing a state of consciousness. A spiritual system will become evident by a visible play of forms. It will be like an *affirmation*. A step that leads from confusion toward the clarity of geometry. At the dawn of modern times, when after the Middle Ages peoples stabilized their social or political forms, an adequate serenity sharpens a lively appetite for spiritual light. The big Renaissance cornice insists on stopping against the sky its profile derived from proportions based on the ground (71). The equivocal oblique of the sloping roof is repudiated (72). Under the Louis and under Napoleon, the will to make the "point of relations" evident shows itself more and more strongly (73).

It is the period of classicism, strengthened by its intellectual epicurism; devoted to the purification of the exterior signs of architecture, it took its distances from the alert Gothic loyalty. Plans and sections are depraved; a dead end is near. We have stumbled against it: academism.

Reinforced concrete brings the roof terrace (74) with rainwater draining toward the inside (and many other constructive revolutions). One can't really draw cornices any more; it is an architectural entity that has ceased to live; its function no longer exists. But the sharp and pure line of the top of a building outlined against the sky has come from it.

Finally, here is the useful organ that the designer seizes: the pilotis. A marvelous means for carrying up in the air, seen from all its four sides, the "point of relations," the "point of all dimensions"—this elevated prism legible and measurable as it has never before been legible. The boon of reinforced concrete or of steel (75).

Thus *simplicity is not poverty*, but simplicity is a choice, a discrimination, a crystallization having purity itself for object. Simplicity is a concentrate.

No longer a spiky agglomerate of cubes, an uncontrolled phe-

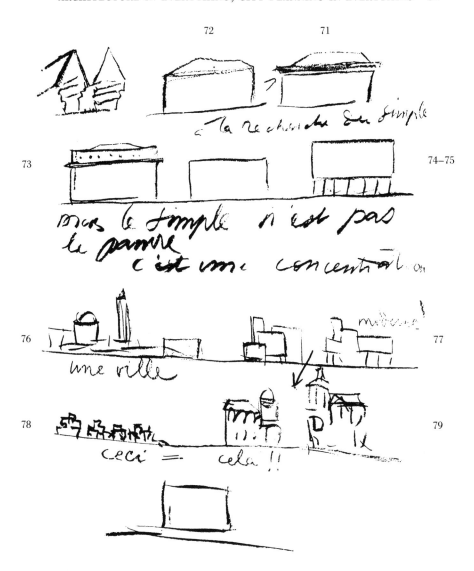

71, 72 à la recherche du simple/searching for simplicity // **73** mais le simple n'est le pauvre, c'est une concentration/but simplicity is not poverty, it is a concentrate // **76** une ville/a city // **77** moderne/modern // **78, 79** ceci = cela!!/this = that

nomenon, but organized, a fully conscious act, a phenomenon of spirtuality.

Another word still, with the intention of disciplining these dashes often full of imagination but which in fact are the disorderly kicks of a pony: I sketch the vision of a beautiful city seen on our study trip (76); here is the dome, there the belfry or the bell tower, here the square palace of the ruler. I have shown the *silhouette of a city*. By what lack of proportion and ignorance of consequences shall we (as is now very much the fashion) silhouette the house as the city is silhouetted (77)? If I multiply houses so deformed, in a street or in a city, the effect will be miserable: tumultuous, cut-up, dissonant (78). What then is the difference between the results of so many undisciplined good intentions and the appearance of the streets with which Buenos Aires, like many European cities, swarms—these atrociously commonplace bazaars, full of laziness and of academic pretensions (79)?

*
* *

Let us reserve that indispensable diversity to our intellect for the time when the symphony of the city will be in preparation. The immense contemporary problems of planning and architecture will bring to the city, in extent and in height, the elements of a new scale. Unity will be in the details; the clamor will be in the whole.

*
* *

I have made the space around the house intervene: I have taken into account its extent and what rises above: dimensions, time, duration, volumes, rhythm, quantities: city planning and architecture.

Planning in all. Architecture in all. Reason, passion, whose synthesis results in an inspired work.

Reason seeks the means.

Passion shows the way.

From the plan of the machine for living—city or house—the architectural work enters into the plane of sensitivity.

We are moved.

Allow me to conclude with a quotation from my latest work, *A House, a Palace:*

> For architecture is an undeniable event that surges in such an instant of creation that the spirit, preoccupied with assuring the firmness of a construction, of satisfying the exigencies of comfort, finds itself raised by a higher intention than that of simply serving and tends to manifest the poetic powers that animate us and give us joy.

A DWELLING

AT

HUMAN SCALE

The urgent problem in all countries is that of building houses for the crowds that the industrial revolution has concentrated in big cities. Descriptions are unnecessary: the facts are there; the problem of quantity presents itself. In addition, strict economy is necessary, we know why.

But only architecture has kept away from industrial methods. The explanation: teaching in these schools is dictated by Academies. They cultivate the past. A desperately backward concept of architecture, and their diplomas, are imposed officially by governments on a public opinion occupied until now with other concerns than verifying current credos. Opinion accepts, at least it tolerates. Professionals build; a number of trades live from it; their lobbies constitute a mass of pressure on parliaments and ministers. The ministers, leaning on the Institutes (sacrosanct authority), give out the official commissions that—it will certainly not astonish you—determine the value, the standards, the dogma of architecture in the town halls and prefectures, in the schools, everywhere. The vicious circle closes tightly on itself. Buddha contemplates his navel.

Ah, but excuse me, the people are not housed! for with such an architectural dogma and such practices, *it is impossible to build houses at prices compatible with a country's economy.* Here too it is useless to insist.

The economic system answers the Institutes: "No, I don't have any secret extravagant funds for you!"

We have our noses at a dead end, we must find a way out. If not? Revolution.

We may just as well make a revolution in architecture.

*
* *

It is, in fact, a question of housing men. In principle, households. To house someone is to assure him certain elements of vital importance that have no legal relationship with Mr. Vignola of the Renaissance, with the Greeks, or with the Normans of Normandy. It is to ensure

a) well-lit floor space,

b) shelter from intrusion: of people, of cold, heat, etc.,

c) the most rapid circulation possible between the different parts of the apartment,

d) a choice of objects in the dwelling adapted to our times.

These different elements make up a physical organism that I baptized in 1921 (*L'Esprit Nouveau*) "a machine for living." A phrase that caught on fast and that I am beaten with today, on both sides of the barricade: by the *academicians* of course (horror, my dear colleague, horror and abomination), and (misunderstanding, because I find the accusation singularly false in its assumptions) by the avant-gardes ("this man, fallen into lyricism, has betrayed the machine for living"). But never mind, it is of no importance.

If the expression has infuriated, it is because it contains the word "machine," representing evidently in all minds the idea of functioning, of efficiency, of work, of production. And the term "for living," representing exactly the concepts of ethics, of social standing, of the organization of existence, on which there is the most complete disagreement.

In the world, among the different social classes, we do not agree on an intellectual point of the greatest importance: *the reason for living*.

How can one take up this subject in the restricted time of a lecture; it is impossible. It is nevertheless the most beautiful of subjects. However, at many points of my previous lectures I have touched on it (and it will be the same for the following). When my ten lectures have been given, you will have added up and found my thinking on the subject.

For today, in the systematic search for a dwelling at human scale, I shall analyze some cases; some guidance may derive from them.

But to begin with, a few words on life on an ocean liner: for fifteen days between Bordeaux and Buenos Aires, I am cut off from the rest of the world, from my barber, my laundress, from my baker, my greengrocer, and my butcher. I opened my trunks, I settled in my house, I'm in the skin of a gentleman who has rented a small house.

Here is my bed, like a raised couch. I'll sleep in it; I shall nap on it when we go through the tropics. There is a second berth, but I am alone. Here is the wardrobe with its mirror (a piece of furniture as accepted in the life of peoples as Mr. Vignola in the life of Academies; it is just as much an anachronism. However, here the manufacturer of the Faubourg St.-Antoine had to stay within limited dimensions, for we are on the sea . . . and room is expensive). This wardrobe could be infinitely better designed; it is nevertheless very useful. Facing it, between the two beds, the desk (or dressing table, as one likes), with three precious drawers; the carpet, pleasant to bare feet (very pleasant, the bare feet). I go through a small door: a big washbowl, a cupboard for underwear, drawers for toilet articles, mirrors, a lot of hooks, a profusion of electric light.

I go through a second door: a bathtub, a bidet, a toilet, a shower, the drain directly in the floor.

I have a telephone within reach of my bed or of the desk.

That's all. Dimensions: 3 meters by 3.10 meters for the bedroom. For the whole: 5.25 m × 3 m = 15.75 m². Retain this figure.

These are what are called "luxury" quarters in which important gentlemen travel at ease.

A man is happy, carries on all the functions of domestic life, sleeps, washes himself, writes, reads, invites his friends, within 15 square meters. You'll interrupt me to say: "Well, and eating? the kitchen? and the cook, the valet de chambre, and the femme de chambre?" I was waiting for you! In fact, that's what I wanted to bring you to.

Food? I'm not concerned by it. It is the job of the dining room, using refrigerators, kitchens, cookers, washing machines, etc., etc., and an army of employees. We are fifteen hundred to two thousand inhabitants on this boat. If there are fifty men in the kitchen, my housework, just mine, employs 50 ÷ 2000 = *a fortieth of a cook*. Ladies and gentlemen, I employ a fortieth of a cook; I've found the trick to have at my service only a fortieth of a cook. Oh servant crisis, how you are made easy! But, pardon, that's not all: *I am not concerned by my cook, I don't have anything to do with him, I give him neither orders nor money to go to the market.* I can even, if you agree, invite you all to dinner after the lecture, and you may eat Moscow caviar, Argentine *putchero*, Bresse chickens, and drink stout or Munich beer or make Veuve Cliquot pop! It would not bother me at all!

At seven in the morning my valet de chambre, who is extraordinarily polite and helpful, wakes me; he opens the blinds and the window. He brings me my chocolate. Then, I write or I read. I go for a stroll. My valet has done the room, the toilet, and the bath. In the afternoon, he brings me tea and the ship's paper with the latest news. He has prepared my dinner jacket discreetly at 7 P.M., and when I return at night the bed is ready, the night-light lit. God, how easy life is.

My valet de chambre cares this way for about twenty travelers. I have thus at my service *one-twentieth of a valet de chambre.* How the cost of living goes down! In such conditions one can really afford servants. Till now, I have employed only the fortieth of a cook and the twentieth of a valet de chambre; total: three-fortieths of a servant! How much lower the cost of living gets, I repeat it, and repeat it to myself. I repeat it so often that I finish by thinking the problem over and perceiving the white and rounded dome of Christopher Columbus's egg.

Let us continue the discoveries: "John, here is my laundry, have it washed for me for the day after tomorrow, but have my trousers ironed while I am at the barber's."

Etc., etc. I shall spare you the rest, but I have the figures.

A traveler satisfied with the benefits of the Company, classified in the category "deluxe," I occupy 15 square meters. I employ three-fortieths of a servant. I have no problems concerning him. I don't have to know whether John smokes cigarettes and reads novels, or wants to go to the movies. At two in the morning, I call John on the telephone: "John is in bed, I'll send you someone." Here is Paul. "Paul, be so good as . . ."

There are refrigerators, there are kitchens, there is heating. There is an abundance of hot water and cold. I have iced water in my thermos. There is a showy dining room for which one dresses. As that bores me, most of the time I eat in the small dining room of the recalcitrants. There are quantities of maitres d'hôtel, of waiters, of wine-waiters, who spoil you as if you were a bride. There is a laundry, there are ironing rooms. There is a telephone switchboard that answers every request and sends you personnel. There is a post and telegraph office. . . .

In this liner that contains two thousand inhabitants within its seven to ten floors, I note something else of importance: from the apartment described above, one arrives, by a small private corridor, to a big promenade *that is like a boulevard*, the deck.

There one meets the crowd, as on the boulevards or in your city on Florida Street (89). Another boulevard (encumbered with lifeboats, it is true) is on top of the liner, as a big roof terrace would be above an urban building. Inside the liner, there are many streets, two per floor, named Rio, Buenos Aires, Montevideo, with numbers on the cabin doors just as there are on all the houses of cities everywhere. These streets, which are not on the ground, delight me; they are in the same spirit that led me to create, by another line of thought, the "elevated streets."

What I am telling you is extremely ordinary: usual in all the hotels on the earth and the sea. But *what is prodigious* is to evoke our home life; what seems unqualifiable insolence is to dream of integrating the things described above in the purgatory of the daily life of modern men imprisoned in the houses of the preindustrial age.

Thus, *liberty appears*, to us who are slaves; the solution is there, within reach of the hand. Economy, sociology, politics, city planning, and architecture push us toward it. But I confess that there are solemn idiots (I insist on the term) who are indignant about such suggestions. Proclaiming the Rights of Man, they invoke *"liberty"*!!!

I have just explained to you the problem of public services. A unit at human scale: 15 square meters. Let us take, to be at ease, a surface ten times bigger: 150 square meters. And let us get rid of everything not needed inside.

The conditions of life are falsified by outmoded conceptions, we attribute false surfaces to our homes; we raise rents by two times or by five. To this cost we add that of servants and the frightful cares they cause. In our home do we have a baker to make our bread and a pastry cook to make our cakes? The example applies to my demonstration above. We haven't thought, we aren't adapted; we have remained in the academic thoughts and the customs of the preindustrial age.

Here we arrive at the heart of the question of public services. It is on their precise organization that both modern planning and the modern dwelling must be founded. The scale of architectural problems will change. A building with a facade of 10, of 20, of 30 meters built privately is an anomaly, an anachronism. It means investing one's money in unfavorable conditions (despite appearances), it means obstinately increasing inefficient means that after us may hardly be used.

On the contrary, the dwelling, the office, the workshop, the factory (architectural events that can be generalized under the simple heading of lighted floor space) will use new forms of standardization, of industrialization, of efficiency. Not only shall we reduce building volumes infinitely, and economize for each household and each business enormous general expenses, but by these methods we shall reduce the cost of construction by half. And by this method, in city planning, we shall solve the problems of circulation (which is like a system of rivers, or arteries, with brooks, rivers, and estuaries on one hand, and autonomous landing ports along the rivers (car parks)). In architecture, we shall give cities immense and majestic perspectives covered by the most beautiful and useful vegetation. Going to the limit of our ideas, we shall tear the building industry away from its preindustrial methods; building will no longer be a seasonal industry, paralyzed by the effect of bad weather. We shall get to the house assembled from standard components, prepared in factories, made perfect by industrialization, like an automobile body, and put up on the site by *assembly workers* and no longer by discouraging crowds of masons, carpenters, sheet metal workers, roofers, plasterers, joiners, electricians, etc., etc. . . .

Ah, but what will the Chambers of Commerce think?

The *dwelling at human scale* is the basis of this evolution.

Let me show you by what ways, through twenty years of attentive curiosity, certitudes have come to us.

The beginning of these studies, for me, goes back to my visit to the Carthusian monastery of Ema near Florence, in 1907. In the musical landscape of Tuscany I saw a *modern city* crowning a hill. The noblest silhouette in the landscape, an uninterrupted crown of monks' cells; each cell has a view on the plain, and opens on a lower level on an entirely closed garden. I thought I had never seen such a happy interpretation of a dwelling. The back of each cell opens by a door and a wicket on a circular street. This street is covered by an arcade: the cloister. Through this way the monastery services operate—prayer, visits, food, funerals.

This "modern city" dates from the fifteenth century.

Its radiant vision has always stayed with me.

In 1910, returning from Athens, I again stopped at Ema.

One day in 1922, I talked about it to my associate Pierre Jeanneret; on the back of a restaurant menu, we drew up spontaneously the *immeubles-villas* [townhouse buildings]; the idea was born. A few months later their detailed plans were shown at our big stand on city planning at the Salon d'Automne ("A Contemporary City of Three Million Inhabitants"). Then, in 1923–24, we pushed the idea further. I explained the mechanism in the book *Urbanisme* (City Planning), in which dwellings were already agglomerated into urban neighborhoods. Objections were made to the fragility of the suspended gardens, their lack of sunlight, etc. In 1925, at the Decorative Arts exhibition, despite the refusal of the Governing Board, despite the traps untiringly laid before us

by the direction of the Exhibition, we built in *real full-size* a whole
unit of our townhouse buildings, the Esprit Nouveau Pavilion,
which, with its big rotunda on city planning (the diorama of the
city of three million and the diorama of the center of Paris named
the Voisin Plan), made up a protest against the dim program of
the Exhibition (decorative art) and offered solutions to the imminent crisis of big cities. This done, we pushed our studies further,
we "pushed the motor," extracted the essence of our solution,
transferred the problem into the field we dreamed of: the *prefabricated house*. And in 1927, as a result of the battle on the League
of Nations building, a young and energetic Geneva businessman,
Mr. Wanner, asked us to help him apply our principle of "dwellings" in a factory and put everything to work, patiently, meticu-
lously, to achieve—finally—a production worthy of the machine
age.

An idea needs time; its supporters need perseverance, stubbornness: 1907–27!

During this time, at the moment of the first destructions in
Flanders in 1914, I had had a sort of clairvoyant vision of the
problems of contemporary housing. The question was the following: the war would last three months (for the means were too
powerful for it to last longer. The governments saw clear!). Reconstruction would not take longer than six months. After which, life
would go back to normal!

To respond to this program, at a moment when, except for the
magnificent aesthetic inventions of Lloyd Wright and the healthy
creations of Auguste Perret, current architectural aesthetics
sought a precarious renovation in traditional construction methods, I imagined something entirely new, something that was conceived whole, functioned socially, industrially, and aesthetically,
and already proposed, in their totality, the principles laid out before you in the lecture "Techniques Are the Very Basis of Poetry."
I confess nevertheless: the full awareness of this system has come
to me only recently, at the moment when a host of problems proposed by us, villages, rental housing, town houses, the League
of Nations building, the Centrosoyuz of Moscow, the World City,
led us to a general theory, "in the pursuit of architectural unity"
(the subtitle of *A House, a Palace*). Here again, a long period:
1914–29.

Here you see that solution of 1914 called "the Dom-Ino houses." I study the famous old houses of the architecture of Flanders; I draw them schematically; I discover that they are glass houses: fifteenth, sixteenth, seventeenth century (80). Then I imagine this: a construction firm will pour, without formwork but by means of ingenious site machinery, the framework of a house: six columns, three floor slabs, and the staircase. The dimensions: 6 × 9 meters. Standard columns at a standard span of 4 meters; on either side, on cantilevered ribs, an overhang of $4:4 = 1$ meter. Is this surface appropriate (81)?

I tried innumerable combinations of plans within these structural frameworks. Everything was possible (82).

Automatically I had made ribbon windows or window walls (83). But I didn't realize it.

Future perspectives appeared: once the skeleton was poured by a construction firm, the bombed-out inhabitant, with the burnt materials of the original, would finish his house in accordance with his own ideas. He would buy from a parent construction company standard combinable windows, wardrobes (84), combinable drawers, doors. Everywhere, modular dimensions would allow innumerable combinations. And this would be quite new: the doors and windows would not be set into holes in the masonry. No, the doors, the windows, the wardrobes, which the standard height of the floors and spans of the columns made easy to do, would be set in first. These elements placed, the wall would be *built around them*, that is to say, filled in.

Well, there it was, the complete hypothesis of the mass-produced house with a standard framework and a free plan that we are finally able to carry out, today, after fifteen years. I had not realized it, for we were absorbed by other difficult tasks.

Today, here we are on the way. In 1928, Mr. Loucheur, Minister of Labor, asked us to study a small house of 45 square meters, the "Loucheur [low-cost housing] Law" model.

Classification of events:

1) To support the floors: a "diplomatic" party wall (see the second lecture); two steel columns per house, which go through the building and carry the roof. The village mason had fixed two sets of two steel brackets in his wall (84a).

2) For outside walls: a window wall or a ribbon window.

80 1914 // FLANDRES/Flanders // **84** la thèse de la maison à sec/the hypothesis of the house assembled from standard components

Around it, like a "lizard" skin, sheets of galvanized sheet metal that furnish the impeccable solutions of car body bent sheet metal for the running off of rainwater (85).

3) The walls and partitions in compressed straw, in agglomerated wood shavings, or in cork; the interior faces and the ceiling in plywood. A sanitary block in the middle (standard shower, washbowl, toilet). The rest at will by means of standard metal casework, of which I shall speak another time.

The minister is delighted. We had met the illusive cost ceiling, which seemed impossible to achieve. *We had used only very expensive materials:* steel, galvanized sheet metal, cork, plywood; the windows were the patented model produced by Saint-Gobain for our luxury villas.

Well, let us not have any illusions. Workingmen, whose clearsighted spirit I often love, will loathe our houses; they'll call them "boxes." And for the moment, we build these "low-cost houses" of the Loucheur Law by combining several frameworks (86) for aristocrats and intellectuals. One can't skip stages: look rather at the pyramid by which I express the hierarchical nature of society; despite revolutions it will not change (87). The base of the pyramid, the good people, is for the moment wrapped up in the most typical romanticism; its idea of quality is based on the forms of luxury of the generations preceding 1900. It is for this group that enormous Henri II buffets and mirrored wardrobes are still being made. These mastodons of ancient times cannot even get through the doors of our houses. Here is a dwelling of modern times still waiting for those for whom it is designed.

Before I tear off this sheet, note again the stage that we have reached: houses produced in a factory, standardized, massproduced, efficiently. They leave on railway cars and go *anywhere*, assembled by specialists. A numerous dispersed small clientele can be serviced. The pilotis adapt it to any terrain. Inside, the plan *is free*, at will.

These methods of industrialization by standardization lead us naturally to the coming skyscraper: its form is determined by the superposition of cells at human scale. The ground is free. Later we shall be able to speak of city planning (88).

*
* *

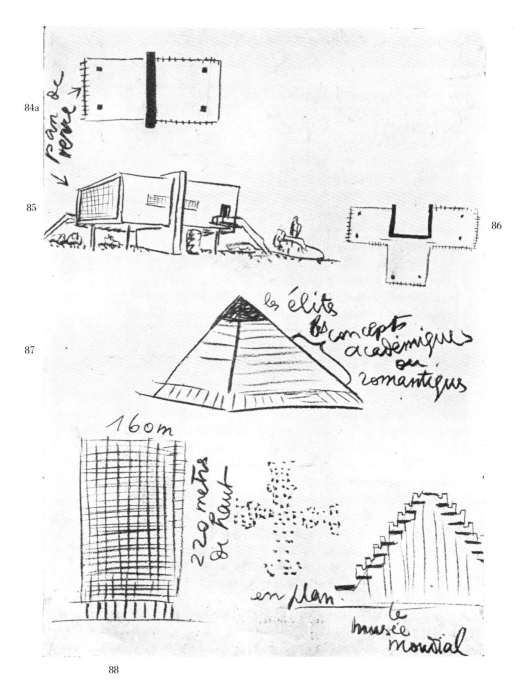

84a

85

86

87

88

84a pan de verre/window wall // **87** les élites/the elites // les concepts académiques ou romantiques/academic or romantic concepts // **88** 160m/160 meters // 220 mètres de haut/ 220 meters high // en plan/in plan // le musée mondial/the world museum

Let us go back to the monastery of Ema and to our "townhouse buildings," two forms of dwelling at human scale. If you knew how happy I am when I can say: "My revolutionary ideas are in history, in every period and every country" (the houses of Flanders, the pilotis of Siam or of the lake-dwellers, the cell of a convent monk being sanctified).

I imagine therefore a cell whose section is characterized thus: it has two floors, two stories. In the lower part, toward the back, I cut out a *street*. This street will become a street raised above the ground, which is something else than a street on the ground. This "elevated street" will be repeated, one over another every six meters; therefore, elevated streets at 6, 12, 18, 24 meters above the ground (92a). I maintain the name "street" rather than corridor because it is in fact an organ of horizontal circulation entirely separate from the villas that line it and whose doors open onto it (90). These elevated streets end, at appropriate distances, at groups of elevators, at ramps, or at staircases establishing the connection with the ground (92). The connection to the roof garden is also found there, with its solariums, its swimming pool, its gyms, its walks amid the vegetation of hanging gardens (91). In some cities with a complicated topography (I shall speak of them), there will be an expressway.

By one of these doors, we have entered inside a villa. The interior plan is chosen by the occupant (free plan due to the independent skeleton structure). Nevertheless, on the front elevation, one comes against a window wall. Subtle combinations allow a perspective on a double height, while the living and dining areas are set one over the other.

At this vital point of the villa, a door opens onto a garden. This garden is "suspended." It is enclosed on three sides. We had produced the Esprit Nouveau Pavilion in 1925 to show that this garden is magnificent. I insist: the hanging garden seems to me the modern formula for a practical intake of fresh air, close to the center of family life; one walks on it with dry feet, avoiding rheumatism, sheltered from the vertical sun and from rain. We built a similar one at the villa in Garches and that in Poissy, which are demonstrations. An efficient garden, with no maintenance. This garden for *taking in air*, multiplied along vast blocks of buildings, is in fact a real sponge for air.

A garden isolates a villa from its neighbor. Let us multiply

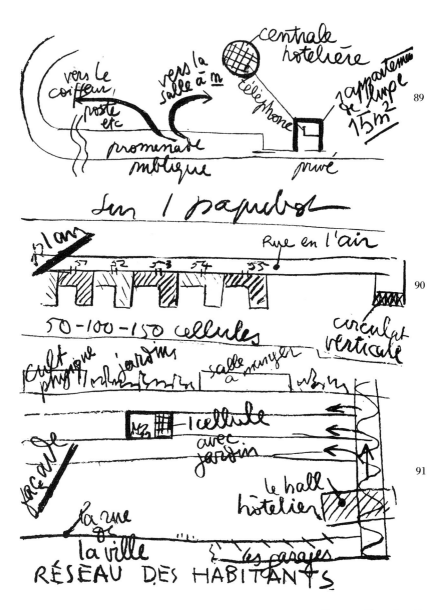

89 vers le coiffeur, poste etc./toward the hairdresser, the post office, etc. // vers la salle à m./toward the dining room // promenade/promenade deck // centrale hôtelière/central hotel services // téléphone/telephone // 1 appartement de luxe 15 m²/a luxury apartment, 15 meters square // publique/public // privé/private // sur 1 paquebot/on an ocean liner // **90** plan/plan // rue en l'air/elevated street // 50–100–150 cellules/50–100–150 dwellings // circulation verticale/vertical circulation // **91** cult. physique/gym // jardins/gardens // salle à manger/dining room // façade/facade // 1 cellule avec jardin/a dwelling with garden // le hall hôtelier/hotel lobby // la rue de la ville/the city street // les garages/garages // RÉSEAU DES HABITANTS/network of inhabitants

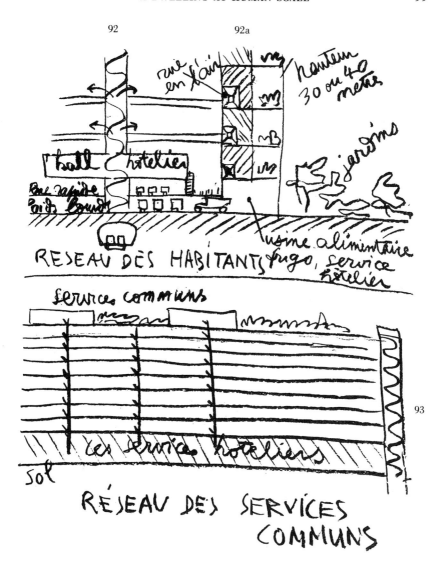

92, 92a rue en l'air/elevated street // hauteur 30 ou 40 mètres/30 or 40 meters high // hall hôtelier/hotel lobby // rue rapide, poids lourds/expressway, trucks // jardins/gardens // usine alimentaire frigo, service hôtelier/food factory, refrigerator, hotel services // RÉSEAU DES HABITANTS/network of inhabitants // **93** services communs/public services // les services hôteliers/hotel services // sol/ground // RÉSEAU DES SERVICES COMMUNS/ network of public services

the standard elements of a dwelling. In elevation, you see the window walls join up vertically; beside them, the powerful architectural effect of the lateral separations that interrupt the window walls.

Let us draw the sections. The green chalk indicates the gardens, the red the habitable volume of the villas, the yellow the elevated streets connected by walks, above the streets, to the vertical circulation going down to the big public services hall. Further still below, the garages, where everyone will find his car (92, 92a).

On the same cross section let us read another yellow part, which is the public services factory. Here it is (93), drawn along the whole length of this new section. *The public services factory.* I have described the advantages of the ocean liner to you. You understood me! Let us indicate in violet the vertical connections carrying these services to each of the villas.

I cannot insist further, but let us notice this: with such buildings, a new module determines the facade. These window walls, enlivened by the big holes of the gardens (six meters), bring a new architectural vision. The appearance of the city will change; the scale of city plans will be based on an architectural module of six meters instead of the present one of three.

Retain this important fact for the day when I shall show you how money can be earned in planning a big city (instead of being spent) by adding value to the ground and how one can find the key to solving traffic in big cities with a complicated topography, and how finally one can, in this way, create relationships between nature and architecture as majestic as they are unexpected.

We have noted, haven't we, that the construction industry should harmonize its methods with the spirit of the machine age by giving up *small* private constructions. Dwellings should not be made in meters, *but in kilometers.*

*
* *

The pursuit of the ideal of economy, in the design of the standard dwelling, leads us beyond the simple shell of the human snail. This dwelling has to be combinable by millions; this obligation will lead us to unexpected solutions. To live, to move on "lighted floors," to breathe in the "air intake" gardens, to live in the liberty of centrally serviced villas, to circulate rapidly and efficiently in the "streets off the ground" is already to be in great progress compared to the present state of things.

Modern life—office and factory—by its sedentary regime, its reduction of physical effort, weakens organisms and makes the nervous system anemic. Sport has developed, spontaneously. If it occupies many spirits, it is practiced by only a few bodies. In reality, what is it? The answer is disarming: sport, at present, is fifty thousand anemic persons who, under very poor conditions, get together in stadia to watch the biceps and calf muscles of twenty strong boys work out: such is the role of stadia. Having built a stadium, the city fathers say: "Now we have paid our tribute to sport."

Sport should be regular, daily, or at least semiweekly. If one does not wish to evade urgent realities, one must *lay out sports grounds at the foot of dwellings*. In addition we shall see, in studying modern planning, that a healthy city requires generous traffic networks. Modern techniques, by building high-rises or in "kilometer" lengths, give us all of the ground free and also, by increasing the density of population, reduce distances.

New conceptions are needed, flexible and inventive. Here is one I like, for it brings admirable possibilities from the social point of view:

I draw a square of 400 square meters, as often allotted by planners to each house in a new garden city (94). Lots are laid out along straight or curved streets, the small houses are the multitude of red dots. I call that shrapnel development (95) because of its chaotic appearance; later on, vegetation saves everything and we are reassured. The governing boards are satisfied: "We have accomplished a work of philanthropy," they think.

Profound error, pure illusion: the worker and his wife have been forced into martyrdom. Their garden? Extra housework duties, very serious, serious for the body they deform; the movements of gardening are *poor movements;* tasks of gardening, wear of the body. "To cultivate one's garden!" There is quite a lot of literature about that . . . and good business. So many posters streaming with color, so many flyers, so many beautiful books and fine speeches maintain the illusions and the rheumatisms.

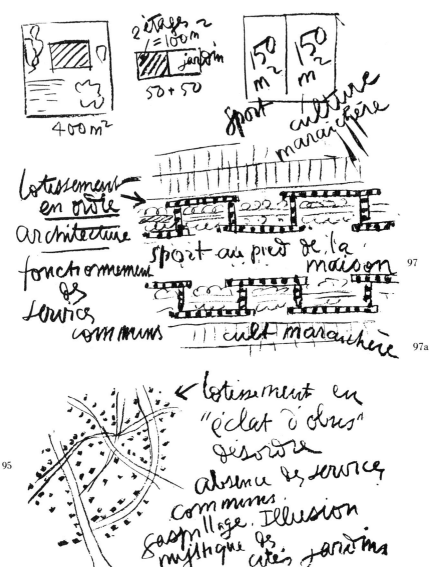

95 lotissement en "éclat d'obus" désordre, absence de service communs, gasspillage. Illusion mystique des cités jardins/ "shrapnel" site plan, disorder, no public services, waste. Mystical illusion of garden cities // **96** 2 étages/2 floors // jardin/garden // **96a** sport/ sports // culture maraichère/allotment gardens // **97, 97a** lotissement en ordre/orderly site plan // architecture/architecture // fonctionnement des services communs/operation of public services // sport au pied de la maison/sports at the foot of the dwelling // cult. maraichère/allotment gardens

The human dwelling should be extended by *public services*, and sport become a daily home activity. Here is a solution completing the dwelling on the *elevated street* and the air intake garden: I suppose 50 square meters for the dwelling (on two levels = 100 square meters) and 50 square meters for the hanging garden (96). I have piled them one on another up to 30 meters high, the dwellings and their gardens. Of the 300 square meters remaining, let us take 150 for sports. The 150 square meters belonging to each dwelling are combined for the advantage of sport (96a) and allow us to lay out *at the very foot of the buildings* an uninterrupted series of playgrounds. A worker comes home, he puts on his gym suit, facing his home he finds his team or his instructor; his wife and children do as much. Soccer fields, tennis and basketball courts, children's playgrounds follow each other on the boulevard between the setbacks of the garden dwelling units (97).

In the same way, the remaining 150 square meters have been added together for use as allotment gardens. A farmer manages a hundred or a thousand lots, plows them with a tractor, spreads fertilizer, proceeds to sprinkle automatically by opening a set of valves. And this vegetable gardening is productive. Workers will pick their pink radishes or carrots there, after having developed their muscles and lungs, and so, *infallibly*, their optimism (97a).

*
* *

What I call searching for the "dwelling unit at human scale" means forgetting all existing houses, all existing building codes, all habits or traditions. It is to study pitilessly the new conditions in which our existence goes on. It is to dare to analyze and to draw conclusions. It is to feel behind one the support of modern techniques, facing one the inevitable evolution of the building industry toward more intelligent methods. And it is to aspire to appease the hearts of machine age mankind, and not to pamper some romantics of "old roofs" who, while fiddling away and without even noticing them, would witness the breakdown of a people, the discouragement of the city, the lethargy of a country.

THE UNDERTAKING

OF FURNITURE

The renewal of the plan of the modern house cannot be under-taken efficiently without laying bare the question of furniture. This is the Gordian knot. It must be cut; if not, all efforts at modernism are vain. We must "put the helm hard over": a machine age has succeeded a premachine age; a new spirit has replaced the old.

Let us try one day, in a house—in our own homes for instance—to examine our surroundings and to ask ourselves the questions "how" and "why"; to insist on knowing *what these mean.*

We shall find ourselves in general really *facing a most bewil-dering nonsense.*

If we consent to undertake a timely meditation, we shall come out transformed, cleaned out, and—evidently—quite decided to throw off the yoke, quite decided to efface so much evidence of the ridiculous adventure we have been made to undergo. We shall be overwhelmed, we shall ask ourselves: "How has this been possible? How could this have happened here *without my realizing it?* After all I am not crazy, etc., etc."

Very moved, we shall feel ready to act. . . .

But no! We shall fall quietly under the spell of normal life, by the pressure of opinion, throttled by the all-powerful brake of custom. It is not for nothing that we are part of a codified society: we are governed by the thinking of others. To react? To act alone, in accordance with the honest impulses of one's mind and one's heart, that is a serious matter. It requires certain conditions to be able to do so.

Listen: *a new period has begun, animated by a new spirit.*

The hour is favorable. Clean away. On this void let us build something new, animated by a new spirit.

Today, we see clearly!

*
* *

What is this talk about? About *our furniture, our knickknacks, our works of art.*

Custom, fashion, and a hundred years of bourgeois life have falsified assumptions. We are in a compromising and compromised situation. Academism still!

New joys await us, real spiritual joys. Let us take back our free will. Let us create a home that will interest and excite men as well as women.

*
* *

Women have preceded us. They have carried out the reform of their clothing. They found themselves at a dead end: to follow fashion was to give up the advantages of modern techniques, of modern life. Renounce sports, and, an even more material problem, be unable to take on the jobs that have made women a fertile part of contemporary production and allowed them to *earn their living.* To follow fashion: they couldn't have anything to do with cars, they couldn't take the metro or a bus, nor move lively in an office or store. To carry out the daily *construction* of a "toilette," hairdo, boots, buttoning a dress, they would not have had time to sleep.

So women cut their hair and their skirts and their sleeves. They went off bareheaded, arms naked, legs free. And get dressed in five minutes. And they are beautiful; they lure us with the charm of their graces of which the designers have accepted taking advantage.

The courage, the liveliness, the spirit of invention with which women have operated the revolution in clothing are a miracle of modern times. Thank you!

We men? a sad question! In dress clothes, we wear starched collars and resemble the generals of the Grande Armée. In street clothes, we are not at ease. We need to carry an arsenal of papers and small tools on us. The pocket, pockets, should be the keystone of modern clothing. Try to carry everything you need: you've destroyed the line of your costume; you are no longer "correct." One must choose between working and being elegant.

The English suit we wear had nevertheless succeeded in something important. It had *neutralized* us. In town it is useful to have a neutral appearance. The important sign is no longer in the ostrich feathers of a hat, it is in the eyes. That's enough. Monsieur Waleffe in Paris, disgusted by the English, preached a gigantic crusade: silk breeches and stockings, shoes with buckles and garters, "French" elegance, Latin genius! And samples of all sorts of calves! It failed; everyone laughed.

At Saint-Moritz on the snow, modern man is up-to-date. At Levallois-Perret, at the headquarters of the automobile industry, the mechanic is a forerunner. We office workers are beaten by a serious length by women.

Thus, the spirit of reform has only just appeared. It remains for it to influence all the acts of life.

* *
* *

What then is furniture?

"The means by which we make our social status known." That is, very precisely, the mentality of kings: Louis XIV did it brilliantly. Would we want to be Louis XIVs? That would make a lot of him. If there are millions of Louis XIVs on the earth, there is no longer one Sun King.

Seriously, do we really want to be Sun Kings?

Furniture is

> tables for working at and eating
> chairs for eating and working
> armchairs of different shapes for resting in different ways
> and *cabinets* for storing the objects we use.

Furniture is tools,

And also servants.

Furniture serves our needs.

Our needs are daily, regular, always the same; yes, always the same.

Our furniture corresponds to *constant, daily, regular functions*.

All men have the same needs, at the same hours, every day, all their lives.

The tools corresponding to these functions are easy to define. And progess, bringing us new techniques, steel tubing, folded sheet metal, welding, gives us the means to carry them out infinitely more perfectly and more efficiently than in the past.

House interiors will no longer resemble the Louis XIV style.

There is the adventure.

*
* *

Our needs are the needs of men. We all have the same limbs, in number, form, and size; if on this last point there are differences, an average dimension is easy to find.

Standard functions,

standard needs,

standard objects,

standard dimensions.

The question of *standards* has already made a lot of progress. It is as old as the world and has set the form of each of our civilizations. But the disrupting nineteenth century has passed here: Monsieur Homais. The question of modern standards has already progressed; we have neglected to notice it.

The whole world has agreed on the form and dimensions of letter paper. The industry of office furniture is based on the *format of letter paper.*

The spirit of the machine age has searched ingeniously. What was done for automobiles has been done for office furniture. A revolution was produced; cabinetmakers' shops were closed, and in other parts of town the steel furniture industry was created.

Precision, efficiency, purity of forms and lines have developed.

Ask a banker if he is not proud of his office furniture?

*
* *

He is very proud of it.

When he gets home, he is welcomed by a load of curios capable of exploding the manometer of reason, if one could fix a manometer of thoughts on our skulls. Here, at home, he no longer works, he doesn't produce; he can lose, waste his time, trouble his spirit, wear it out, lie to it. It is of no importance; he is resting, he has no competitors . . . unless some Louis XIV among his friends who would willingly call himself Louis XV if that could give him a higher rating on the scale of ostentation.

*
* *

I draw a plan of furniture and a section through a traditional bedroom (98). The big Normandy wardrobe, the period chest of drawers offer only mediocre storage space. Time lost by the user and space taken up in the room; big pieces of furniture, understandable at the time of castles or in the rooms of country houses, are a disaster in the modern dwelling.

Now I draw a modern arrangement in plan and section: windows, partitions, and built-in storage. I have saved a considerable

98

99

99 casiers/cabinets

amount of space; one can move around easily; gestures are rapid and exact; storage automatic. These are *minutes gained, every day;* precious minutes (99).

I shall declare that in addition to seats and tables, furniture is mainly cabinetwork. But most of the time these cabinets are poorly dimensioned and hard to use; here I denounce wastefulness. I shall push the enemy into his retreat, search what this furniture is really for. I shall acquire the certainty that with the new industries of wood and metal, one can build precise cabinets that work admirably, whose dimensions are not approximate but sure, and I shall be led to conclude that the furniture of cabinetmakers and merchants serves us very badly, that these are cumbersome leftovers, contrary to economical and efficient solutions since they force us to build houses that are too big and since they complicate our existence by preventing the rational organization of households. Finally they have *only an aesthetic purpose.* But if a useful object no longer has a function, if it has only an aesthetic interest, it has become a parasite and is thrown out. We shall see where to find an aesthetic form that will suit us; we shall seek to see what can gratify the heart, the sensitivity of modern men.

Let us be frank:

I draw a shelf with glasses on it; a shelf with plates, soup plates, etc.; a shelf with bottles, pitchers, etc. Drawers with automatic storage of silverware. Here the chapter of instruments for eating is closed (100).

I draw a shelf with linens, sheets, towels, etc., a shelf with underwear, drawers with lingerie, stockings, etc.

I draw a shelf with shoes, a shelf with hats.

I draw clothing hung on a clothes hook; a dress (101).

That's all.

The inventory of objects we use is complete.

These objects are in proportion to our limbs, are adapted to our gestures. They have a *common scale,* they fit into a module. If I study the question, and for twenty years I have been obsessed by the anomaly of furniture (I earned my living in the past furnishing a lot of apartments), I find a common dimension. I find the cabinet that contains these objects efficiently.

I draw this cabinet (102). It is 75 centimeters wide and 37.5 to 50 centimeters deep, or 150 by 75 in front and 37.5 to 75 deep.

100

101

c'est tout/that's all

The variation of the dimension in depth comes from the different ways of arranging the inside of this cabinet.

In 1913, having to design demountable material for a traveling exhibit of decorative art (and decorative art meant everything from the pots and pans in the pantry to the salon and the boudoir), I found this module of 75 centimeters and 150. Then I forgot it completely.

When we were preparing our Esprit Nouveau Pavilion in 1924—where we wanted to demonstrate at the same time the principle of functionalism in furniture and the aesthetic purpose of a dwelling—after a close analysis we again found these dimensions.

In 1925 the Esprit Nouveau Pavilion seemed to throw light—which at the time was found brutal—on this question.

Finally, in 1928, our associate for the interior equipment of dwellings, Madame Charlotte Perriand, also concluded with the same dimensions. While I am speaking to you here in Buenos Aires, we are having a big stand at the Salon d'Automne in Paris showing in an unanswerable manner the principle of the "equipment of the modern dwelling" with standard cabinets.

This said, there is a constructive conclusion, architectural, economic, industrial: it would be timely to create such cabinets industrially, *containers*, mass produced, to be sold to private clients who install their houses or to architects who draw plans. The first would place these cabinets against the walls of their bedrooms or make them up into high or low partitions (see the Esprit Nouveau Pavilion, 1925); the other would build walls and set the cabinets into the masonry.

We still have to equip the inside of these cabinets. This equipment can vary from the simplest of current office furniture to the greatest refinement. As it would come to be placed, after construction, within standard containers, it could be sold in the Bazar de l'Hotel de Ville or on the Champs-Elysées (103).

When the house is finished, at the moment when the painters do the last coat, the evening before the inhabitants bring their books and trunks, one could put into the cabinets the equipment appropriate to the functions to be satisfied; one would install the doors of the cabinets: sliding panels in sheet metal, in plywood, in marble, in plate glass, in aluminum, etc.; a taste for simplicity or opulence would be free to show itself.

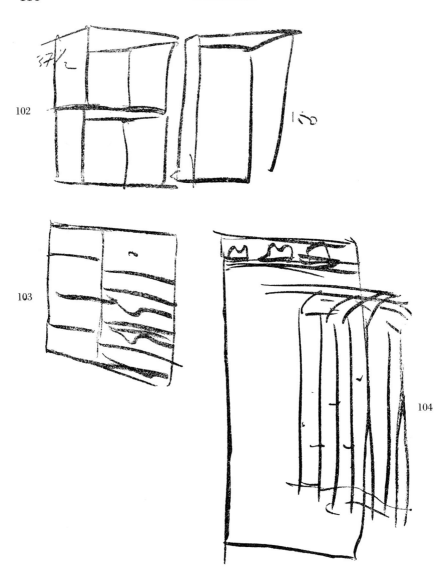

102

103

104

And if the house is prefabricated, you can realize how easy the manipulation becomes.

Try to imagine the new dwelling. Each room is reduced to its *adequate* size and receives a perfect quantity of light (either by a ribbon window or a window wall). Its shape is suited to its purpose; the doors open so that it is easy to get around. At hand in the bedroom, in the library, in the living room, the pantry, the kitchen, blinds go up or down, screens slide. Behind them compartments appear, suited to what they are to contain. Every object is stored as in a jewel case; some equipment comes forward on ball bearings, your clothing is spread out before your eyes, etc. (104).

And thus, there is no more cabinetmakers' furniture in the house! I am sorry to think of all those good craftsmen, but I think one should adapt oneself to the new conditions of modern life.

The reduction of furniture to the state of cabinets making up the wall itself can also be obtained by rudimentary methods of reinforced concrete construction:

I draw the ceiling and the floor of one story; I divide the height in four, for instance, by means of three slabs of reinforced concrete, several centimeters thick, going from one wall to another or stopping halfway. I close one side or the other of my shelves with masonry, depending on needs. A small steel U-shaped track above and below each shelf takes sliding doors in sheet metal, in aluminum, in plate glass, in wood, or in marble. Here you have magnificent closet partitions to be equipped with the same materials described above (105, 106).

In this second drawing, you see the big closed bookcase of a luxurious villa built with supreme economy and whose architectural aspect is, I assure you, imposing and . . . beneficent (107). Here our spirit is free of the hodgepodge of furniture. We are now ready to bring into our home, in the exceptional conditions of architectural calmness, the work of art that will make us think or meditate.

These methods allowed us to install the model offices of the Centrosoyuz (Moscow Cooperatives Office Building). The wall separating the offices from the corridors is designed this way: from one end of the building to the other, the back of each office is a model of storage design. Such also had been the solution planned in the competition for the League of Nations office building in Geneva (108).

Office or living room, pantry or boudoir, always and everywhere, standard and precise functions are accomplished and satisfied; objects put in order at human dimensions, with common sizes. Farewell, the chests of yesteryear!

What will the chambers of commerce of furniture and antiques think, who mass-produce Louis XVI pieces "with nail holes" and "period patina"! (See chapter V, "A Hurricane," in *Decorative Art of Today*, published by Crès et Cie., Collection de l'Esprit Nouveau.)

*
* *

Tables?

I shall explain myself by this simple proposal; why shouldn't we distribute a certain number of tables in our apartments (two or three combinable formats), of different materials if one likes. Their construction in welded steel tubes makes it possible to attach the top with an automatic clamping system. You have a lot of guests? Quick, you bring together a few tables; the tops go through doors vertically; the steel tube frame is raised to go through vertically as well. Everything is easy (109). Who forces you to have a dining room?

*
* *

Seats?

We shall make another shocking announcement: *seats are used for resting.*

I shall not talk about the "style" in which—if it is not according to which—one wants to rest!

On the other hand I notice that, depending on the time of day, depending on one's activities, depending on the position one takes in a living room (and which we change four or five times in an evening), there are many ways to be seated. One sits "actively" to work. Chairs are an instrument of torture that keep you awake admirably. I need a chair when I work.

I sit down to talk: a certain armchair gives me a decent, polite

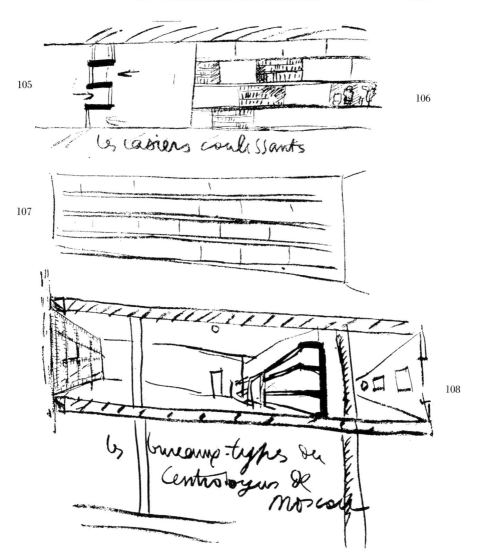

105, 106 les casiers coulissants/cabinets with sliding doors // **108** les bureaux-types du Centrosoyus de Moscou/typical offices of the Centrosoyuz in Moscow

manner. I sit down "actively" to hold forth, to prove a hypothesis, to propose a way of seeing: how this high stool is suitable to my attitude! I sit optimistic, relaxed; this Turkish stool of the *cavedjis* of Istanbul, 35 centimeters high and 30 centimeters in diameter, is a marvel; I could stay there for hours without tiring, *sitting on my behind.* And if we are fifteen in a little house, come determined to do nothing, our hostess has taken fifteen stools nesting in each other out of a closet. I tend to a more total relaxation *kief*; I remember that Noel, the head of the body section at Voisin Automobiles, equipped his 14-horsepower sport with a spring cushion set on the floor; and on it I do five hundred kilometers without a stop, without tiring; I remember it when I furnish my living room (110). But here is the machine for resting. We built it with bicycle tubes and covered it with a magnificent pony skin; it is light enough to be pushed by foot, can be manipulated by a child; I thought of the western cowboy smoking his pipe, his feet up above his head, leaning against a fireplace: complete restfulness (110a). Our chaise longue takes all positions, my weight alone is enough to keep it in the chosen position; no mechanism. It is the true machine for resting, etc., etc.

Modern woman has cut her hair. Our eyes have learned the form of her legs. The corset is out. "Etiquette" is out. Etiquette was born at the court. Only certain persons had the right to sit, and only in a certain way. Then, in the nineteenth century, the bourgeois became king and ordered for himself armchairs infinitely more sculptured and gilded than had the royal princes before. "Good manners" were taught in the convents. Well, today, all that bores us. A distinguished person never loses his distinction, even during Carnaval. Here we are now reassured!

And especially, here we are being better seated!

And the house has been emptied of its furniture.

Space and light abound.

One moves, one acts, rapidly.

And perhaps we shall have the pleasure of thinking about something, during that hour of rest, that hour of relaxation, at home?

That is the root of the matter; *to think of something.*

Of the harmony of proportions,

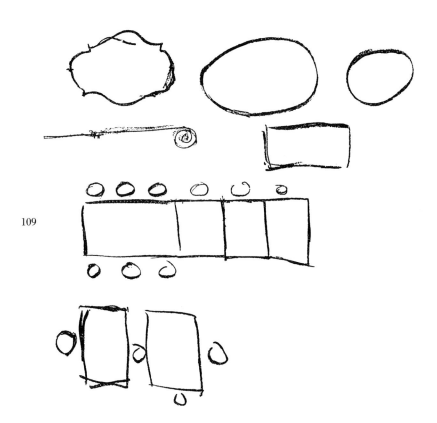

109

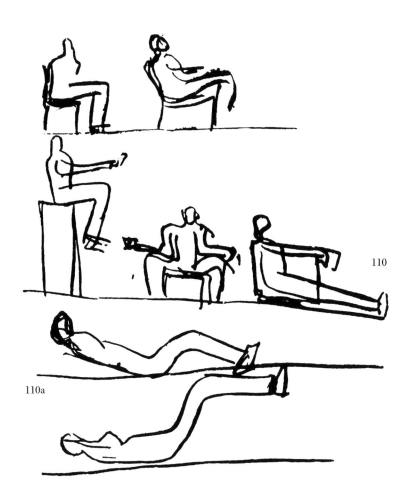

or of some poem on machinery, on the life of peoples ancient
or modern, even of a poem in verse,
　　or some music,
　　or a sculpture, a painting,
　　a graph,
　　or a photo of a simple or a sublime phenomenon, usual or
exceptional.
　　Life is full of opportunities to collect things that are *subjects*
for thought:
　　this pebble from the seashore
　　this admirable pinecone,
　　these butterflies, these beetles,
　　this polished steel part taken from a machine,
　　or this piece of ore.
　　The gods? It is our spirit that shapes them from the things of
the Earth.

* *
* *

The adventure? Oh yes, the adventure of furniture. Events are
unfolding, *the notion of furniture has disappeared. It is replaced
by a new term: "household equipment."*[1]

---

1. See *Cahiers d'Art*, 1926, no. 3.

Fifth lecture
Friday, October 11, 1929
Friends of the Arts

THE PLAN
OF THE
MODERN HOUSE

     We are now tooled to find solutions for the plan of the modern house, if we want to look for them.

     Let me remind you of the "paralyzed plan" of the masonry house and what we arrived at with the steel or concrete one:

> the free plan
> the free facade
> the independent structure
> ribbon windows or window walls
> pilotis
> roof gardens
> and the interior furnished with cabinets and
> rid of the congestion of furniture.

*
* *

A little biology to begin with:

> this skeleton *for carrying*

this muscular filling *for action*
these viscera *to feed and to operate* (111).

A little automobile construction:

a frame
a body
a motor with its organs of feeding and evacuation (112).

Please note, in this last case, with what flexibility the electric cables, the gasoline pipes, the exhaust pipe go around the rigid organs—the motor, the frame, the body, etc.

And in this sketch, in the upper corner, the rigidity of the elements of a masonry house, all slavishly superposed from floor to floor (113), and, next to them, the flexibility of the modern house with its independent structure, its free interior plan independent from floor to floor (114).

*
* *

How to take advantage of these new freedoms?
In favor of *economy*,

of *efficiency*,
of resolving *numerous modern functions*,
of *beauty*.

The *architectural revolution*—for it is a real revolution—implies different acts:

1) *to classify*
2) *to dimension*
3) *to circulate*
4) *to compose*
5) *to proportion*.

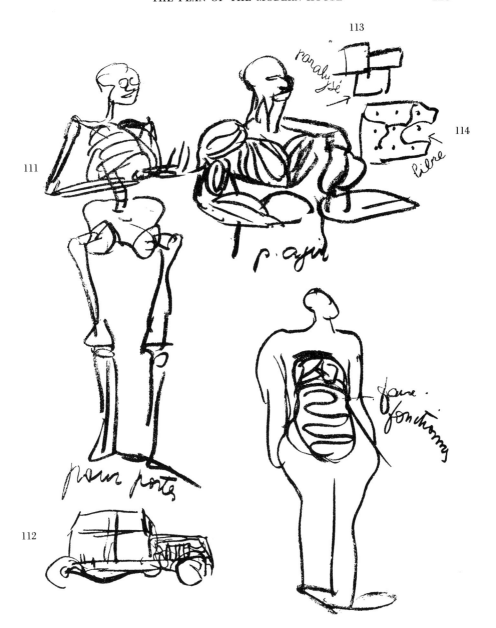

111 pour porter/to support // p. agir/to act // pour fonctionner/to operate // 113 para-
lysé/paralyzed // 114 libre/free

I   TO CLASSIFY

Two independent factors are present, simultaneous, synchronous, inseparable, indissoluble:

a) a biological phenomenon
b) an aesthetic phenomenon.

The biological is the end proposed, the problem stated, the fundamental function of the undertaking.

The aesthetic is the physiological sensation, an "impression," a pressure by the senses, a compulsion.

The biological affects our common sense.

The aesthetic affects our sensitivity and our reason.

The two united in simultaneous perceptions produce the architectural *emotion*—good or bad.

One must therefore recognize the *organs* of the house, list them, classify them;

one must determine the useful contiguities, unfold successive operations in their normal order.

And for each purpose, say to oneself:

> heating: what is it?
> ventilation or airing: what is it?
> daylighting: what is it?
> artificial lighting: what is it?
> vertical connections, elevators, ramps, stairways, ladders; horizontal connections (circulation): what are they?

A cold-blooded examination of these questions can give solutions that will make a revolution in the building industry.

A revolution? Yes, for in current practice, successive inventions have produced innumerable new objects, and no thought has been given to the subject, everything has accumulated in disorder, in confusion, and this confusion *has led us simply to wastefulness.* (An example among hundreds: if I discovered the possibility of living with three-fortieths of a servant, do I not also have the right to want to heat myself with a tenth or a hundredth of a furnace?)

II   TO DIMENSION

I am speaking of the dimensions of rooms in dwellings.

Until now the question has been taken up superficially, since masonry construction, depending on the superposing of rooms from floor to floor, prevented all innovation, contradicted that effort of research into economizing of which we have made a fundamental basis.

Today we can, as we like, introduce the greatest variety of rooms in a house without concern for superposing floors; I have demonstrated it.

Now then, let us analyze these dimensions, let us calculate them in detail. An operation of rationalization similar to dealing out space in modern factories. A toilet would not have more than 8 square meters and a bedroom would no longer have the same form and surface as a dining room for the simple reason—quite unreasonable—that it is just above it.

With my charcoal and my chalks I describe the series of reasoned actions that presided at the construction of a tiny little house on the edge of Lake Leman.

I knew that the region where we wanted to build included 10 to 15 kilometers of hills along the lake. A fixed point: the lake; another, the magnificent view facing it; another, the south, also facing it (115).

Should one first have searched for the site and made the plan in accordance with it? That is the usual practice.

I thought it was better to make an exact plan, corresponding ideally to the use one hoped from it and determined by the three factors above. This done, to go out with the plan in hand to look for a suitable site.

Notice, in this apparently contradictory procedure, the key to the problem of modern living. To plan a dwelling in accordance with the logic of reasonable functions. Then to place one's building; I showed you before that the new elements of modern architecture made it possible to adapt to a site whatever the circumstances.

We calculated thus (116):

entrance	3 square meters
toilet	1
dining room	9
living room	12
guest room, small sitting room	9
bedroom	9
bathroom	3
wardrobe	3
kitchen	4
laundry	4

Total .... 57 square meters

III   TO CIRCULATE

It is an important modern word. In architecture and city planning, circulation is everything.

What is a house for?

One enters,

one carries on methodical functions.

Workers' houses, villas, townhouses, the League of Nations building, the Centrosoyuz of Moscow, the World City, the plan of Paris, *circulation is everything.*

One can line up the functional elements of a house in a circuit, these being dimensioned and the indispensable contiguities determined.

I draw (117):

An entrance; it opens on the left onto the reception area, on the right onto the services.

The dining room and living room are combined; nevertheless a sideboard (in concrete) forms a spine to separate them.

The small sitting room, transformable immediately into a guest room with beds coming out of the floor, a closet hidden by a sliding panel, and a washbowl built frankly outside the volume of the house.

A circulation is created between the entrance and the garden

115

116

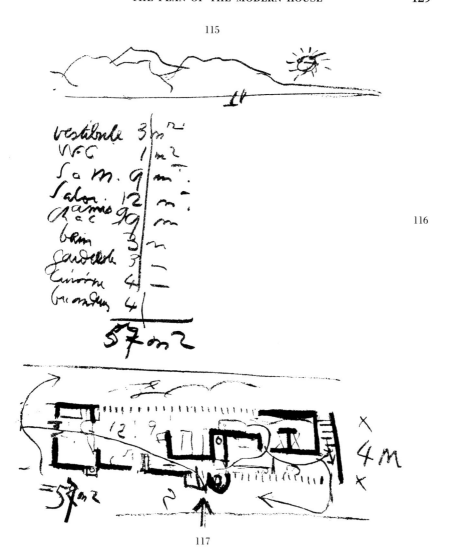

117

116 vestibule/entrance // w.c./toilet // s a m/dining room // salon/living room // ch amis/
guest room, small sitting room // ch a c/bedroom // bain/bathroom // garde-robe/wardrobe //
cuisine/kitchen // buanderie/laundry

to the left, which is surrounded by walls and used as a summer living room.

To the right of the dining area, the sleeping space is near the bath and the toilet.

One single window 11 meters long unites and lights all the elements, making the majesty of the magnificent site enter into the house: the lake with its movement, the Alps with their miraculous light.

To the right of the entrance the kitchen and the laundry, the stairs to the cellar and the service door to the paved courtyard; then, on the other hand, the connection with the bedroom through the dressing room, a second "service" circulation.

The doors are either 75 or 55 centimeters wide. The house is 4 meters deep. Inside, this house of 57 square meters offers a perspective of 14 meters! The 11-meter-long window introduces the immensity of the outdoors, the unfalsifiable unity of a lakeside landscape with its storms or radiant calms.

There is really not a square centimeter lost here; and that's not a small job!

Beauty? But this is the very characteristic of the intention that determined all these operations.

The plan in my pocket, I went off to look for a site. I discovered a little ribbon of shore so small that I should never have thought of buying it, if I had not had in my pocket the certitude that its dimensions were adequate.

Let us go on now to another example of modern circulation inside a house. This scheme corresponds to a particular way of life: I draw only the plan of the bedroom floor (118).

Monsieur will have his *cell*, Madame also, Mademoiselle also. Each of these cells has floors and ceilings carried by freestanding independent columns. Each cell opens by a door on a walkway along the three apartments. Once through each door one is in a complete unit made up of an entrance, a dressing room (storage of underwear, linens, and clothing), an exercise room, a boudoir or office, a bathroom, and finally the bed. Low or ceiling-height partitions, built from cabinets or not, subdivide the space, letting the ceilings through. Everyone lives as if in his own small house.

I also show how with curved partitions (119), easy to build, one obtains two bedrooms with their bath in a space that would normally have allowed only one traditional room.

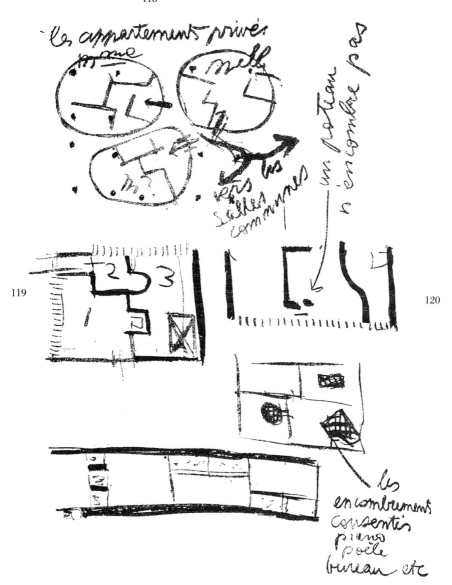

118 les appartements privés/private spaces // Mme/Madame // Mlle/Mademoiselle // M/ Monsieur // vers les salles communes/toward common rooms // **120** un poteau n'encombre pas/a column does not encumber // les encombrements consentis piano poêle bureau etc/ accepted encumbrances, piano, stove, desk, etc.

Again, I show the sort of curved partitions we call "grand piano" giving three bedrooms where normally one would have found only two (120).

It would be easy to multiply these examples, which are prompted by daily problems if one acquires the habit of strolling with one's pencil, step by step, thinking out well the functions by which our occupant will find pleasure in living in his house.

IV   TO COMPOSE

Let us take into consideration the personal qualities of the architect.

It is good to persuade oneself of the existence of certain things, among others this one that is of capital importance and of which I have already spoken:

I draw a personage (121). I have him enter a house; he discovers a certain dimension, a certain shape of room, or a certain arrival of light through a window or window wall. He goes on: another volume, another entrance of light. Further on, another source of light; still further, a flood of light and half-shade just beside it, etc.

These successive volumes lit differently, *one breathes them in:* breathing is activated by them.

I have always liked to cite the section of the Green Mosque of Brousse, which is a masterpiece of rhythm by its volumes and its lighting (122).

As you can imagine, I use light freely; light for me is the fundamental basis of architecture. *I compose with light.*

But some are worried. These vast inpourings of light and especially these window walls arouse murmurs in Buenos Aires, in Rio, wherever, they say, the sun is so strong. (On heating or cooling, I have already explained myself.) When you buy a camera, you are determined to be able to take views in the twilight of Paris or the sparkling sands of an oasis; how do you manage? *You use a diaphragm.* Your window walls, your horizontal windows are all ready to be diaphragmed at will. You will let light in wherever you like. Your window wall will be made of transparent glass, or special glass (which we studied with the laboratories of Saint-Gobain)

mosquée verte/Green Mosque

that will have the insulating value of a thick wall and will stop the sun's rays; or finally, wire-reinforced glass, translucent glass, or glass bricks. Window walls, diaphragms, are new terms in the language of architecture.

V   TO PROPORTION

Everything is geometrical to our eyes (biology exists only as organization, and this is something that the mind understands only after study). *Architectural composition is geometric*, an event primarily of a *visual* nature; an event implying judgments of quantities, of relationships; the appreciation of *proportions*. Proportions provoke sensations; a series of sensations is like the melody in music. Erik Satie used to say: the melody is the idea, harmony (in music) is the means, the tool, the presentation of the idea.

The architectural *idea* is strictly an individual phenomenon, inalienable. It is good to push an idea to a state of purity; I have explained the reason for the regulating diagrams. I have also said that simplicity is derived from richness, from abundance, by choice, by selection, by concentration.

Each of us gives a personal expression to an idea: individual poetry. Each one has the right to observe himself, to judge himself, to know himself, and to act with clear-sightedness. We, Pierre Jeanneret and I, have built quite a lot of houses. Studying our own production, I manage to discern the general intention that determined the tendency of our work. With similar methods of *classification*, of *dimensioning*, of *circulation*, of *composition*, of *proportioning*, up to now we have worked on four distinct types of plans, each expressing characteristic intellectual preoccupations.

The first type shows each organ rising up next to its neighbor, in accordance with an organic reasoning: "the inside takes its ease, and pushes out to form diverse projections." This principle leads to a "pyramidal" composition, which can become busy if one doesn't watch out (Auteuil; 123).

The second type shows the compression of organs within a rigid envelope, absolutely pure. A difficult problem, perhaps a spiritual delight; spending spiritual energy within self-imposed limitations (Garches; 124).

The third types furnishes, with a visible framework (skeleton structure), a simple envelope, clear, transparent as a network; it allows the creation of useful volumes of rooms different on each floor in form and quantity. An ingenious type appropriate to certain climates; such compositions are easy, full of possibilities (Tunis; 125).

The fourth type attains, on the outside, the pure form of the second type; inside, it has the advantages, the characteristics of the first and the third. A very pure type, very ample, also full of possibilities (Poissy; 126).

It is not useless, I repeat, to read constantly in one's own work. The consciousness of events is the springboard of progress.

*
* *

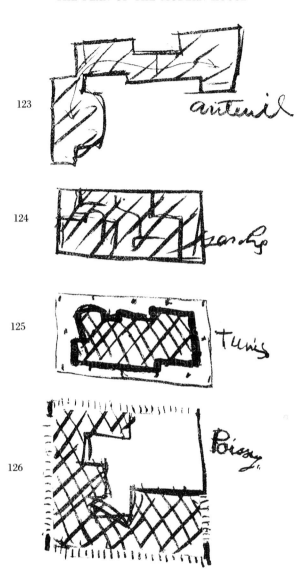

123 Auteuil // 124 Garches // 125 Tunis // 126 Poissy

To conclude, let us analyze that construction going up in Poissy, near Paris.

The visitors, till now, turn round and round inside, asking themselves what is happening, understanding with difficulty the reasons for what they see and feel; they don't find anything of what is called a "house." They feel themselves within something entirely new. And . . . they are not bored, I believe!

The site: a big lawn, slightly convex. The main view is to the north, therefore opposite to the sun; the front of the house would usually be inverted (127).

The house is a box raised above the ground, perforated all around, without interruption, by a long horizontal window. No more hesitation about architectural plays of voids and solids. The box is in the center of fields, overlooking orchards (128).

Under the box, going through the pilotis, a carriageway arrives turning in a hairpin whose curve encloses, exactly under the pilotis, the door to the house, the entrance, the garage, the services (laundry, linen room, servants' quarters). Automobiles drive up under the house, park or drive off (129).

From inside the entrance, a ramp leads easily, hardly noticed, up to the first floor, where the life of the inhabitants goes on: reception, bedrooms, etc. Receiving views and light from around the periphery of the box, the different rooms center on a hanging garden that is there like a distributor of adequate light and sunshine.

It is on the hanging garden that the sliding plate glass walls of the salon and other rooms of the house open freely: thus the sun is everywhere, in the very heart of the house (130).

From the hanging garden, the ramp, now on the outside, leads to the solarium on the roof (131).

This is connected by a spiral staircase three stories high down to the cellar dug out in the earth under the pilotis. This spiral, a pure vertical organ, is inserted freely into the horizontal composition.

To finish, look at the section (132): air circulates everywhere, there is light at every point, it penetrates everywhere. Circulation furnishes architectural impressions of such diversity that they disconcert visitors ignorant of the architectural liberties brought by modern techniques. The simple columns of the ground floor, by

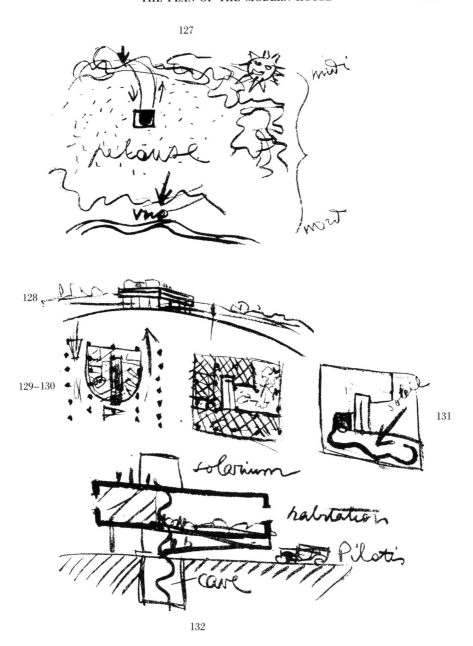

127 pelouse/lawn // vue/view // midi/south // nord/north // soleil/sun // **132** solarium/solarium // habitation/dwelling // pilotis/pilotis // cave/cellar

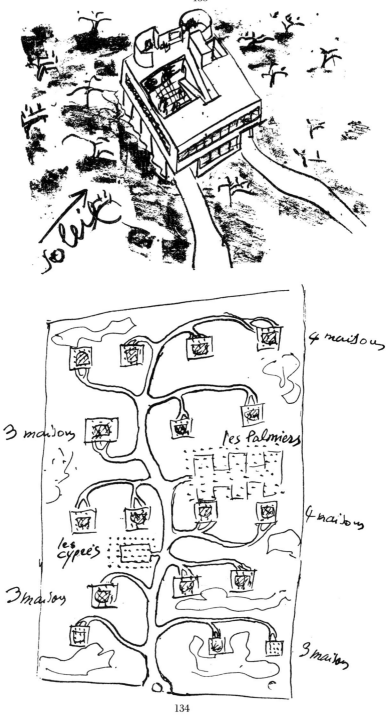

133

134

133 soleil/sun // **134** 4 maisons/4 houses // 3 maisons/3 houses // les palmiers/palm trees // les cyprès/cypresses

their suitable plan, frame the landscape with a regularity that suppresses all notions of "front" or "back" or "side" of the house.

The plan is pure, made exactly in accordance with needs. It is in its right place in the rural landscape of Poissy (133).

But in Biarritz, it would be magnificent. If the view is elsewhere, on another side, if the orientation is different, the hanging garden would simply be turned around.

This same house, I should set it down in a corner of the beautiful Argentine countryside; we shall have twenty houses rising from the high grass of an orchard where cows continue to graze. Instead of laying them out along the customary detestable garden-city streets, which result in destroying a site, we shall build a handsome traffic system, poured in concrete, into the grass itself, in full nature. Grass will grow along the edge of the roads, nothing will be disturbed, neither trees nor flowers nor herds. The inhabitants, who came here because this countryside with its *rural life* was beautiful, will contemplate it, maintained intact, from their hanging gardens, or through the four sides of the long windows. Their home life will be set in a Virgilian dream (134).

You won't hold it against me, I hope, that I have gone at length before your eyes into this example of *liberties taken*. They have been taken because they were *acquired*, torn out of the live resources of modern materials. Poetry, lyricism, brought by techniques.

Sixth lecture
Monday, October 14, 1929
Friends of the City

A MAN =

A DWELLING

DWELLINGS =

A CITY

A CONTEMPORARY CITY
OF THREE MILLION INHABITANTS
IS BUENOS AIRES A MODERN CITY?

The moment has come to explain the "law of the meander." Big cities are in an inextricable situation. Mechanization has precipitated them into it. The sharp violent hour of crisis is everywhere. A thousand and one *small* solutions are proposed that would make everything worse; besides, they are so expensive they cannot be undertaken. Nevertheless, a miracle can happen. The

disturber itself offers the *continuity* of the phenomenon and its
solution; every obstacle is dissolved and diluted, and, flexibly, the
solution appears, simple and efficient. Miracle? Not even that!
The disturber, mechanization, gives us elements of construction
or reconstruction. The abscess is pierced, the way is clear straight
ahead. It is the lesson of the meander, victory over oneself, a
consoling lesson. Here is the *"law of the meander"*:

I draw a river (135). The goal is precise: to get from one
point to another: river or idea. A slight incident takes place, the

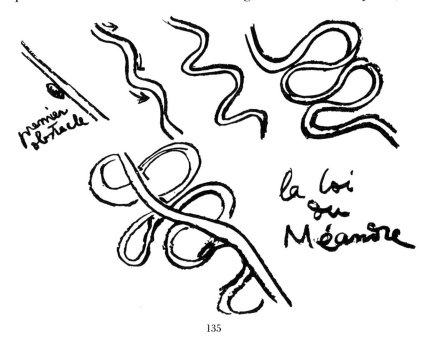

135

premier obstacle/first obstacle // la loi du méandre/the law of the meander

incidents of the spirit: immediately, a small slight bend, hardly
noticeable. The water is thrown to the left, it digs into the bank;
from there, by reaction, it is thrown back to the right. Then the
straight line disappears. To the left, to the right, always deeper,
the water bites, hollows, cuts away; always wider, the idea seeks
its way. The straight line has become sinuous; the idea has acquired incidents. The sinuousness becomes characteristic, the

meander appears; the idea is ramified. Soon, the solution has become frightfully complicated, it is a paradox. The machine works, but it is slow and its mechanism has become delicate and awkward. The objective is respected: one moves toward the goal, but on what a path!

The loops of the meander have made something like figure eights, and that's stupid. Suddenly, at the most desperate moment, there they are touching at the outermost point of their curves! Miracle! The river runs straight! Thus a pure idea has burst forth, a solution has appeared. A new stage begins. Life will be good and normal again . . . for a short time only. But lengths of old meanders remain, inert, unused, marshy, stagnant: bushes invade their banks. Social, mental, mechanical organisms remain that are parasitic, anachronic, paralyzing.

Thus ideas follow the law of the meander. Moments of "simplicity" are the unknotting of acute and critical crises of complication.

*
* *

The cities, the big cities of the world are growing without a doctrine. I have already defined the temporal basis of a doctrine (and I mean by that a sufficient period, which may be that of a generation, say twenty years). To know where one is going, because one knows where one has been.

The planning practiced today is rather aesthetic—beautifying, gardening. It is "playing at sand piles" while the house burns.

I replace the word "urbanism" by the term "equipment." I have already replaced the term "furniture" by that of "equipment." Such stubbornness shows well that we are purely and simply claiming tools for work, for we do not want to die of hunger facing the embroidered flowerbeds of aesthetic urbanism.

*
* *

We do not know where to go because we do not know where we have been. We need a diagnosis and a line of conduct.

In 1922 I tried to delve into an analysis, I did some laboratory work. Isolating my microbe, I watched it develop. The biology of my microbe appeared in indisputable clarity. Certitudes acquired; diagnosis. Then, by an effort of synthesis, I drew up the fundamental principles of modern city planning. This was our big exhibit on city planning at the Salon d'Automne with the diorama of a "Contemporary City of Three Million Inhabitants."

In 1924–25 I published the book *Urbanisme* in the Esprit Nouveau Collection at the moment when our city-planning rotunda of the Esprit Nouveau Pavilion at the International Decorative Arts Fair brought analytical studies of the dwelling of modern man, and of the grouping of these dwelling units into a city neighborhood. This exhibit repeated the diorama of 1922 and presented the Voisin Plan for Paris, accompanied by a big diorama showing the entire city with its new business *center*. After analysis, after diagnosis, after the work "in the moon," it was finally a formal application to a concrete case: Paris. In 1928, the Redressement Français published a proposition of program for a planning commission, with the title: *Toward the Paris of the Machine Age.*[1]

So much attention applied to planning would seem to give me the right to address you on this throbbing theme: contemporary cities.

*
* *

Around a river (136), with a few concentric lines of charcoal, I make you witness the foundation of the first small town, the market town, the city, its fortified walls, the suburbs with the second city wall, the third, the fourth, etc. We have gone from the time of the Romans to modern times. And we haven't moved from our center.

On the left, on the right, to the north, to the south, I show some abbeys founded in open country. The roads that connect them to the city have remained throughout the centuries; they

1. *Vers le Paris de l'époque machiniste*, by L. C. (Redressement Français, 28 rue de Madrid, Paris).

136

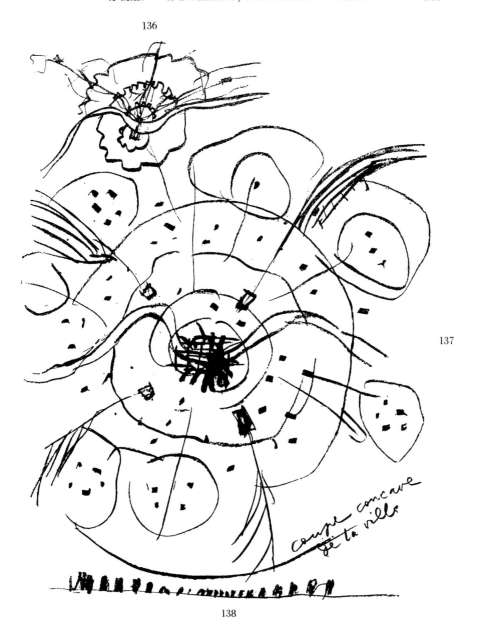

137

138

138 coupe concave de la ville/concave section of a city

have remained one of the essential arteries of the city. These country roads are today raised to the rank of a great urban artery!

Then, on the second drawing, I show the railway, the stations. And the suburbs and greater suburbs that the railway has created. The circumference of the city has become gigantic (137).

I wonder why this gigantic disk has developed? In yellow, I sow the powder of men spread all over; I see these yellow dots join the radial canals descending to the heart of the city; all that yellow powder accumulates there in the daytime. In the evening, it returns out there to its near and far suburbs. I note that there are two periods in the functions of a city: a concentration in the center; then a dispersion on the periphery. I also notice that the city is a gigantic wheel all of whose radial organs lead to the hub, from the four horizons, from all around the enormous surface governed by a *radial system*.

When, above, I draw the section of the city, I see that the tendency of centuries has been to widen the streets, to increase the volume of the buildings. And if I summarize this tendency by a scheme, I draw the profile of a city that is *concave:* rising at the edges and widely spaced, lower at the center and concentrated (138).

I try to read still more clearly. I express the state of facts by a new scheme: the circle formed by concentric rings closer and closer together is irrigated by rivers of circulation, which I draw in blue and which are wide at the periphery and narrow in the center. I express this state of concentration by a new scheme made up of concentric circles: at the center the circles nearly touch. I say, here is a *characteristic state of congestion* (139).

I classify historically by underlining: *the age of the horse, up to 1850*. And repeating my scheme, I express *the age of the railway*. I have drawn the stations (140).

What do the stations do? They pour crowds into the heart of the city. They *pour* crowds. Yes, for the historical rates of speed of mankind have changed; look! From the most ancient times, my line of speeds starts: it slides between the speed of men's footsteps and that of the horse; prehistory, the Romans, the Huns, the Crusaders in Palestine, the armies of the Thirty Years' War and those of Napoleon, walked at the rate of men or horses walking.[2]

---

2. If a Herculean novelist could narrate this to us!

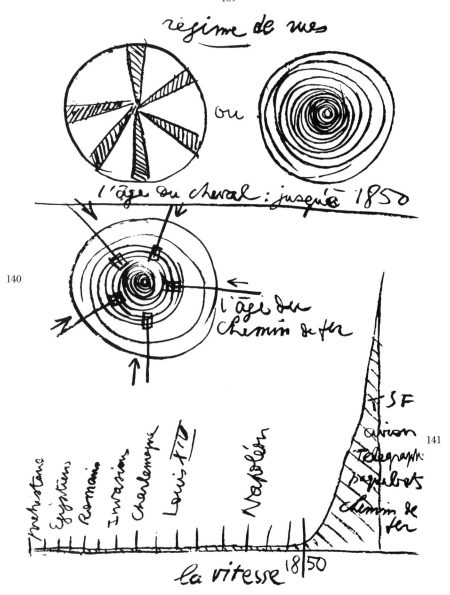

139 régime des rues/street network // ou/or // l'âge du cheval: jusqu'à 1850/the age of the horse, up to 1850 // **140** l'âge du chemin de fer/the age of the railway // **141** préhistoire, Égyptiens, Romains, Invasions, Charlemagne, Louis XIV, Napoléon/prehistory, Egyptians, Romans, invasions, Charlemagne, Louis XIV, Napoleon // TSF, avion, télégraphe, paquebots, chemin de fer/radio, plane, telegraph, ocean liners, railways // la vitesse/speed

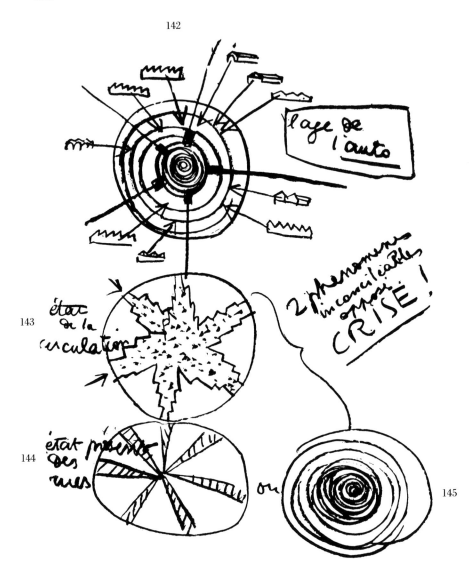

142 l'âge de l'auto/the age of the auto // **143** état de la circulation/existing circulation // 2 phénomènes inconciliables opposés. CRISE!/two irreconcilable opposing phenomena, crisis // **144** état présent des rues/present street network // **145** ou/or

I draw a vertical line, I write: 1850. Then, in eighty years, the curve goes up prodigiously, gigantically. I write: railroads, steamboats, airplanes, dirigibles, automobiles, telegraph, radio, telephone (141).

And again I draw the same circle of the *state of the city*. I place the stations. But I show the automobile factories in the sub-urbs; I send automobiles into the city, I write: *the age of the auto* (142).

And I still try to understand.

A circle; the red pencil draws the matter that is rapidly pre-cipitated into the city (143). It arrives from every side. Where to? Into the center. The scheme is meaningful. Below I repeat the previous scheme of the *rivers of circulation*, in blue (144). By a bracket I join the state of circulation to the previous scheme of congestion, which I repeat (145).

Trying to superpose the red on the blue, I write *convinced*; facing the bracket that joins the state of fact (the traffic) to the existing state (the present city) I write: "IMPOSSIBILITY = CRISIS."

With a horizontal line, I classify these existing events and draw the only possible truth: a blue river of traffic whose star is similar to the red star of the invading flow (146). And this necessity of decongestion I express by these concentric circles that are very far apart at the center and can almost touch at the periphery (147).

There! I have studied, understood, and proposed.

So then, in blue, I draw the face of the contemporary city of the age of the auto (148), the plane, and the railroad: wide streets in the center. Powerful penetrations in the country; less important streets in the periphery; then green spaces. Green spaces? Yes, that is to say, a zone of protection, an escape valve for extension. And then, far off, tiny traffic networks.

I think of the yellow powder of men of awhile back, I said that these men had two periods: they come from the periphery to work in the business district of the center; they return to the periphery to rest.

Am I *stuck* in my schemes? I have no more room in the center, between my immense blue rivers of traffic, for that sudden mass of yellow men. Let us be reassured: modern techniques have taught us to build two hundred meters high. *The city center will be two hundred meters high.* Doing this, I shall increase enormously, by four, even by ten, the density of the center, and distances will be reduced by four.

You will say: What a breathless race for rapidity, for speed!

Yes, for business is in the hands of those who act fastest. Be so good as to meditate on this: every morning, at the opening of the stock exchange, world markets face each other; the price of work is decided. It is decided every morning. It must be adjusted every day. To win the match—for they are thousands who want

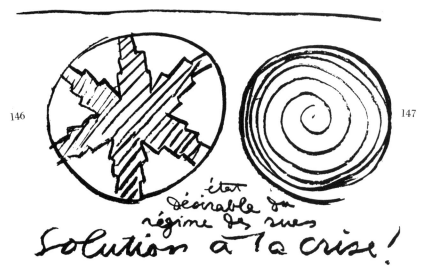

état désirable du régime des rues/desirable street network // solution à la crise!/solution to the crisis

to get an order—to win the match, one must be the fastest, the most direct, the most precise. One must be tooled to "play at business."

He who is well tooled will win. The city that is well tooled will win. The country that has a well-tooled capital will win.

If a city is poorly tooled (151–153), you will see, in the depth of the provinces, the woodcutter idle, the pulleys no longer turning, sadness in the homes, poverty and discouragement.

Again you will object: how does it happen that your diagnosis concerns a circular radial system and that you propose a rectangular one, on two perpendicular axes?

Because I've left the field of the economist who uses symbolic figures and have become an architect again. Architecture is run

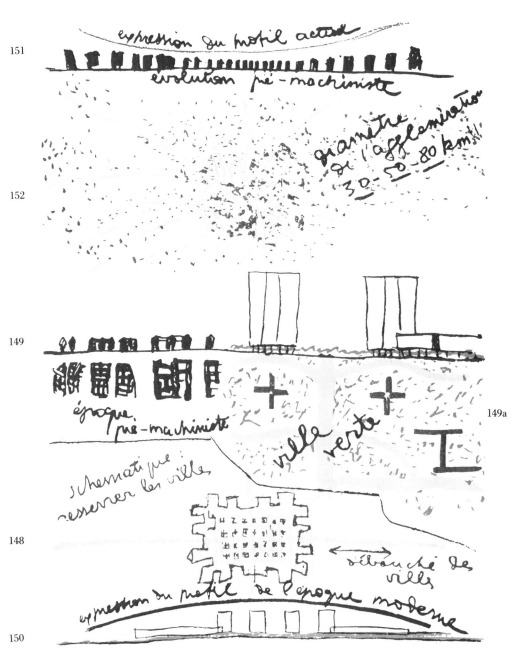

148 schematique: resserrer les villes/schematic diagram: contract the city // débouché des villes/openings around cities // 149 époque pré-machiniste/preindustrial age // 149a ville verte/green city // 150 expression du profil de l'époque moderne/profile of modern times // 151 expression du profil actuel/present profile // évolution pré-machiniste/preindustrial evolution // 152 diamètre de l'agglomération 30–50–80 km!!/diameter of the urban center 30–50–80 kilometers

by the right angle. It is dangerous for architecture to leave this firm and magnificent terrain, to be defeated by the acute or obtuse angle: everything becomes ugliness, constraint, wastefulness.

*
* *

Buildings two hundred meters high, gigantic avenues. We have thus changed the *scale of the city*.

Let us go back in history:

Here (149) are the narrow streets of the Gothic town, serried within its walls, and its tiny city blocks; streets cross every 20, 40, 50 meters.

Here under Louis XIV a new discipline. The carriage has just appeared. First the curved streets are straightened. The streets are widened and much bigger blocks of buildings are designed.

Here is Haussmann who amplifies this tendency. The courtyards open wider. Hygiene, police, and urban dignity have progressed.

Remember my prodigious graph of speeds a while back. I draw skyscrapers 200 meters high, 150 to 200 meters long, and I build them every 400 meters. These are good street intervals for subways, automobiles, buses: a street crossing every 400 meters.

I write (because I have calculated it) built surface: 5 percent; free ground available: 95 percent.

I refer to my second lecture ("Techniques Are the Very Basis of Poetry"): one can circulate under the pilotis of the buildings. The streets have no connection with the buildings. The buildings are above the ground, in volumes occupying space and visible to our eyes; the volumes are arranged in accordance with the inevitability of the right angle which is order, calm, and beauty: the streets will be whatever they wish, curved or straight. They are rivers, great branching rivers following an exact arithmetic. Their junctions are junctions of free-flowing rivers, large junctions. The course of a river should never be blocked, encumbered, for its width would be modified at such points and deplorable disturbances would result. The boats on our rivers full of traffic—automobiles in this case—must dock *at ports*, in harbors *outside*, to the left or the right. There is room to build the ports, the harbors.

And the whole city will be covered with vegetation (154). Air and light will be abundant. *There will be no courtyards, for courtyards are harmful.* Men who work in full daylight work well. Those who see things from above, at 100, 150, or 200 meters, are happier than those who live in holes and see only prison walls.

If I draw a section through a modern city, it is not concave; it is convex. That is sure (150).

Besides, here, on these different schemes, there are many certitudes. These certitudes make up a doctrine. *A doctrine of city planning.* Is there no doctrine of city planning today? There must be a doctrine.

*
* *

Ladies and gentlemen, have I barely approached my subject? It is immense. But the other lectures will come bringing their lights. It is enough to join together the certitudes thus acquired.

I have written a book on the subject; I have made a lot of detailed studies. I cannot repeat the demonstrations already made. But I can assemble all this in a few essential ideas. The following, which are fundamental:

City planning is a question of equipment, of tooling. If one says tool, one says good work, output, efficiency.

City planning is a matter of aesthetics, only if at the same time it is a matter of biological organization, of social organization, of financial organization.

Aesthetic urbanism is expensive, leads to immense expenses, is a terrible drain on taxpayers. Furthermore, it is inappropriate, or unethical, since it is of no help to life in the city. Real city planning finds the means in modern techniques for solutions to the crisis. It finds in economic problems, which are its essence, *its own financing.* I shall prove this another time. From this automatic financing a big financial profit comes that makes it possible to spend money on social peace. For this financing to exist, to arise, the intervention of a strong authority is necessary.

Another time I shall show how the financing of projects comes from government intervention. We shall determine the point at which authority must intervene and we shall see which authority must intervene and how.

Everything that has preceded in my demonstrations brings its support to the solution of the urban crisis. The problem well propounded in everything—in the dwelling or the collection of dwellings—and the call for the new means of the machine age undo the terrible rings of the meander, more precisely they pierce the meander from side to side, and life can again begin its wide course. There is no miracle. There is clearing up, maturity, there is fruition. What would academic thinking or artificial sentimentality do here?

City planning is a question of synthesis, of composition *on the ground and above the ground*. What makes solutions abort is that one has thought *in one dimension* and not synthetically in *extent* and in *elevation*, that is to say, in soil to plow with all the tools of speed and in *volumes of buildings to fill with people* in optimal conditions of health and joy.

Noise must be conquered. A healthy doctrine of city planning and a doctrine of the "machine for living" gets rid of noise.

Do not imagine that our ears will get used to the racket of modern life. Besides, there is noise only where the solution is contradictory, from a mechanical or planning point of view. The tendency of a good machine is not to make noise but to be silent. We suffer from noise, noise is abnormal, its effects are disastrous. Soon millionaires will offer their friends *hours of silence*. Unless modern planning triumphs, bringing peace. A capital will be found to claim praise because it has become silent.

From all we have already said, it is evident that the modern city will be covered with trees. It is a necessity for the lungs, it is balm to our hearts, it is the very spice of the great geometric aesthetic introduced into contemporary architecture by steel and reinforced concrete.

I submit the following idea to the ministers of public education: a law would oblige each schoolchild to plant a tree, somewhere in town or outside. This tree would have the name of the child on it. The expense would be insignificant. *But it would require plans!* And in fifty or sixty years, a lovely act of piety would lead these men and these women, become old, to the foot of a big tree that had accomplished its immense ramification. This is just a little idea, in passing, to show how indispensable to our bodies

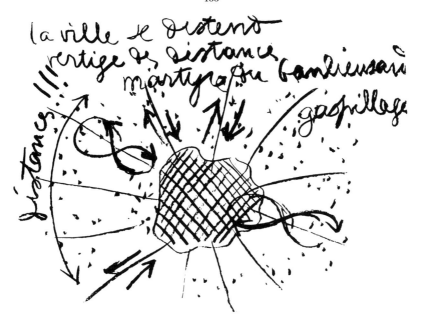

153 la ville se distend/the city spreads // vertige des distances/dizzying distances // martyre du banlieusard/martyrdom of suburbanites // gaspillage/waste // distances!!!/distances // **154** la ville doit se resserrer par la valorisation de son sol/the city should contract on itself by the valorization of its ground // adaptation des services communs à la vie moderne/adapting public services to modern life // la ville peut devenir une VILLE VERTE/the city can become a green city

155

155 les gratte ciel de verre/the glass skyscrapers // les rues superposées/the superposed streets // l'autostrade/the expressway // les redents/the zigzag buildings // les bases nouvelles de la composition urbaine/the new bases of urban design // un nouveau lyrisme de l'époque machiniste/a new poetry for the machine age // **156** LA VILLE VERTE/the green city

and to our hearts is the nature that we can no longer do without, nature in the hearts of our inhuman cities.

*
* *

I finish by setting forth the terms of the *visual elements* of city planning and its *poetic elements*.

First, in plan: diversified spaces (149a).

Then in elevation (155) what I draw here:

the ground first, covered with vegetation; the rivers of traffic crossing it, and the parking harbors surrounded by trees.

Here is an expressway on its pilotis disappearing in the distance.

Dominating the trees, or in the midst of their branches, between leaves and lawns, the "elevated" streets, buildings with two or three setbacks, with cafes, shops, pedestrian walks.

Here, the big housing blocks with their public services, without courtyards, and opening onto parks.

Here is the skyscraper all in crystal and shining in the atmosphere.

But we have remained men, the men of all times with their eyes at 1 meter 70 above the ground. Here is the real view of the intense, the ardent modern city: a symphony of greenery, of leaves, branches, and lawns, and flashes of diamond through woods. A symphony! See with what poetry progress has animated us, with what tools modern techniques have endowed us. This has never been seen before. No, never, for a new period has begun, animated by a new spirit (156).

A HOUSE
—A PALACE

THE PALACE OF THE LEAGUE OF NATIONS IN GENEVA

The purpose of this lecture in the series now reaching its end is to determine an honest meaning to a term that, to us, mean lies, pretentiousness, vanity, wastefulness, and profound imbecility. This term is set forth: *Palace*.

We have advanced enough on the loyal ways of architecture to feel ourselves capable of judging. Let us evoke your palaces: that of the Congress, that of Justice. Ours: the Grand Palais Exhibition Hall in Paris, the Palace of Justice in Brussels, that of Rome. Finally, a high proportion of those projects that came from all countries regimented under the sign of academism, on the occasion of the big international competition for the construction of the palace of the League of Nations in Geneva.

You imagine them; it is as if they rose before your eyes; I do not add a word; you have judged. What use are they? To show ostentation. The functions that their program implied? Practically impossible to carry out.

Last year, I wrote a whole book on this subject: *A House, a Palace*. I subtitled it "in search of a unified theory of architecture."

I went into a lot of detail to explain myself. Nevertheless I shall again go through the technical aspects of our project for you. You will find the elements of what it is useful to emphasize here. What should be understood and brought to the attention of honest people, in this rigorous series of functions that made up the very reason for propounding the problem, is this:

Architecture is a series of successive events going from an analysis to a synthesis, events that the spirit tries to transmute by the creation of relations so precise and so overwhelming that deep physiological sensations result from them, that a real spiritual delectation is felt at reading the solution, that a perception of harmony comes to us from the clear-cut mathematical quality uniting each element of the work to the others and the whole to that other entity which is the environment, the site.

It is then that everything that serves, everything that is useful is transcended. An overwhelming event: creation. A phenomenon of poetry and wisdom that is called beauty.

And, from the moment that we have based the notion of *Palace* on indispensable functional elements—on utility—and have claimed to tend toward the sublime as a consequence of a high intention, we feel, we architects and planners, empowered to design the city. The city is a whole. A city must be beautiful because a high intention . . . , etc., raises above the brutal satisfaction of functions elements that . . . etc.

From such sights, the healthy man—an ordinary or a highly cultivated one—draws a galvanization, a sustaining incitement to joy (happiness is not material; it is a feeling of something).

Only someone who is saturated with the spirit of academism does not understand, one who has lost his *original sensitivity* by the artifices of learning and of laziness. He understands nothing of the new sight unrolling before his eyes.

All the great traditional works, those that without exception constitute the classical chain, link after link, were revolutionary when they first appeared.

The essence of creation is necessarily to equate new relationships, since one of the terms is fixed—human sensitivity—and the other is always moving, the contingencies, that is to say the *environment* produced by technology in every field of a society in permanent evolution.

At this summit of architecture where the word "Palace" becomes honest again, a spirit dominates that I call the *spirit of truth*. The spirit of truth is a rigid measure diving to the very foundation of a work, crossing it, feeding it, carrying it without weakness all the way to its appearance, which wears the quiet smile given by the assurance of being true and the satisfaction of having overcome difficulties.

*
* *

I have drawn the hut of the savage (157), the primitive temple (158, 159), the house of the peasant (160), and I have said: these organisms created with the authenticity that nature itself places in its works—economy, purity, intensity—it is they that, one day of sunshine and clear-sightedness, became palaces. I have shown the house of the fisherman built with a clear-cut truth, indisputable; my eyes, diving one day into architecture, into the eternal facts of architecture, suddenly discovered it. "This house," I cried out to myself, "is a palace!"

I then sketched and explained our project for the League of Nations:

the help brought to the problem of circulation by the pilotis (161);

the design of a modern office building (26, 27, 30, 31);

the greatest problem of the palace, the vertical and horizontal circulation in the big committee meeting rooms and the General Assembly Hall;

the problem of building such a big space (162–164);

that of the eye and the ear, visibility and acoustics, in a place where, as in a Tower of Babel (165), people of all countries and languages are united in debates of which the stakes are world peace. To hear with one's own ears is the only path that heart or reason can take (166–169);

the lighting of the Assembly Hall, day or night. *To see clearly,* to decide world affairs and to take advantage of the optimism of the sun's rays (170, 171);

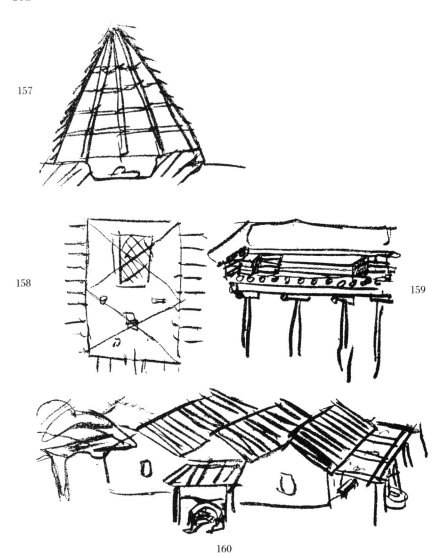

157

158

159

160

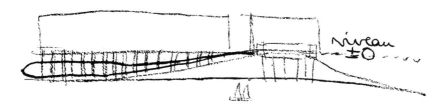

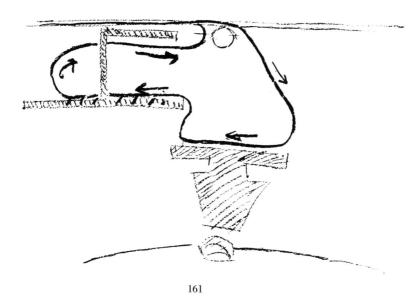

161

niveau/level

162

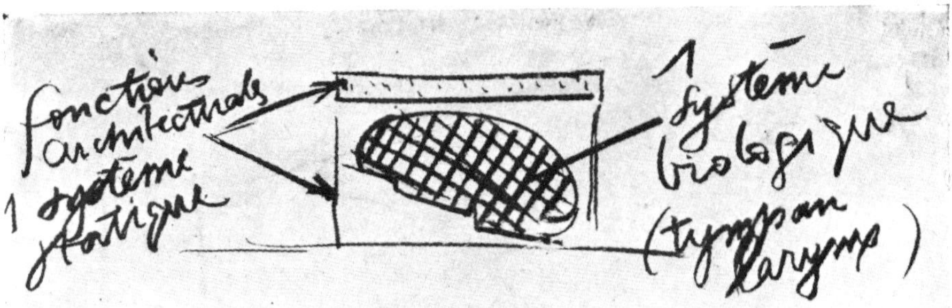

163

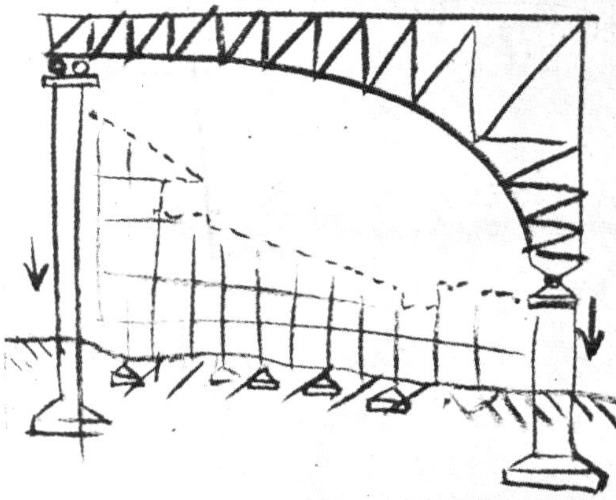

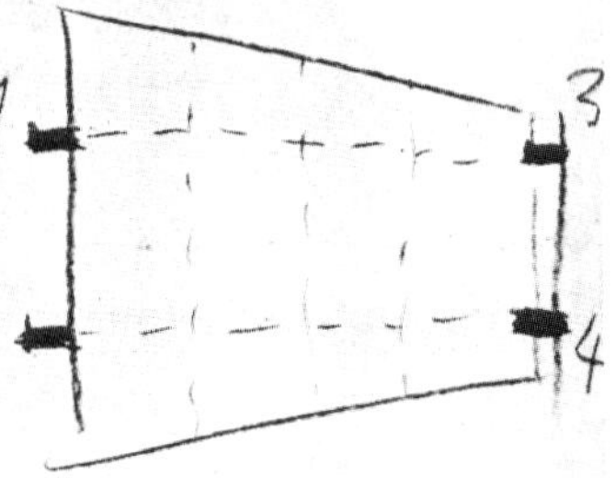

164

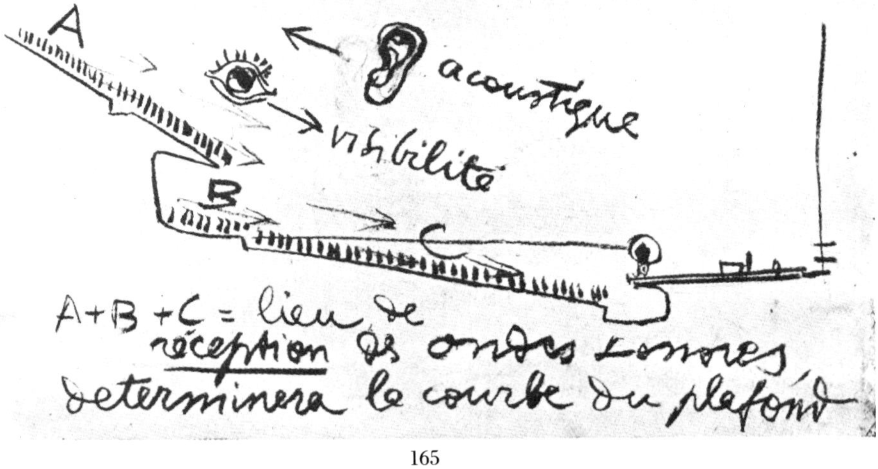

165

162 fonctions architecturales, système statique/architectural functions, constructive system // système biologique (tympan larynx)/biological system (eardrum, larynx) // **165** acoustique/acoustics // visibilité/vision // lieu de réception des ondes sonores déterminera la courbe du plafond/the point of reception of sound waves will determine the curve of the ceiling

AUTHOR'S EXPLANATIONS: 162. Two independent functions clearly determined: static and dynamic. 163–164. Solution of the static problem. A new analysis: the $\frac{1}{2}$ arch of a bridge carries the roof terrace of the hall (4 points of support); a forest of small columns carries the floor of the hall (the audience). 165. The shapes given to the floor to ensure visibility will influence the acoustic curve of the hall.

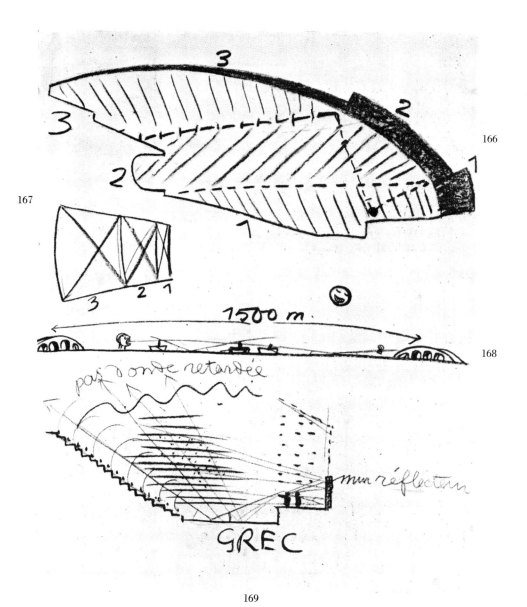

166

167

168

169

169 pas d'onde retardée/no retarded waves // mur réflecteur/reflecting wall // GREC/ Greek

AUTHOR'S EXPLANATIONS: 168. Experiment by Gustave Lyon, making it possible to hear at a distance of 1,500 meters (see *A House, a Palace*). 169. The Greek theater has a reflecting wall, an orchestra level that throws back sound waves on a tangent to the tiers of the spectators. No ceiling in the Greek theater, therefore no waves sent back or echoed. 166–167. Each segment 1,2,3 plays exactly, in relation to the speaker and the auditors, the role of the reflecting wall in the Greek theater; but (especially in 2 and 3) this wall is inclined in order to "shower" the corresponding sectors 1, 2, 3 of auditors with sound waves. As the intensity of the wave projected diminishes with the square of the distance, the surfaces of "reflecting walls" 2 and 3, especially, are enlarged in the same proportion (the square of the surface, 167).

to breathe; first creation of our "neutralizing walls" (172, 173);

finally, the *summing up*, that is to say the architectural synthesis of all the parts in the most loyal spirit of truth and animated by a strong desire: to create a work of harmony.

*
* *

What happened then? We were thrown out of the League of Nations. We were erased, completely disqualified, despite the jury and the experts who had named us to build the Palace.

This important competition, mobilizing 377 architects' offices of the entire world, sending to Geneva fourteen kilometers of plans, was faked.

Why was it faked? The academic spirit reigns at the summit of the establishment, there, very close to the government, in the Institutes. The people at the League of Nations are sincere. They still think "royalty." To govern with ostentation. To impose by the appearances that *in the past were used to impose.* What a phenomenal mistake of judgment, what a misunderstanding of the weight of the moving world!

The best of men reacted. How many memoranda, how many open letters were addressed to Geneva by professional associations. Overwhelming things took place there, in silence. What disillusion among the young of the League of Nations not yet in a position to decide!

Storms in the great European press; anxious questions addressed to the supreme institution in which so many had placed their hopes.

Two years have passed since that arbitrary decision. It is still not possible to see plans of the "academic" Palace that satisfy the program, at the serious moment when it is a question of building and when watercolors and charcoal drawings with clouds are no longer enough.

That June 5, at the League of Nations council in Madrid, we almost won. We lost.

But who knows?

I believe this with conviction: "A new period has begun, ani-

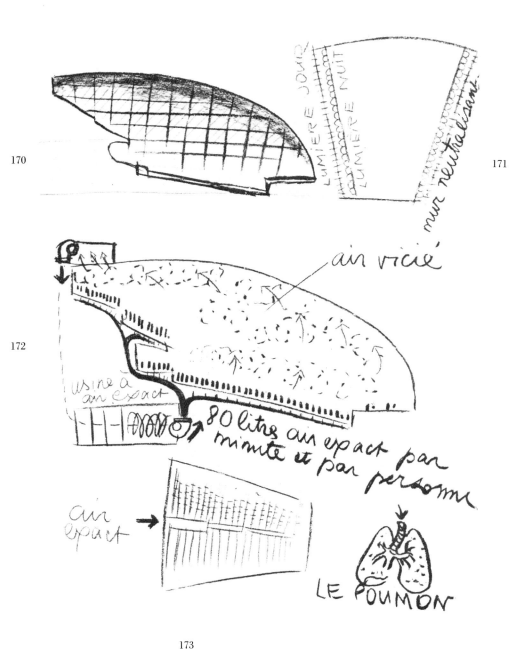

170   171

172

173

171 lumière jour/daylight // lumière nuit/artificial light // mur neutralisant/neutralizing wall // **172** air vicié/used air // usine à air exact/air conditioning plant // 80 litres air exact par minute et par personne/80 liters of treated air per minute per person // **173** air exact/treated air // le poumon/the lung

mated by a new spirit." (I have already said that, haven't I, but may I not repeat it?)

Is such a conviction contrary to the idea of the League of Nations?

*
* *

Ladies and gentlemen, we have nevertheless had the joy, a great joy, after three months of hard work, when we had finished our project, to find that we had proceeded in exactly the same way as if to design a factory, a city plan, a house, a piece of furniture.

And the luxury, or better still, the reason for the existence of our palace, was just that line of conduct animating our work; that spiritual quality expressing itself in the whole of our project, whose lines are pure and sharp, calm and smiling. Once the functions were satisfied, we did not need to add a cubic centimeter to it.

Ninth lecture
Friday, October 18, 1929
Friends of the Arts

THE VOISIN PLAN FOR PARIS

CAN BUENOS AIRES BECOME ONE OF THE GREAT CITIES OF THE WORLD?

Let us clear the ground first:
The "corridor street" must be destroyed.
We shall not really enter into modern city planning until we have first made this decision. The corridor street, born at the time of the horse or the ox-drawn cart, was lined by ground-floor houses, sometimes with one upper floor; the main windows opened on a quadrangle formed by four streets and gave on gardens.

As concentration developed one day, in the hearts of cities, seven stories were built on these ground floors; then the gardens were filled with buildings just as high; only the narrow courts required by regulations on public hygiene remained. Then, even here, almost everything was built up, despite the regulations; electricity had arrived. "Too bad," they said; "to make money, one can just as well light artificially." All this was peopled with men and women. The automobile was born. It invades the street. A devilish hellish noise arises, which would be painful in an empty countryside but is frightful in the corridor street, whose walls are prodigious acoustic amplifiers. Nothing is livable any more (174).

The corridor streets produce *the corridor cities. The whole city is a corridor.* What a sight! What aesthetics! We say nothing, we submit. How quickly we are satisfied! What would you say of an architect who proposed to you a house made up *entirely of corridors?* From time to time, the aesthete-kings built noble rooms, rooms for show, magnificent; they have become the sentimental escape valves of the city: the Place des Vosges, the Place Vendôme, etc. (175).

We could, we can get rid of all the corridors!

To do so, it is enough to invert the problem: the solution will be to "tuck in" everything; taking up everything that is along the streets, reducing the courtyards to zero, piling up high the volumes of the buildings, placing these in the form of crosses, of stars, or the cross of Lorraine or whatever one wishes that effaces the courtyards; one can go toward the light, one can leave the street, one can add up the surfaces of courtyards and spread them as open space to the left and right of the streets, around the buildings, between the zigzags of the dwellings (178). It is in these recovered surfaces that automobiles will come to park; their noisy current will flow regularly at the greatest distance from the houses. The surface of the ground built on will be reduced by as much; one will get away from the street, since modern techniques allow us to rise higher with our buildings; that is the point of the problem. The buildings will no longer be lips pinching the edges of streets. They will be isolated prisms far from each other. The ground of the city will be recuperated. Modern life needs it!

*
* *

It is still necessary to clear the ground and to decide between what one may, in terms of planning, call "medicine" or "surgery."

It has been proven that the street I am drawing here, among others that cross it, has become inadequate. The city fathers, following the usual practice, decide to *enlarge* it. The operation is made by encroaching on the right and left, or sometimes on only

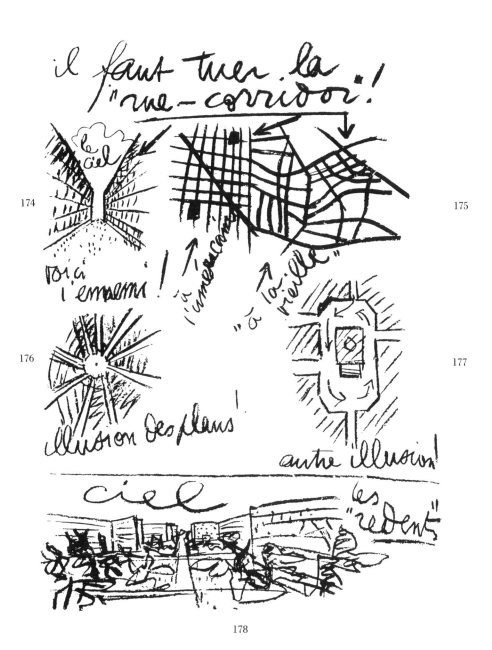

174, 175 il faut tuer la "rue-corridor"!/the corridor street must be destroyed // le ciel/ the sky // voici l'ennemi!/here is the enemy // à l'américain/American style // "à la vieille"/ old-fashioned // **176** illusion des plans!/the illusion of plans // **177** autre illusion!/another illusion // **178** ciel/sky // les "redents"/zigzag buildings

one side. One side of a street for instance is expropriated (supposing that this solution is the most economical; 179); the owner makes a lot of noise (because he was in business on a very busy street); he gets paid dearly. Result:

an old street become wider,
it is very expensive.
That is "medicine."
Here is "surgery":
We leave the crowded street as it is (180). A new network of wide streets is invented corresponding to modern city planning. The new street crosses blocks of secondary, of minor importance. Expropriations are not expensive. Result:

an old street remains,
a new wide modern street adds value to areas previously undervalued.

Total: two streets,
at low cost,
valorization of a poor neighborhood.
Here is another typical example:
Here is a suburban street (a former donkey path) that has become very lively with its activities necessary to neighborhood life.

The automobile has come; numerous accidents multiply along this "old donkey path" raised to the rank of a national or local highway. Its sharp curves are dangerous too. It is decided to widen and straighten it. Both sides are expropriated (181). But along it are found the baker, the butcher, the hardware store, the paint shop, the small department store, etc. Dear, very dear, the expropriation! "Medicine."

Result: *automobiles will continue to disturb dangerously the perfectly balanced network of the good old days; a network of habitation and not circulation.*

Let us see "surgery":
One lays out a big new road behind the houses of the town, in the fields of cabbages, of beets, or through pastures (182).

Result: *few expropriations;*
two roads instead of one.
The conclusion is simple: *in city planning "medical" solu-*

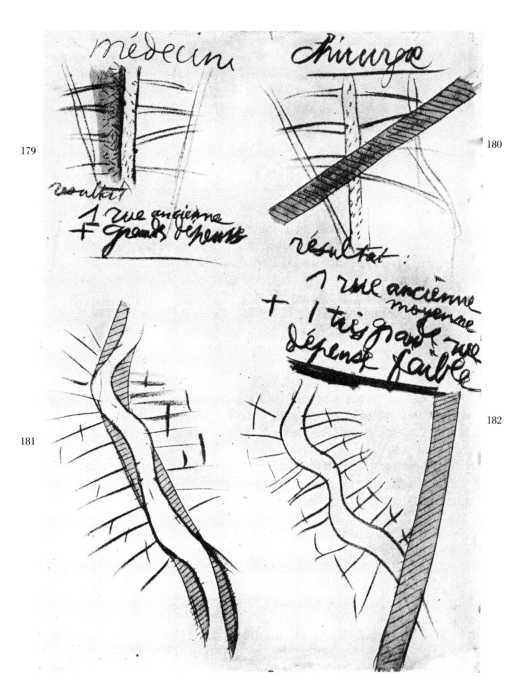

179 médecine/medicine // 180 chirurgie/surgery // 181 résultat 1 rue ancienne + grandes dépenses/result: one old street plus great expense // 182 résultat: 1 rue ancienne moyenne + 1 très grande rue dépense faible/result: one average old street plus one very big street at little expense

tions are a delusion; they resolve nothing, they are very expensive.
Surgical solutions resolve.

It is useful to know this well!

*
* *

I shall now speak to you about the Voisin Plan for Paris, the
project for the creation of a central business district in the very
heart of the city.

"You have the pretension to touch Paris, to demolish, to rebuild, to annihilate the treasures of the past, to impose a new
silhouette on a sublime city?"

Let us get past the obstacle of this unthinking and academic
protest. Let us consider the proud beauty of Paris. Let us talk of
the beauty of the city. Addressing myself to the academicians, I
ask: "What is Paris? Where is the beauty of Paris? What is the
spirit of Paris?"

I draw the medieval city, Notre-Dame in the Cité surrounded
by water, and these bridges covered with houses, these highways
leaving the gates and leading to the provinces; and these abbeys
marking the first stops: Saint-Germain des Prés, Saint-Antoine,
etc. First sketch (183).

Now I express an important event: the building of the Louvre
colonnade by the Sun King. What pride, what contempt for what
exists, what a break with harmony, what insolent sacrilege! Facing
the sawteeth of the gable roofs, facing the maquis of the alleys, the
torment of the medieval city compressed on itself, the magnificent
intellectual artifice of the Grand Siècle! Second sketch (184).

The King continues! Here are the Invalides and a dome in
the country of Gothic spires: indifference to national traditions,
violation of the site, coup d'état! Third sketch (185).

The face of Paris has acquired precise features, a real song
in stones. Soufflot camped the Pantheon at the top of the Mon-
tagne Sainte-Geneviève, another dome! Poets proclaim the radiant
and decent harmony of the stones of France. Boom! Here is Eiffel.
Bang! here is the Tower! This is Paris! It is still Paris! The Tower
is dear to Parisians; beyond the most distant frontiers, it is set in
the hearts of those who dream of Paris. Fourth sketch (186).

The other hill is crowned: the Sacré-Coeur. One sees the Arc

183 St Denis // route de l'est/road east // route d'Espagne/road to Spain // route du midi/ road south // 184 Roy-Soleil/Sun King // 186 ça c'est Paris!/this is Paris

at the Etoile, Notre-Dame. In the whole world, the Tower has become the symbol of Paris. I write: "It is still Paris!" Fifth sketch (187).

So now I design this contemporary event: the Paris business district (188). Immense and magnificent, shining and orderly. Sustained by the history of the city, its vital power, its sense of the appropriate, its lively and creative spirit, even its quick and revolutionary mind, sustained by chronology, by the faith I have in the present time, by the ardent realities of impending morrows, I say coldly, with conviction and decision: "That, that is Paris!" I feel that the whole world has its eyes on Paris, hopes from Paris the gesture that commands, creates, and raises in order, the architectural event that will enlighten all the other cities. I believe in Paris. I have hope for Paris. I beg of Paris to make, once more, its historical gesture: *to continue.*

....

Academism shouts: *No!*

*
* *

A wise caliph of the *Thousand and One Nights* would bring together the academicians, the fanatics among the protectors of the old Paris, the sensitive souls, trembling at the sound of the pickaxe of the demolisher, and finally the conservationists of old wrought iron.

"Have you been in the city," the caliph would ask, "where they are talking of tearing down and rebuilding, there, in the center of Paris? No? Well then, go there where there is talk of tearing down and rebuilding. You will count the old wrought iron. If there is not a certain quantity, I shall cut off your head. For if it is not there, I shall consider you the enemies of life, of the city and of the country. If there is not that quantity, I shall condemn you for *false witness,* like the carrion beetles who smother every spark in the articles of a credulous or dangerously careless press, the sparks that should turn on the light of today over the city!"

All of the big cities of the world are on the edge of a great crisis today. Time is passing. To let the right moment pass may be tragic for Paris!

187 c'est encore Paris!/it is still Paris // **188** l'académisme dit Non!/academism says No!

*
* *

Do we want to see how a state that *wishes* to can earn billions, to tell the truth can *make billions*? And how, having made billions by undertaking development, it can use these to carry out works that will bring the country indispensable means for working?

This demonstration that I shall make for you has something magical about it, something miraculous; one would say juggling and yet it is not.

Does one find it miraculous that violent activity develops around a diamond mine or oil well *that has just been discovered?* More precisely, does one find it miraculous, crazy and senseless, inadmissible and unreal, that *one day a diamond mine or an oil well are discovered?*

I shall show you that the machine age that provoked the birth of big cities, and the congestion at the center of big cities, has created, at the same time, a diamond mine in the center of these cities. And that a method exists—a financial conception—efficient and infallible, that manufactures these diamonds by simple decrees of the state: a paper with a signature! I am not crazy, I speak quietly. I shall prove it.

The idea launched in 1925 in *Urbanisme* touched, or didn't touch, that indeterminate elite that reads the Esprit Nouveau collection. But in 1927, it struck the captains of industry and economists like Ernest Mercier and Lucien Romier, president and director of the Redressement Français. Field Marshal Lyautey, who understood the problems of planning perfectly when he governed Morocco, praised these suggestions. Then, in 1929, Mr. Daniel Serruys, retired director of trade relations at the League of Nations, a matter-of-fact economist in full action in the present hubbub, sustained these propositions. Mr. Loucheur (who knows the building industry) has been interested for a long time in the research we are carrying on and had them ask me: "Where will you get the money?" He had not read my description of the "machine for making money";[1] our plans seemed rather impractical to him.

1. Translator's note: A reference to Alfred Jarry's satire *Ubu Roi*.

I cite these names to show you that we are not at all in utopia, but in the heart of a great contemporary problem.

I present these bases; I insist on these bases; they are fundamental; they are contrary to all the propositions presently before us. This is the point where a modern conception and customs, traditions, habits are projected against each other. First of all this: *city planning is not beautification: it is equipment; urbanism is not gardening, it is tools.*

Then, taking modern techniques into account, the new means for building that are the great modern event, the means of salvation, the door suddenly open on tomorrow, I say with force:

Urban development is not spending money,
> *it is earning money,*
> *it is making money.*

In other words:
Urban development is not depreciation or devaluing, it creates value.

I explain:

As long as the state of techniques didn't introduce any change in the possibilities of construction, in the efficiency of construction, city planning was only sumptuary (Louis XIV).

When the state of techniques offered an efficiency equal in quantity, but of better quality, planning was practical, sumptuary, and profitable (Haussmann, masonry construction, the same number of floors as before).

But as soon as technology allowed the construction, instead of to a limit of 20 meters (a prudent limit for buildings in wood or stone), of *buildings of 200 to 250 meters high* (easily done in steel or reinforced concrete), the problem changed color. *The situation is reversed; the problem is entirely new; it is positive and no longer negative. It is constructive. It leads to operations that revalue city land.*

So, *urban redevelopment valorizes.*

That is all there is to it.

There is a moment when the elements are available, when an operation presents itself.

The moment is now. It is the undoing of the meander, it is today's solution of our inextricable chaos.

Let us stop for a moment on a nearby example of valorization: Sao Paulo of Brazil is a city in intense development; its suburbs extend far onto the surrounding plateaus. There are no arteries to this spreading of a formless suburb. An English company said the following: "I shall build a magnificent highway that will extend from the city into the countryside." Yes, charming; and with what money? The company went to see the landowners along its projected route (I shall call them A.B.C.). "Your land is inaccessible, *it is worthless*. If our highway passes it or crosses it, your land connected to the city by a magnificent expressway *will acquire a certain value*, it will be valorized. We shall ask you something in exchange: that you give us a strip of land along the highway, of a depth *n*. We shall build the road. Your land will be valorized, we shall be paid with this strip of land *n* that you give us. But if you are not willing, we shall not go past your site. Your property will rest inert and worthless as it is today." Naturally everyone agreed, the reasoning being unanswerable. The company, with its brief under an arm, its plan of the road, its property of a strip *n* along the left and right sides, went to see the bankers. With one blow, by an *artificial act,* value was added, *money was drawn from an inert site,* by the simple exchange of the signatures of the company on the one hand, the neighboring property owners on the other. That is planning! *Not a cent was spent. The hour was ripe and the useful elements present.*

But let us get back to Paris. *Where* does the hour ring? *Where are the elements present?*

No matter how well, how generously, how selfishly, how carefully the world is organized (or one tries to organize it—the League of Nations, the International Labor Office, international conferences, etc.), a vital phenomenom exists, persists, and will never disappear: that of *competition*, which is the unavoidable nerve of action, the impetus for production. Competition is between diverse existing powers; there will not be, there cannot ever be only one single power, for, the day after its advent, a new force will surge forth.

Therefore, a country, or a concept of "country," or a region, or an administrative unit will always delegate its powers to a command center. And these centers, spread over the "round machine," will face each other, oppose each other, play their matches.

A tough, intense, violent game, one must not fool oneself; it is a question of one's daily bread.

At the opening of the stock market, every morning, every time the sun rises again, the ratings of the world are given, and the work of the whole world is *conditioned every day by stock market quotations.*

What is needed, between the hour of knowing the rates and the sending in of orders that will adjust operations and make contracts possible, *what is needed is speed.* It is a race to the finish line; whoever arrives faster, better informed, consequently better placed, better equipped, is the one who wins. Ill luck to him who sleeps.

Mechanization, which has transformed the idea of time and imposed rapidity, demands the creation of *business districts.* Intensity, capacity, rapidity, silence (for noise perturbs organisms incurably). The business district will be at the point that is closest to all the parts of an urban agglomeration; *this point is the center.*[2]

I explained my ideas carefully in my book *Urbanisme* of 1924–25. I cannot begin again here, for, to be truthful, I should like to bring you to the burning crossroads of decision, there where the question of money comes up.

Nevertheless those are numerous who want to evade realities, to shift, to desert, and who propose like children to go build a business district outside the city.

It is still and always the fear of great solutions and the fallacious caress of delays and "seesawing" that lead to turning one's back on a solution. And yet, before our eyes and under our eyes, in all the cities of the world, the phenomenon happens unfailingly; the strata of the business districts are built up slyly, creating the most tragic menace to the cities. What menace? Suffocation, traffic jams, paralysis. Follow my charcoal:

Here is a city center, its streets. At the busiest points, the

---

2. In the big cities with a radial plan, if, despite all hope, the reconstruction of the city were requested, the new plan would certainly not be radial and there would not be a literal geometric center.

most vital, one finds buildings, new or under construction. They
are the offices of big companies that are *equipping themselves* for
the struggle of business: with order, organization, clarity, coherence, efficiency, etc. They equip themselves *inside*, within their
buildings, as they are prevented from doing so outside since the
city officials do not act and do not prepare the necessary plans. I
draw all these buildings at the strategic points. This exists; it is
quite recent; it is being done today under our eyes. It is the great
abomination, the outrageous crime against the life of the nation.
But why so? What then? Is it possible? Let us not be naively
astonished: the city officials are persuaded that to plan is to beau-
tify. Under this sketch I write: *cancer* (189). I figure the cost of
each operation: the purchase of the site by a big company, at a
high price; the concentration of personnel in an already over-
crowded area: congestion, traffic jams. I see with terror that *the
street cannot be widened*. I am overcome. I do not believe in the
two or three meters of widening of the street foreseen on the city
plan. *I need rivers of circulation and harbors of parking*. It is thus
*a dead end toward which the city councils and the absent-minded
parliaments are pushing us!* Under "cancer" I write *dead end* and
enormous expenditures. Let's get down to the point; I promised to
make billions.

The business district will be in the *center of the city, there
where the price of land is very high*.

A limit precise, real, and not approximate will determine a
sufficient surface—the perimeter ABCD. It will be the site of the
first operation of development (190).

On this surface will be built office buildings up to 200 or 250
meters high. The density of this part of the city, already high, will
be multiplied by four, perhaps by ten. But the new buildings will
cover only *5 percent* of the surface of the ground (I have explained
this); it will therefore be easy to build them without disturbing
work in the center. Once the offices are built, the leases transferred, the new density achieved, the enterprise will be finished
by the demolition of all that remains in the sector ABCD (except
some valuable old constructions): 95 percent of the ground will be
given over to circulation.

Result: the solution of the problems of the big cities by the
concentration of the business district, the shortening of distances,

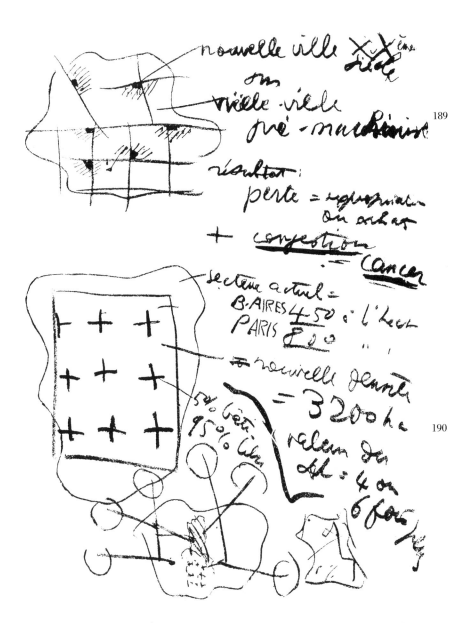

189

190

189 nouvelle ville XXème siècle sur vieille ville pré-machiniste/new twentieth-century city on old preindustrial city // résultat: perte = expropriation ou achat + congestion = cancer/result: loss = expropriation or purchase plus congestion = cancer // **190** secteur actuel = B. AIRES 450 à l'hectare, PARIS 800 à l'hectare/present surface = Buenos Aires 450 per hectare, Paris 800 per hectare // nouvelle densité = 3200 ha/new density 3200 per hectare // 5% bâti, 95% libre/5% built, 95% free // valeur du sol = 4 ou 6 fois plus/value of ground 4 to 6 times more

the rapidity, the creation of a harmonious working day, in pure air, in daylight, far from noise.

The site ABCD contains four to ten times more occupants than before. *Therefore it is worth four to ten times more.* We have earned billions. More than that, these neighborhoods, up till now obsolete and unadapted to modern life, have become the most beautiful in the world. *We again double the billions earned.*

When then did the miracle take place? It took place at the exact moment when the creation of the business district *stopped being the result of arbitrary day-to-day decisions and became a planned operation.* That is the margin between losing and winning. A planned operation, that is to say an enlightened act of organization, of coordination, on the horizontal and the vertical planes, all at the same time.

Is it therefore necessary to buy, to expropriate all the buildings within ABCD? Yes. What shall we pay them with? With the billions won. But how, materially, objectively, will these billions be earned? That is to say, created? *When the government, the highest authority, has decreed the valorization.* There is therefore intervention of authority, of the highest authority. A signature will be given that will make the miracle of the spontaneous birth of billions.

I must explain that miraculous capacity of the government to make billions with a signature.

I draw this rectangle: it is a hundred-franc bill. Inside a frame is written Bank of France (191). Above, this affirmation, gratuitous: 100 francs. Gratuitous? No, one reads "payable in cash to the bearer" and it is signed "the chief cashier," "the general secretary"; the signatures are more or less legible. There you are! A virtual value has been created, a piece of paper has been created thanks to a *hypothetical* pact. And the whole country works in full confidence in this virtual value; it receives and pays with this virtual value.

One can therefore have confidence in the highest authority (for the Bank of France is guaranteed by the state), one can therefore engage all the enterprises of a country by an *agreement*.

An agreement! Let us not tire of being precise; in our business of city planning, a question of *time* will come up. Here is another agreement. I draw a new rectangle; it's a draft (192). On it is written: "I shall pay to Mr. X at the date of . . . the sum of . . ." It is signed; the payee also signs it. With this second signature,

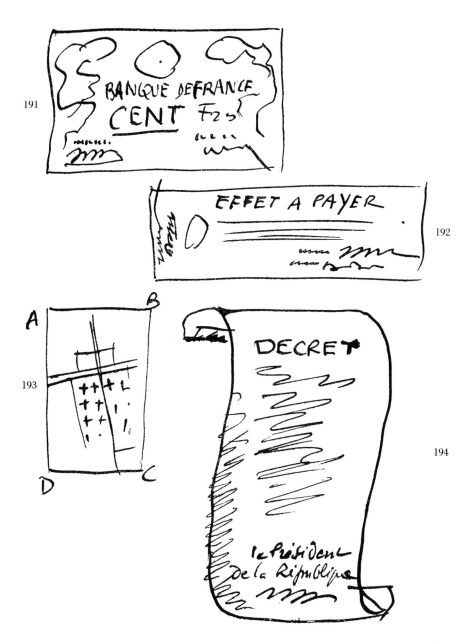

191 BANQUE DE FRANCE CENT Frs/Bank of France 100 Francs // **192** EFFET À PAYER/Draft payable // **194** DECRET/Decree // le Président de la République/the President of the Republic

he goes to the bank with his paper. If the bank has confidence in the two signatures, it discounts the draft, that is to say that it pays out the amount right away, before the date indicated. And all the important businesses in the world are based on the same principle of confidence.

So, to create the Paris business district, I present the question of confidence: does the government have the confidence of the firms that can carry out the business district (the financiers, the contractors for roads or buildings, for electricity, compressed air, transports, etc.)? The confidence of those who will occupy the business district (the merchants, the companies who will be owners or tenants when the district is ready)? To be clear: if the state, the highest authority, puts its signature on the bottom of a draft, will the citizens have confidence in the state?

It is impossible to envisage the contrary, for, if that were the case, it would mean that the country no longer recognized its authority; this doesn't happen even on a day of revolution; it would mean that the country is bankrupt and consequently that all activity would be annihilated.

So, here:

I draw the periphery of ABCD. It expresses the exact site of the business district in the heart of Paris (193). I draw another rectangle; it is a parchment, it is a *government decree* (194); on it is written:

Decree of urbanization of the zone ABCD
of the region of Paris

With the agreement of the state,

Under the control and the supervision of the state, which solemnly engages itself to require its realization, the following work will be undertaken by private initiative . . . starting from . . . and within the final date of . . . in order to build the central Paris business district.

Description of project:

....

....

....

Etc.

As a result of the constructions listed in the present decree, the density of the zone ABCD will be carried to 3,200 occupants per hectare and all the means of rapid access and evacuation, of healthy living conditions and of circulation of this population will be assured in accordance with the project approved by the Parlement.

In the name of the French people,
> *The President of the Republic.*
> *signature:*

....

This time, the billions are created, the valorization is effected.

Notice this well, it was necessary to fix the limits ABCD. The operation must be as precise as the figure written on the draft or the bank note. An annex to the decree on the day of its promulgation blocks the price of the properties on the site; the prices are thus immobilized or in a state of immobilization from that day on. They will be determined, case by case, by experts, after the promulgation of the decree.

Speculation is stopped at once on the zone ABCD. Committees of experts, arbitration commissions, will function. Wholesale expropriation? All right. But the right price can be paid, since the value of the ground has gone up from four to ten times *because of the engagements of the decree*. The owners, for *reasons of public welfare*, will be expropriated, but well compensated. The lots *will be regrouped*. The technicians will be able, sheltered from pressure, to seek pure solutions and the exact sites to carry them out. Developers will organize companies to build such and such a skyscraper. Agencies will organize the transfer of inhabitants, the permutations; they will establish new leases. There will be a lot of calm financial, technical, administrative movements, on paper, sheltered from gold rushes. There will be organization.

Gold will go to the state, the profits due to the valorization of the site ABCD. But the state has taken on responsibilities: those of assuring the means of access and of evacuation, etc. That will be expensive: metros, expressways, streets, "elevated" streets, parks, sewage, etc. The means of transport and many public services are conceded to private firms. The state will say to them: You will have to transport 400,000 more persons every day. Gross profit m. Part of the gross profit represents the interest and depreciation of a fair part of the investment of your network; I, the state, will pay the rest in accordance with expert judgment; I shall subsidize. I have at hand the enormous profits of the valorization. With another part of these profits, I shall pay for the technical equipment, sanitary and aesthetic, that it is my duty to provide. With the remainder, I shall provide the access from the outside to the business district, and in this way shall prime the rational redevelopment of the greater Paris. Etc., etc.

But be so good as to hear still more: *what is true for the center of Paris is also for all of the city* and all cities. *It is by classifying and valorizing that present problems will be resolved.* It will be neither by the conservation of wrought iron, by gardening, or by pretended beautification. Nor, besides, by sterile appeals to philanthropy, nor by raising taxes that would be crushing. The problem must develop from itself: the cause, mechanization; disastrous consequences, mechanization; new bases for planning, mechanization; the miracle of a solution, mechanization.

City planning is equipment. A cathedral or Versailles were, for the needs of their time, equipment; agree that retrospectively we even draw pride from them.

Listen again to this which is of capital importance, which is all of the question in its most irrefutable seriousness: what the state will do for the business district, *it should do for the city, for the suburb, for the industrial zones, for the canals and the locks, the roads and highways, the airlines, the harbors, the production of energy,* white or green or blue coal. *In a word, all of the country needs to be equipped if one wants to face up to modern problems.*

The decree of mobilization of the ground should therefore extend to the whole country, and once more for motives of public welfare. Long minute technical studies would be made calmly and not feverishly. I proposed this in my report to the Redressement Français in 1928: *Toward the Paris of the Machine Age.* The *rois-fainéants,* the lazy proprietors whom destiny will find sitting at the very edge of the works of valorization, will not cash in alone on the profits; the state will kindly share in them; its enormous profits will be used to fill in the "holes" that a healthy revaluation will inevitably leave; these holes are certain open spaces, certain areas to be protected by intelligent *zoning*. Thus the unification of real property can be made. What urgency for the country!

*
* *

And by the way, this still: do you not think that in each country prudence would advise setting up urgently a *ministry of national equipment*, with a minister safe from parliamentary ups and downs? The most beautiful of all Ministries! For years I have been pursued by the shadow of Colbert! May the country give us a Colbert!

*
* *

Ladies and gentlemen, I have told you *how* to realize the business district of Paris. I haven't told you what that district would be, nor where, nor of what will be made its anatomy, nor what would be its beauty. I don't have the time. The problem is too vast. You will see some projections of it on the screen shortly. Imagine that I had to write a book of 300 pages in 1925 to justify, to explain the Voisin Plan of Paris, and to make it respectable. I have spoken finance to you who are more moved by debates on proportions and on harmony. But, before, I had analyzed before you what in my mind the modern city should be. In 1922 I was considered crazy. Today, not at all. The only objection that is made to me is: "And the money!" It was this I had to answer.

The Voisin Plan of Paris was the result of laboratory studies in 1922 for the Salon d'Automne: "a Contemporary City of Three Million Inhabitants." In 1922 I was asked: "You must have crazy clients?" Nevertheless, for three years it was impossible to make any technical objections against me; but I was insulted, called barbaric and heartless, iconoclast and anti-Christ. In 1925 came the International Exhibition of Decorative Arts. We were not at all interested in dealing with frivolities. We made the Esprit Nouveau Pavilion with this program: *reform of the dwelling*. And we went

from the useful object to the design of big cities. Our undertaking
was enormous, we didn't have a cent. The direction of the exhibition forbade us to carry out our program; it took away our site.
Then it built—at our expense, they said amiably—a six-meter-
high fence, painted leaf color, which put our pavilion outside the
exhibition and hid it completely from view. A minister was needed,
Mr. Anatole de Monzie, to get the fence torn down.

A watchword had appeared to us:

The automobile has killed the big city,
The automobile must save the big city.

I went to see the big automobile manufacturers, to help us in
our need. Nothing doing! But Mongermon, Gabriel Voisin, and
Henry Frugès of Bordeaux understood and helped us to start. The
name "Voisin Plan of Paris" comes from there. Our pavilion was
paralleled by a vast rotunda on city planning: the detailed plans
of a *dwelling at human scale*, the urgent problem of architectural
renewal, and the 1922 studies with the diorama of 100 square
meters; then the plan of the Paris business district, and to make
it perfectly understandable, another diorama of 100 square meters
showing the city, from Vincennes to Maillot, with the Seine in
front, and all of historical Paris preserved and free of modern
congestion.

Paris, the spiritual home of the world,
Paris, the business center of France,
the site of the government of a country.
Will Paris survive?
Or will it die out softly, slowly, in the mirage of its inherited
strength, in the complaisant contemplation of what was, but is no
longer: that constructive energy that conquered all obstacles and
put the city in tune with new circumstances; that constructive
spirit that was always revolutionary, always on the barricades;
the Romanesque, the Gothic, the Renaissance, the great kings,
Haussmann and Eiffel.

Will Paris survive by continuing its historical traditions? Such
was our question in 1925.

The years have passed. In the relatively quiet Paris of 1922,
I had counted on *what would happen*, with the certainty of the
hour that would sound one day. The hour has sounded: Paris is in

agony. I had thought that it would take ten to twenty years. In seven years the disease has taken over the city.

Our "lunatic" ideas have spread:

from 1920 to 1925, by the *Esprit Nouveau,* our magazine on contemporary activity;

in 1925, by the Esprit Nouveau Pavilion;

in 1925, by the book *Urbanisme* (today in its twentieth edition);

in 1928, by the same, translated in Germany;

in 1929, by the same, translated in England and in America, and being translated in Japan and in the USSR.

An intense elite, dispersed, isolated, each for himself, which thinks it is alone and which is an army, has been convinced.

The press, the big press, the dailies, the weeklies, the magazines, the professional reviews, the seminars have commented on the problem.

L'Action Française has said: this project is our program.

French fascism in 1926 said exactly the same thing.

L'Ami de Peuple, in a recent editorial, denounced me as a tool of Lenin, a destroyer.

L'Humanité, the French communist daily, accused me in 1923 as the agent of French capitalism for strangling the "Grand Soir."[3] "He brings," it said, "a solution for the housing problem, and thus the working class masses will be sufficiently comfortable to no longer wish to take the risk of a revolution."

The President of the Soviet of Moscow, in June, closed a discussion lasting many hours by the decision to build our Centrosoyuz Palace on pilotis, *in order to start the redevelopment of Greater Moscow.*

The Redressement Français, an economics study group of big French industrial firms, published my *Toward the Paris of the Machine Age,* and under its patronage the idea stirred up new circles intensely.

Finally, Mr. Daniel Serruys declared, in a lecture on Paris at the Geography Hall this spring to an audience of senators, of deputies, of city councillors, of manufacturers, that the Voisin Plan was the only solution that dared to call for energetic measures,

---

3. Translator's note: The romantic nineteenth-century communist and anarchist dream of the outbreak of "the revolution."

and that only far-reaching measures could prevent the imminent disaster.

At the moment of printing this book, Lieutenant Colonel Vauthier submits to me a work to be published by Berger-Levrault: *The Aerial Danger and the Future of the Country.*

This study, written by a specialist in aeronautics attached to the Aerial Defense Headquarters, shows that the Voisin Plan, by its high buildings, its wide spaces, ITS PILOTIS, its parks with their ponds, ANSWERS POINT BY POINT the anguishing questions raised by the coming war, which will be AN AERIAL WAR, A CHEMICAL WAR.

Here is an unexpected remark. Here are singularly serious conclusions. In substance, Lieutenant Colonel Vauthier concludes: "If the state does not take useful measures with urgency and unshakable firmness, Paris will be simply and purely annihilated in a future war . . . ."

I haven't made these citations out of vanity, but to show that the technical idea, outgrowth of the industrial revolution, in agreement with the sociological and economic phenomena due to it, rises to the political level, questioning the principle of *authority*.

Everywhere the same question: *Who could envisage such a decision?*

A king?

A political leader?

Parlement?

People's commissars?

A crisis of authority. Politics devours energies. Politics is not a constructive function; it is a strainer, which only acts by elimination; it is an oven, a fire. What is burned? Passions, currents of ideas. What is strained? Ideas. What ideas? Those that arise daily and whose fate, at a moment of their development, is to concern the stability of society. When do these ideas submit to the test of the burning strainer? When they are ready. A day comes when an idea is ripe. But a more serious question: in the lives of men as of communities, *an hour rings, and passes*. Do not imagine that that hour comes back! Events roll on, destiny passes. Happiness or unhappiness slide by; one catches Luck by the hair as she goes by. Happiness or unhappiness comes from that hour that is gripped in passing, or allowed to flee.

In city planning, there is a moment when there is still time; the hour also comes when there is no longer time. And, in the trajectory of the life of a people, there is a favorable hour when everything is possible; more than that, when everything is easy, because everything is alert, moved, tense, open to solutions. But the hour past, everything has little by little closed up; one can no longer go back. And mediocre destinies set in. It is a hundred years later that it is recognized.

The quality of a ruler is precisely to recognize the hour.

*
* *

One might believe in a certain unanimity among "professionals" on the reasonings I have just exposed. Don't think so! The most diverse opinions are current, sown broadcast. I have obliged myself to see to the essence of the problem; I have gotten away from architecture. In general, professionals tend to search for solutions more directly translatable in pencil, in wash drawings and watercolors, for it is with wash drawings and watercolors that the consent of governing boards and councils is obtained. A concrete objective is proposed and one is considered closer to the possibilities of realization. I belong to the Committee for a New Paris, founded by a big Paris daily. I met with it for the first time May 1 of this year. I found twenty highly competent professionals sewing the last threads on the project to which they had rallied: the Triumphal Highway. The problem was Paris. Paris with its obsolete center, impenetrable by cars, completely jammed, surrounded by an immense undisciplined suburb dramatically cut up, or rather inorganic, unorganized—born from day to day.

I draw (195) the urban phenomenon of Paris: the successive walls, the sprawling suburbs, the radial railway lines, the radial national highways, squeezed within a belt of suburbs, an organism eminently concentric, radial stratification, indisputable biology. Alas, everything has surpassed the means of modern times: one doesn't circulate, one loses one's time in circulation. The life of workers becomes a calvary. It is necessary to clean up, to classify, *to revive, to harmonize.*

The Triumphal Highway? Starting from the obelisk of the Place de la Concorde, one sights the Arc de Triomphe, one crosses Neuilly all the way to the monument of the Défense (all this exists, created by Louis XIV) . . . and from there, one continues for 24 kilometers to Saint-Germain-en-Laye, and one baptizes it Triumphal Highway. Does the *word* transcend *city planning?* Will Paris escape from Paris? One of the best known of my colleagues, a man I have always admired for his flexible ingenuity as a builder, cries out, facing me, laying his hand flat in the middle of the plan of Paris: "Let them stop bothering us once and for all with the 'center of Paris.' We shall build the Triumphal Highway. The city will develop itself along this Highway. We shall empty the center of Paris: we shall make a garden for nursemaids out of it, and we shall go there just for fun!"

Valorization? A completely safe operation? The city and the region of Paris will leave their enormous radial plan to line themselves up?

I know very well that along those completely new 24 kilometers we shall be able, we architects, to build admirable buildings. But for what category of people? What other category will settle around them? It is my turn to ask the question: "where will you get the money?"

And this other question: the center, an immense virtual fortune—because of its central location—shall we with a careless gesture count it for nothing?

I try to sketch the itineraries of buses, of the metro, of automobiles that will connect the Paris *region* with the *new business center*, and I compare them with the length of the existing itineraries, radial ones: calculate, please, by day and by year, the gasoline lost and the time lost.

And when the Triumphal Highway will be built, automobiles will unfurl on Paris; starting at the Porte-Maillot, bottlenecks will begin: the Avenue de la Grande-Armée, today too narrow; the Etoile, the perfect *obstacle* to circulation (the illusion of plans); the Champs-Elysées congested, impracticable, today, for people in a hurry; the gigantic vase that will absorb the waves of the Triumphal Highway: the Place de la Concorde? It is already dangerous to drive there now. To get away? The Place de la Madeleine? The Chamber of Deputies? a bottleneck. Take the Tuileries? the Arch of the Carrousel, bottleneck; the Louvre, bottleneck; Place des Pyramides, bottleneck; Pont-Royal, bottle-

195

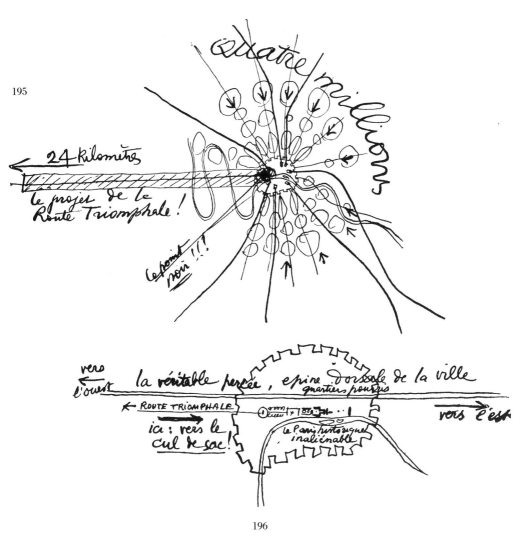

196

195 quatre millions/four million // 24 kilomètres/24 kilometers // le projet de la Route Triomphale!/the Triumphal Highway project // le point noir!!!/the black spot // **196** vers l'ouest/toward the west // la véritable percée, épine dorsale de la ville/the real breakthrough, the backbone of the city // quartiers pourris/rotting neighborhoods // ROUTE TRIOMPHALE/Triumphal Highway // ici: vers le cul de sac!/here: toward the dead end // le Paris historique inaliénable/the inalienable historical Paris

neck; Saint-Germain l'Auxerrois, bottleneck; City Hall, bottle-neck. All of historical Paris condemned or cast into a feverish atmosphere!

Five hundred meters to the north, close to the Opera, *parallel to the Triumphal Highway, through rotting neighborhoods* ready for the pickaxe, the Voisin Plan of 1922–25 proposed the *great east-west slash*, without an obstacle, *coming from outside, leading outside*, ventilating Paris all of a sudden, the *spinal chord* of Paris. Gigantic valorization (196).

And since they seem to insist on it, it would also go to Saint-Germain-en-Laye.

The region of Paris menaced with its population, and its sick common people, are waiting to be saved by us. Shall we answer only: "Triumphal Highway"?

It was May 1, 1929; when I left the Committee, the boulevards were deserted at 6:30 in the evening; the taxis, in accordance with their custom, hid themselves on this day when those who consider themselves disadvantaged by their present social standing demonstrate solemnly. The police were innumerable. This silence was anguishing. I thought of our Triumphal Highway. The late newspapers announced that the previous evening the Minister of the Interior, foreseeing trouble, had had 3,500 known communists arrested!

To free oneself of all academic spirit . . . even in baptizing streets!

*
* *

To compensate in this book for the persuasive arguments of slide projections, lacking here, I give a description of the business district that appeared in the *Intransigeant* of May 20, 1929:

THE STREET

What follows is a free description of precise plans of urbanism and architecture established on the realities of statistics, on the resistance of materials, of social and economic organization, on the rational valorization of real estate.

Definition up to this time:

A roadway; most of the time, sidewalks narrow or wide. Above, a wall of houses; their outline against the sky is an absurd cut-out of gables, chimney pots, metal pipes. The street is the lower depth of this adventure; it is in permanent shade. The blue of the sky is a hope, very far, very high. The street is a drain, a deep slit, a narrow corridor. One touches its two sides with the two elbows of the heart; the heart is always oppressed . . . although this has existed for a thousand years.

The street is full of people; one has to watch one's way. Recently, it has become full of fast cars; death menaces between the two edges of the sidewalks. But we are trained to face being crushed.

The street is made up of a thousand different houses: we have become used to the beauty of ugliness, it means taking evil well. The thousand houses are black and their proximity disturbing; it is awful, but we don't mind. Empty, on Sunday these streets flaunt their horror. Except for these discouraging hours, men and women are crowded elbow to elbow, the shops are lit up; all the drama of life swarms everywhere. And if we know how to look, we have a good time in the street; it is better than the theater, better than in a novel: faces and desires.

*
* *

Nothing in all this exalts in us the joy that is the effect of architecture; nor the pride that is the effect of order; nor the spirit of enterprise that is born in open spaces.

But pity and commiseration are awakened by the shock of the faces of others. And "hard labor" oppresses.

*
* *

The street can sustain its human drama.

It can once more sparkle in the new glare of lights.

It can laugh at its multicolored signs.

It is the street of the thousand-year-old pedestrian, it is the residue of centuries; it is an unused organ, on the wane.

The street wears us out.

Finally it disgusts us!

For why does it still survive?

*
* *

These twenty years of the automobile (and many other things, since for a hundred years the machine age has precipitated us into a new adventure), these twenty years of the automobile have led us to the eve of decisions. A congress on "The New Paris" is now being prepared. What will happen to Paris, what streets will we be given? May heaven preserve us from delegates, followers of Balzac, avid of the drama of faces in the black valleys of the streets of Paris. Reason, already and alone, urgently forces dazzling solutions on us. But if an appropriate poetry raised the rational design to the level of the benefits of architecture? The Paris of tomorrow could be prodigious, at the scale of the events that lead us, day by day, to a new cycle of civilization.

Specialists in planning have sought, sometimes have proposed, fortunate solutions. Discussion centers on circulation: the horse-drawn stream has swollen into an Amazon of automobiles. Therefore: size, width, and classification: the pedestrian, the automobile.

And many other things still that planners must organize.

*
* *

I should like to do the portrait of the contemporary street. Readers, try to walk in that new city and let yourselves benefit from nonacademic initiatives. Here:

You will be under trees, surrounded by lawns. Immense green spaces are around you [see 154–156]. Healthy air, almost noiseless. You can no longer see any buildings! How is that? Through the branches of the trees, through the charming scrollwork of the leaves, you can perceive in the sky, at great distances from each other, masses of crystal, gigantic, higher than any other buildings in the world. Crystal that reflects the sky, that shines in the gray skies of winter, that seems rather to float in the air than stand on the ground, that sparkles at night, the magic of electricity. There is a Metro station under each of the limpid prisms; this shows you the distance that separates them. These are office buildings. The city is three or four times denser than today, distances to be covered are thus three or four times less and fatigue is reduced by three or four. The buildings cover only 5 to 10 percent of the ground of this neighborhood of the city; that is why you are in a park and why the highways are far away.

An ideal office consists of one side of glass and three walls. A thousand offices: *the same*. Ten thousand offices: *the same*. Therefore from top to bottom on the facades of the buildings everything is in glass. And there is no more stone visible on these immense buildings, but only crystal . . . and proportions. Architects no longer use stone to build; a palace, a house are no longer in stone.

At the time of Louis XIV, it was a good idea to limit the height of buildings to the limits of the resistance of masonry construction.

Today, engineers can do anything, as high as one can wish. But the regulations of Louis XIV remain: 20 meters to the cornice!!! You won't go higher! And there you are, building on all the surface of the city, not 5 or 10 percent, but 50 to 60 percent. And you perpetuate automatically the black clefts of the streets, the shame and disaster of our cities. Your density is four times lower.

As you have just seen, the street will not be that of New York, that frightful misadventure.

When one has dug up the deep foundations of the office buildings, mountains of soil will come up from the excavation. It is then, stopping the unceasing disappointing game of tumbrels going to barges and barges going to pour out in distant suburbs (and thus the whole surface of Paris went to fills *next to* the city), that we shall let the heaps accumulate between excavations, in the middle of parks, we shall plant these mountains with trees and sow them with lawns. Go and see, in the Jardin des Plantes, next to the Museum of Natural History, a tiny artificial hill that creates an astonishing little bucolic site and presents a point of unexpected perspectives.

Through the branches, rising behind the hills that seem like the distant views in a film, one sees the crystal prisms of the immense office buildings. Every 400 meters they rise regularly, without paying attention to the directions taken by the automobile roads or the pedestrian paths. Here, all of a sudden, one is facing a charming Gothic church, cradled in greenery: there are Saint-Martin or Saint-Merry of the fourteenth or fifteenth centuries. There is a club installed in a townhouse of the Marais built under Henri IV; sanded footpaths lead to it.

Then the pedestrian esplanade rises in an easy ramp. We arrive at a terrace that disappears for 1,000 meters before us: cafe terraces cradled in the foliage of the trees, dominating the ground of the city by one story. But a second ramp brings us to a new street, this one raised two stories. On one side are the displays of luxury shops: a new Rue de la Paix; on the other, the distant spaces of the city. And the third ramp carries you to a promenade with club rooms and restaurants. One is almost above the foliage; it is a sea of trees, and here and there, far away, the majestic crystal in pure and limpid prisms. Stability, immobility, space, sky, light! Lightheartedness.

Beautiful works of architecture appear above the foam of the trees. Look there, that is amusing, that golden cupola above a Greek fronton is the X Theater, the latest work of Mr. Nénot, member of the Institute! It is of no importance whether it is really Renaissance or fake; that doesn't disturb the architectural symphony: it is only a question of personal ethics.

These three successive terraces, which are gardens of Semiramis and restful streets, stretch their ravishing horizontal lines, tiny and low, disappearing between the big vertical crystals. Far away, there, see that line disappearing from view, on a line of columns (what a colonnade, my God, 20 kilometers long), that is the one-way elevated highway, which allows automobiles to cross Paris like racing cars.

Thus office work is no longer done in the permanent twilight of joyless streets, but as under the open sky, in the open air. Do not laugh, the 400,000 employees of the business district let their eyes roam on a fully natural landscape; as, from the high cliffs of the Seine near Rouen, you see at your feet the swell of trees, like an undulating herd. There is absolute quiet. Where would noise come from?

Night has fallen. Like a hive of meteors at the summer equinox, the lights of the cars along the expressway.

Two hundred meters above, on the roof terraces of the skyscrapers (real gardens, planted with spindle trees, arbor vitae, laurels, ivy, enameled with tulips or geraniums in embroidered flowerbeds, or crossed by paths bordered with flowers), electricity spreads a calm joy; the night is the ceiling; there are armchairs, conversation, orchestras, dancers. Calm. At this same level of 200 meters above the ground, other roof gardens, very far, all around, look like suspended golden dishes. The offices are dark, their facades extinguished, the city seems to be sleeping. The distant rumble of the Paris neighborhoods remaining in their old crusts is heard.

That is the intense business district, the *City*.

*
* *

Figures confirm this hypothesis. To create the business district of Paris is not a fanciful conception. It means, for the State, winning billions in valorizing the center of Paris. To take over the center of Paris in a planned operation is to make billions.

*
* *

Streets will no longer exist.

*
* *

And for the residential neighborhoods as well, the street cleft has ceased to be the solution.

....

Ladies and gentlemen, so much for Paris. Now as for Buenos Aires:

I gave this lecture a subtitle:

"By an ardent and clear-sighted civic sense and as a consequence of ice-cold reasoning, can Buenos Aires become one of the great capitals of the world, one of the most worthwhile cities of the world?"

I shall say all I think with force and conviction. Buenos Aires? It is one of the most beautiful subjects of my life.

Buenos Aires is one of the most inhuman cities I have known; really one's heart is martyred. For weeks I walked its streets "without hope" like a madman, oppressed, depressed, furious, desperate. Nevertheless where does one feel as here such a potential of energy, such power, the strong and tireless pressure of an inevitable destiny? A great destiny. I have often been told that I was born under a lucky star; my life has been extremely troubled, dangerous, but I have never capsized. At the very edge of an open abyss, I always saw the solution. It is my famous "meander." Well, in coming here I had providential luck. Our steamer, after fourteen days at sea, lost an hour or two at Montevideo. So that instead of arriving at Buenos Aires by day, I arrived at night. And when a man with some sense of poetry has lived fourteen days in the solitude and silence of the ocean, and when he is on the deck at nightfall above the bridge, scrutinizing the impassibility of the fallen night and seeing the city so long awaited approaching, he is in a state of grace, his spirit tense and his sensitivity on edge.

All of a sudden, beyond the first beacon lights, I saw Buenos Aires. The smooth sea, flat, unlimited to left or right; above, your Argentine sky so full of stars, and Buenos Aires, that phenomenal line of light beginning at the infinite right and escaping to the infinite left at the level of the water. Nothing else, except, in the center of the lights, the trembling glimmer of electricity that expresses the heart of the city. That is all! Buenos Aires is not picturesque or varied. The simple meeting of the pampa and the ocean, in one line, lit up at night from one end to the other. Mirage, miracle of the night: the simple, regular, and infinite punctuation of the city lights shows what Buenos Aires is to the eyes of the traveler who has been alone for fourteen days on the ocean.

This image has stayed with me, intense, masterly. I thought: There is nothing in Buenos Aires. But what a strong and majestic line.

The next day I awoke in the heart of the city. During eight days I went about my business. I suffered in your town as never before. One day, I burst out: "There was nevertheless a sea when I came! Where is the sea? I haven't seen the sky since I have been here. I want to see the sky!" We went, crossing railway lines and the huts along the harbor—an immense harbor but that isn't noticeable, so strangely is it placed—to the Costa Nera, your big new promenade above the Rio. There, an immense sky, the sea pink with the mud of the Parana (a magnificent color that is like richness dripping from a horn of plenty). Oh, how one is alive here, how one breathes, how happy one is, how one shakes off the frightful vice of your inhuman city!

A sort of saintly enthusiasm seized me. I thought: "I shall do something, for I feel something." The memory of my arrival—the remarkable horizon—and this sky and this sea heightened and broadened my perceptions. A constructive rhythm began to shake the amorphous reality of your amorphous city.

I studied the geographical maps of Argentina, measured the lines of the rivers, the great stretches of plains and plateaus, the barrier of the Andes, studied the network of railroads that already irrigate your country. I knew for the first time that Argentina is immense, that it begins at the latitude of the Chaco whose Indians are naked and that it goes all the way to the icebergs, to the Tierra del Fuego. I learned what one did in Argentina: cattle raising; what will be done: extensive agriculture, then the exploitation of the inexhaustible reserves of ore and oil. That some day you would have the hydroelectricity of the Andes instead of English coal. I flew far over your country by plane. I saw that it was empty, that there was enormous room for a fantastic expansion. In the city, I felt the concerted effort of two million men come to "make America." In offices, I saw that the Germans, the British, had sent technicians to equip the country; and above all I felt the enormous financial and industrial power of the USA. Here, people come from all over the world, for all efforts are useful. Your port is the fifth in the world. I had the joy of discovering the gold mine that a distinguished society is for a prospector in ideas, educated, well-bred, devoted to the cult of the spirit; I even was able to feel that passion for certain things that are the glory of the young French and are so dear to me. I felt strongly that your city is an American city with all its naivetes, its fears, the terror of making mistakes that leads to pastiches of Louis XVI or the Renaissance, but also an explosive city with an entirely new motor and a soil encumbered by the tools, now unusable, of a rapid colonization. Your elegant stiffness, your reserve, due in part to the dominating spirit acquired by the government of the big ranches of the campo or the administration of big trading companies, and in part to the incertitude that the silence of a great ocean gives you in keeping you far from the world, I realized that it was the trait of a people, and that Buenos Aires, made of all these peoples, was in reality a new one, a monolith animated by a burning civic sense.

Some weeks having passed, my mind preoccupied by architectural questions and living in violent stress with or against you in the lectures that I gave, the desire, then the decision inscribed themselves in me *to do something important*, magnificent. I had thought so much about theoretical problems of city planning! I was charged as full of energy as a dynamo. Buenos Aires appeared to me to be *the site for contemporary city planning*. One day, on my first image of the city stretched out on the edge of the Rio, I built the city that Buenos Aires could be, if an ardent and clear-sighted civic sense, if ice-cold reasoning could raise the necessary energies. I even felt profoundly that these energies would arise soon, so great is the danger for you, so great the pride, so long has the hour of architecture rung for you, so much has the machine age, bursting out everywhere and in everything, sounded an alarm, a real call to action in your inhuman city and your streets without hope.

*
* *

Look at the map of North and South America. The cordillera of the Rocky Mountains here, the cordillera of the Andes there, barring the horizon of the Pacific. Plateaus and plains here extend now to the Atlantic beyond which, in Europe, is a world full of culture, of experience and still of energy. Converging on a point that has been definitively chosen, I trace the lines along which products are shipped and received in a perpetual exchange (197). Everything happens in this place, center of command, seat of headquarters, the site of a great modern city, New York. New York is the symbol of energy, of courage. New York is built of skyscrapers dominating the sea. But New York is only the first gesture of contemporary civilization; built in improvisation, in confusion, it is a paradox, a sad example; it is a stage that has been lived and should not be relived. New York is an example of action. What will be the fate of this city born at a time of haste (198)? I won't go into it, not wanting at all to prophesy. I draw the skyscrapers and I write: *Pitiful paradox*.

Here, further down, on the southern continent, everything invited me to draw a similar network of convergent lines. It is all embryonic, but all will be thus, soon. A site is predestined, on the shore of the Rio de la Plata, in the back of the giant estuary. An immense city is spread out there, trembles there, the enormous head of a body barely formed. It is Buenos Aires, Buenos Aires whose destiny will inevitably be that of New York, seat of command in order, in organization, in reflection, in greatness, in splen-

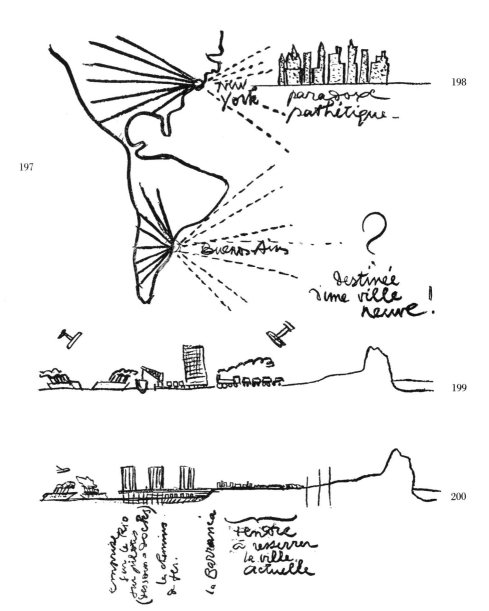

197, 198 New York // paradoxe pathétique/pitiful paradox // Buenos Aires // ?destinée
d'une ville neuve!/destiny of a new city // **200** emprise sur le Rio sur pilotis (dessous =
docks) le chemin de fer/extension on the Rio on pilotis (below = docks) the railway // la
Barranca/the Barranca // tendre à resserrer la ville actuelle/try to contract the present city

dor, in dignity, in beauty. Imagine: we of the old world, we have crossed the ocean, and we arrive in our boats in sight of the city of modern times. The city of modern times to which nature has offered nothing. It is a void. But no, nature has brought this meeting of the pampa and the ocean, in an infinite low line. Man is here to act, to show himself. So, Buenos Aires, a purely human creation, a pure creation of the spirit, an immense mass raised by man in the waters of the Rio and upright in the sky of Argentina. There is something intoxicating, ennobling, in that hope. What an incitation, what an invitation to travel!

But other equally true events also show us the form that the city will take:

Let us draw a section across America (199). The Pacific Ocean here. Then the Andes. The destiny of Argentina begins, turned toward the east: plateaus and plains, cattle raising, wine, wheat, and the ores of its earth: I draw a merchandise train on the way to the delta of the Rio, and airplanes. I come to the city, I cross it, and I *get to the sea*, for it is at this point that all the different events giving the city its reason for being are crystallized. I go over the customs warehouses and the docks, over the railway lines, and I continue, you can see, on the soil of Argentina and that of the city all the way to the sea, above the sea, at the limit of the sea, in reality the Rio. I draw the cargoes at the docks, steamers arriving and others leaving, planes arriving from Europe or on their way, others that go to Santiago de Chile, to Rio de Janeiro, and to New York (200).

I draw your attention to two singularly fortunate events. The ground of the pampa and of the city are not on the level of the Rio; it falls almost vertically with what you call the *Barranca*, a steep slope, so steep that the original city stayed behind it. But with our reinforced concrete, we are going to bring the ground of the city *above the Rio*, far forward on piles founded in the compact clay of the estuary, a good soil for founding skyscrapers. This soil is only at eight or twelve meters below the level of the water (201).

Let us now see in plan the succession of events (202).

Let us trace the limits of water and land. To the west on the land, on ground flush with the water, already acquired from the Rio by fill in recent years, I draw the existing Retiro railway terminal in a dead end (the northern railway network) and the lines of freight trains going to the rather out-of-date docks; to the south, slightly southwest, the other terminal, the Constitucion, also in a dead end (the southern railway network). I break through the dead ends, I draw at the foot of the Barranca a network of freight and travelers, *a network that goes through*, connecting the north to the south and the southwest to the northwest. All of this is *under the new ground of the city*, in reinforced concrete twelve or eighteen meters above. There is no longer a terminal, but rights-of-way; there should not be dead end terminals in the center of cities: trains *pass* but are *not made up there*.

Why have I made this enormous platform in reinforced concrete raised on piles in the waters of the Rio? Because I feel a great pity for the people of Buenos Aires blocked in a city without hope, without a sky, and without arteries (I shall explain this) and because I find it the most elementary wisdom to open a city onto the sea. The view of the sea and the sky are a beneficent sight and a city should be saved from neuraesthenia.

I plant the skyscrapers of the business district in majestic alignments on the reinforced concrete platform. They cover 5 percent of its surface. The 95 percent remaining are reserved for circulation, and for parking cars. The whole city, till now cloistered in its depressing streets, *opens onto the sea*, in full light, in full liberty, in full joy. From the edge of the platform the planes and steamers will be seen arriving. At that site conquered at little expense on the Rio, I put 3,200 inhabitants to the hectare and not just the 400 given in your statistics in the present center. *What valorization!* What a deal! What billions created by the miracle of modern techniques!

I arrived from Europe the first time by steamer, I was intensely moved by the infinite line of lights and the little twinkling that indicated the center of the city. Today, in this new hypothesis, I am facing a human creation of contemporary times. It is worth the trouble to design something so pure.

I have prepared this big sheet of blue paper, the upper part darker, slightly lighter below. I imagine myself at the bow of a steamer with all its travelers, also with its emigrants about to land at the promised land. With a stroke of yellow pastel, I draw the infinite line of lights I had already seen. With the same yellow pastel, I draw the five skyscrapers 200 meters high, lined up in a

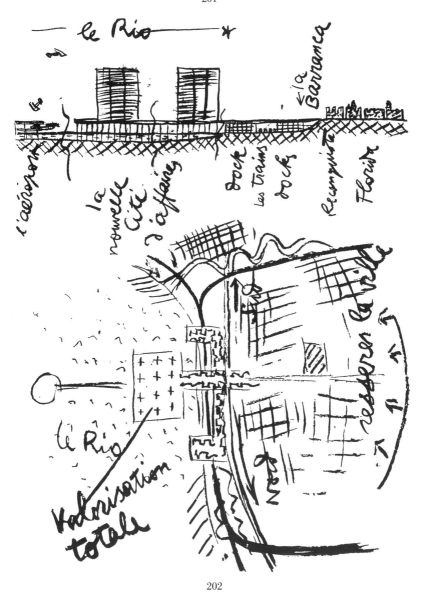

202

201 le Rio/the Rio // l'aéroport/the airport // la nouvelle cité d'affaires/the new business district // dock, les trains, docks/dock, trains, docks // la Barranca/the Barranca // Reconquista // Florida // **202** le Rio/the Rio // valorisation totale/complete valorization // nord/north // resserrer la ville/contract the city

striking front, streaming with light, surrounded by a vibration of
yellow. Each contains 30,000 employees. A second line of skyscrapers behind them, perhaps a third. In the waters of the Rio I
draw the lighted beacons, and in the Argentine sky the Southern
Cross preceding the millions of stars (203). I imagine the wide
esplanade above the Rio, with its restaurants, its cafes, all the
places of leisure where, finally, the men of Rio have regained the
right to see the sky and to see the sea. . . .

I came back a second time to Buenos Aires, by day, in a
hydroplane, coming from Montevideo. At 4:30, my friends of Montevideo in a group at the end of the harbor waved their hats; at
6:15, I was in my hotel room in Buenos Aires telephoning to Garraño to have dinner with him; an hour and three quarters to go
from one capital to another, to land, be transported in a motorboat,
go through customs and passport control, take a taxi, the hotel
elevator, and to telephone, to do what until now just for the ship
it took ten hours! In sight of Argentina, at 500 meters altitude, the
city appeared: the shores soiled with shanties, the heart of the
bristling city far from the river bank, tumultuous with this disorder
typical of America, sign of a prodigious vitality, but also of improvisation, of incoherence. Against this painful sight of an overpow-
ering nightmare, I oppose a new state of consciousness, these
glass prisms, shining, geometrical, under an intense light; cold
reasoning (billions earned) and poetry (love of order and of beauty,
or organization and of harmony). A pure human creation.

The flat and expressionless shores of Argentina would carry
the sign of the creative spirit. Here would be a general headquarters. Here, really, everything already exists for raising a monument of the contemporary spirit: a great city of the world.

*
* *

How good it would be to go into all this, to fix the details, to explain
numerous concomitant reasons. We would spend hours on it; it is
not possible. Nevertheless I have the duty of explaining the tragic
point of Buenos Aires, that which laid the *streets without hope* on
a surface 14 kilometers wide by 20 kilometers deep. It is an object
lesson, an analysis of related events.

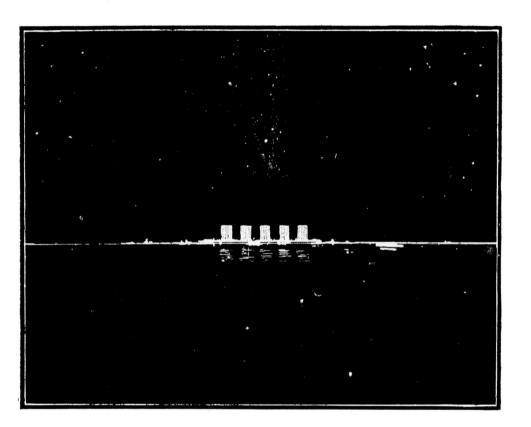

203

All of Buenos Aires is planned on the *Spanish square*, on the settlers' layout. Period of the ox-drawn carts and the gaucho. The Spanish square is the module of 120 meters for the sides of a city block. An old module of the time of slow travel (oxen or horses). Streets are 10 meters wide, no sidewalk; they are dirt roads. The houses on either side have only ground floors, sometimes a first floor. The lots are 8 to 10 meters wide and their depth goes to the middle of the block, therefore 50 meters. The houses turn a blank wall toward the streets; inside the lot, they open on pleasant gardens. Life is good there, in *quiet*, in *privacy*, and in good light (205).

Thus, since Columbus, all of America has been settled. By plane, one sees it well at river bends or in the middle of prairies. This is permissible since men think in geometry. I saw the Spanish square in a village of the pampa, San Antonio d'Areco, neat, amiable, noble—quiet in the streets, the sun in the gardens, and the balusters outlined against the sky; one would have said Palladios.

But Buenos Aires?

Toward 1880, the city pulled itself together. Toward 1900, it grew enormously.

In extension first. The square of 120 meters, originally, *could be policed*. It was order and organization (the Roman spirit); at the end of the streets, as far as one could see, the countryside spread away. Suddenly, an irresistible push, a fever of growth, the town surveyor hurried to lay out more squares: 120 by 120, almost to infinity! He is still going on today! The sight of the plan of Buenos Aires gives a shock; one is suffocated. I saw this plan on the boat, off the Canary Islands (204). I cried out to myself: "Oh, is it possible? What an adventure!" You number your houses with a figure that expresses their distance starting from the east for the streets perpendicular to the sea, and from the central Avenida de Mayo for the streets parallel to the sea; you have houses numbered 25000, which implies a street in a straight line 25 kilometers long. But your streets cross every 120 meters. It is enough to drive one crazy! Look backward at the development of the city from its beginnings: from *organic* when it was made up of 10 squares in one direction and 10 or 15 in the other, when it contained 100 or 150 squares, *it has become inorganic* with its 10,000 or 20,000 squares. From something representing a spirit of order and orga-

204 Buenos-Aires // le damier maniaque/the crazy checkerboard // **205** "le carré espagnol"/the Spanish square // plan/plan // 120 m, jardin au milieu, coupe/120 meters, garden in the center, section // **206** la rue/the street // aujourd'hui! la nuit partout! tout est rempli/ today! darkness everywhere! all built up // **207** le ciel argentin/the Argentine sky // la mer/ the sea // **208** voici du terrain à bâtir!! pas de lumière!/these are building sites!! no light

nization, it has become perfectly amorphous, a primitive system
of aggregation. It is no longer an organism, *it is no more than a
protoplasm*.

How then insert in this protoplasm a cardiac system (aorta,
arteries, and arterioles) indispensable to the circulation and the
organization of a modern city? How to use the speed of automobiles when that of oxen or horses has been imposed, when, *in
every direction*, a stop every 120 meters is necessary!!!!!

And now, in elevation. The countryside is no longer within
sight at the end of the street. The business district has been built
up. Everything happened at the same time; trolleys and automobiles in streams, in rolling floods, on roadways less than 8 meters
wide. In this city, a sidewalk of 1.20 meters has been reserved for
pedestrians; the sidewalks are full of people, they have to cross
each other in 1.20 meters; trolleys shave the sidewalks like guillotine blades. You know I am not exaggerating: danger is permanent
for the pedestrian; he can't look up, he watches his step. And why
are they rushing in such numbers? Because the Spanish squares
have been filled with buildings; buildings of seven floors on the
street side (206); and having covered the gardens entirely they now
can, thanks to a new regulation, go up in pyramids of 30, 40, and
50 meters, playing at baby skyscrapers. Your city bristles like a
young New York. Every building here is an office or a shop. That
is why the streets burst with pedestrians, with autos, and with
trolleys. Then they said: "We shall open up." And now two *diagonals* are opened, the well-known diagonals from which salvation
is hoped. At each crossing, every 120 meters, the diagonal will
bring definitive confusion. The sky? It can no longer be seen;
besides, one has to watch one's step tirelessly. The noise is frightful, the walls rising straight up from the street are the most beautiful magnifiers of sound. To sleep at a hotel? Yes, with cotton
stuffed in one's ears.

And human beings in all this? I am not talking about the
enormous proportion of space always lit artificially (208). I am
concerned by the pedestrian on his sidewalk, in his prisoner's
round. The term is not metaphorical. Walking in a crowd on the
sidewalks of Buenos Aires is depressing; energies are worn out by
it. One walks, one walks. I seriously believe that in a laboratory
of biology, animals that were put in a state of strangulation similar

to the pedestrian of Buenos Aires would be mentally deformed, they would acquire twitches or neuroses. Thus, pedestrians would acquire them also, in your city as much as in Paris, even more so despite its paradoxical air of order. In Paris, there are frequent stretches of sky, lakes of sky, different ones; here, it is pitiless monotony. I think: the city has arrived at a dead end; it would be useful to take decisions; but a doctrine is needed to know how to decide. One feels in you an energy too great to capitulate to this cataclysm created by the machine age: the irrational growth of big cities.

I repeat that you can, you too, valorize your ground. A praise-worthy concern of citizenship and a success have given Buenos Aires the magnificent Avenida Alvear. Foreigners are led there. I was taken for a walk there the day after my arrival, and I was delighted, enchanted by Buenos Aires.

One evening, worn out, discouraged, I asked: "I want to see trees." We went for a walk on the Avenida Alvear, in the Palermo Park along it; all that I have dreamed of for such a long time in city planning exists there: the wide avenue streaked with automobiles and the park walks branching off it. Palm trees, eucalyptus, gum trees, willows, etc., lawns and crowds at ease. I said to my friend: "Look here, this is the business district of the Voisin Plan, *we are under the trees.* Not a sound, the air is pure, man is no longer harried. The skyscrapers? But you glimpse them from time to time through the foliage. *We, humans, are under the foliage.* The enormous skyscrapers do not bother us at all: an exquisite veil is stretched over them . . ."

Vilar, the architect, led me to a small skyscraper (a very small one) he is building on Avenida Alvear. The two upper floors are his own townhouse, with terraces and roof gardens. Ladies and gentlemen, from there *in the heart of the city one can see the Rio,* a line of pink waves under the blue of the sky. It is a grandiose sight. And this more: at 25 meters of altitude above Buenos Aires, the air is dry. You find the humid air, the humid and hot air of the city a calamity. Many of those who work in town, in the heart of the city, could escape from that steam bath, breathe healthily and see the Rio.

To breathe, to see the Rio, to be under the trees, to see over the rolling sea of the trees, such is the gift of modern technology.

To make of Buenos Aires, a city with a constrained motor, one of the most beautiful cities in the world. To make it a city of the contemporary epoch. Nature had prepared nothing for it. To raise up a splendid creation of the spirit!

Eighth lecture
Thursday, October 17, 1929
Faculty of Exact Sciences

THE WORLD CITY

AND

SOME PERHAPS UNTIMELY CONSIDERATIONS

Ladies and gentlemen, this lecture will be rather lopsided. The subject announced, "The World City," is in my mind meant rather for the general public than for the professionals in this amphitheater—architects, engineers, students of architecture. It was meant to give me the opportunity to extend the concept of architecture to the very organization of modern times, or, at least, it would have allowed me to show that a certain quality of mind, the result of a period of civilization sufficiently revealed by numerous works, animates all human undertakings, theoretical or applied; it was meant to give priority to the function that is the very origin of the working of life, of harmony and beauty; I mean to say organization.

Now, I am here at the Faculty of Exact Sciences.

Without preparation, I shall change my plans and try to take leave of you with more timely considerations.

Besides, you will see on the screen the plans of the "World City." I shall explain its principle to you in two words; then, leaving this subject, I intend to answer before you a question that was raised the other day by one of the Faculty professors: "What would you do if you were asked to teach architecture?"

*
* *

In evoking the World City, I have brought up the word that is the important word of today: *organization.*

If we are inspired today by the desire for organization, it is because in the past a notion of disorder, or disorganization, of a state of trouble, of perturbation was implied. The universal search for an efficient organization is a positive act, an optimistic gesture; it affirms that a great event has taken place, that a general evolution has been produced, and that if, in the daily lack of consciousness, we have failed to realize this, we have sometimes stumbled—and especially at the present time—to the depths of dead ends and have found ourselves facing a wall that must be overthrown. Danger and salvation!

To organize!

*
* *

What is the World City?

The World City is the business office of the world, the seat of the big corporation of world interests.

It should be the place where statistics and documents are concentrated, a place of debates far from passions, outside of crises.

And also, the center of research and the reception center for suggestions.

One day, decisions will have to be taken, promises, punishments, by organizations appointed for these tasks. It should only be with a profound knowledge of their subjects. Such eventualities demand speed, exactitude, precision, and even a multiplicity and veracity of documents.

Life flows between two magnetic powers each capable of attaining the sublime. One of these poles represents *what a man does alone:* the exceptional, the pathetic, the divine in personal creation.

The other represents what men do, what they undertake in society, men organized in groups, cities, or nations: certain forces, certain specific currents of communities.

Here, individual greatness, the breadth of genius.

There, administration, order, intention, galvanization, civic sense.

Altogether, two contradictory energies but harnessed to the same destiny, the story of the blind and the lame; one cannot manage without the other; but one can revolutionize the other; the other can oppress the first.

Modern organization should, by the rational organization of the community, free, *liberate the individual.*

To make it possible to visualize events, to make them understandable almost instantaneously to the onlooker, a place is needed, a means of explanation—in this case, buildings.

*
* *

Here is the war, then the postwar, the evidence of the end of a world. On all sides, associations are formed, giving themselves the task of solving such or such a problem. Then the League of Nations is born. Actually, the League is political, to tell the truth a lighthouse keeper on duty, a policeman who regulates circulation, a judge who takes into account. The watchman sees what is apparent. The policeman orders the circulation depending on the state of the street; the judge decides according to a code. Who will give the state of the world—the profound state in birth—and who will give the code? The watchman? No! The policeman? No! The judge? No!

The world lives, is agitated, moves, reacts. Every cause has its consequences, every effect its cause. At certain moments, the world expresses itself; on certain occasions, solutions appear to visionary or practical minds. From the colossal mass of forces present, in conflict, propositions appear.

To unite these propositions, to classify them, to coordinate them, make them known, have them discussed, a place is needed, a headquarters, and tools for work; in this case, buildings.

The World City is also the marshalling yard of the ideas of the world; historical documents, contemporary statistics, propositions come to it. A place is needed for this; in this case, buildings.

Thus, after the efforts of practical adaptation by the International Labor Office and the League of Nations, it was felt necessary to go back to essentials: to go to what dominates the equilibrium of the world, to pure idea, to pure thought.

Such was the conception of Paul Otlet of Brussels, the magnificent advocate of the World City.

Thus, a new spiritual renewal appeals to architecture.

The idea is general; once given out, there are no more obstacles, nor mountains, nor seas; neither iron nor glass cages, nor Institutes, nor Academies. It touches wherever there is an antenna.

Architecture is the result of the state of mind of its time. We are facing an event in contemporary thought; an international event, which we didn't realize ten years ago; the techniques, the problems raised, like the scientific means to solve them, are universal. Nevertheless, there will be no confusion of regions; for climatic, geographic, topographic conditions, the currents of race and thousands of things still today unknown, will always guide solutions toward forms conditioned by them.

But the work itself, the spiritual creation that architecture can incarnate so strongly, will never be anything but the product of a man, as writing is the product of a hand, of a heart or a mind. The entire responsibility rests on each of us. At the hours of decision, at dangerous turning points the individual arises, more strongly than ever.

Today the individual is nourished by the work of the world.

We have the task of organizing a new harmony with the risk of the unknown, but also in the great joy of creation.

Architecture magnifies ideas, for *architecture is an undeni-*

able event that arises in that instant of creation when the mind,
preoccupied with assuring the solidity of a construction, with de-
sires for comfort, finds itself raised by a higher intention than that
of simply being useful, and tends to show the poetic powers that
animate us and give us joy.

The plans for the World City have provoked violent criticism
from the far left of architecture in German countries. I was accused of academism. The projects of the buildings are strictly
utilitarian, as *functional* as the rigor of a machine; especially the
helicoidal World Museum, so violently incriminated (210), and the
library and exhibit rooms, and the University, and the building for
the International Associations. They are built according to the
latest technical formulas, their form is in each case an organism.
That organism confers an attitude on them. We have composed
with these different attitudes, placing them together in a vast landscape and uniting them with a concerted, thought-out, mathematical, regulating diagram, bringing harmony and unity (209).

The plans for the World City, with its buildings that are real
machines, bring a certain magnificence in which some wish at all
costs to find archaeological inspirations. But, from my point of
view, this quality of harmony comes from more than a simple
response to a well-propounded utilitarian problem. I attribute it
purely and simply to a certain state of lyricism.

* *
*

Let us now face the impromptu subject of this farewell lecture: *If*
I were to teach architecture?

Your city, more than Paris or any other, gives me a thousand
ideas. I explain the reason to myself thus: first of all Buenos Aires
is in America. And America is separated from Rome and from Mr.
Vignola and the Institut de France by the silence of an ocean.
America—the pampa or the rain forest! You are faced with gigantic problems; you must work fast; you have no prejudices; you will
do things animated by the spirit of the time!

But here is what is strange: in the USA as with you, Mr.
Vignola is God. Your cities show nothing original, if it is not an
extravagant growth of balusters (there is an American syndrome

209

210

210 le musée/the museum // tri-parties/in three parts // 3 nefs parallèles/three parallel bays // coupe sur nef/section through bay // a = objet/a = object // b = temps/b = time c = lieu/c = place // d = entrepôt/d = storage

of balusters) and a blind devotion to the *orders of architecture.*
When I say "to the orders of architecture" I remember my as-
tonishment as an anguished young man, fleeing the beaten paths
of architecture where the professors, the books, the manuals, and
the dictionaries solemnly filed "the orders of architecture." It is
absolutely laughable to give them any attention: "the orders of
architecture"! The orders of whom and of what, the architecture
of what? And to think that for four hundred years the machine of
the world of architecture has been stranded in this disorder! Even
at the edge of the rain forest, at Asuncion! America under the
orders . . . You see, quite sincerely I feel myself faint to dare ask
thus: "Whose orders?" . . . I feel insolent, but I feel honest.

Your city, Buenos Aires, risen under the burning breath of
mechanization! . . . "The orders of architecture!" Besides, one
sees them everywhere in the streets, camouflaging forms and
keeping out light.

"If I were to teach architecture?" . . . A perhaps untimely
question. I should begin by forbidding the "orders," by stopping
that disease of "orders," the scandal of "orders," that unimagin-
able failure of the spirit. I should require: *the respect for
architecture.*

On the other hand, I should explain to my students how, on
the Acropolis of Athens, there are things to move them of which
they will later understand the real greatness, in the midst of other
greatnesses. I should promise them, for later, the explanation of
the magnificence of the Farnese palace, and the explanation of the
spiritual abyss open between the apses of Saint Peter's and the
facade of the same church, built rigorously in the same "order,"
one by Michelangelo, the other by Alberti. And many other things
about architecture that are most pure, most true, but that require,
to be understood, a certain mastery. I should affirm that nobility,
purity, intellectual speculation, visual beauty, the immortality of
proportions are the great profound joys of architecture, perceptible
to everyone.

I should direct my teaching and I should continue untiringly
on a more objective plane. I should try to instill in my pupils a
sharp sense of verification, of free will, of the "how" and the
"why" of which I have already spoken. I should urge them to
cultivate this sense tirelessly, till old age even. This verification I
should want on the very objective plane of facts. But facts are

mobile, changing, especially in our time. I should teach them to despise formulas. I should say to them: *proportion is all.*

To get back to our little sketches:

To the young student, I should ask: How do you make a door? What size?

Where do you put it (211)?

How do you make a window? But, in fact, what is a window for? Do you really know why windows are made? If you know, tell us. If you know, you can explain to us why windows are made under arches, or square, or rectangular, etc. (212). I want reasons for that. And I should add: Hold on: do we need windows today?

At what point of a bedroom do you open a door? Why there and not elsewhere? Ah, you seem to have many solutions? You are right, there are many possible solutions and each gives a different architectural sensation. Ah, you realize that different solutions are the very basis of architecture? Depending on the way you enter a room, depending on the place of the door in the wall, you feel a certain sensation and the wall that you have pierced also takes on a very different character. You feel that there is architecture. For instance, I forbid you to draw an axis on your plan; these axis lines are a formula for impressing fools.

Another equally serious question: where do you open your window? You notice, that depending on where light comes from (213), you feel such or such a sensation? Well then, draw all the different ways possible to open a window and you will tell me which are better.

In fact, why have you given the room this shape? Search other *viable* shapes, and in each you will open doors and windows. Oh, you can buy a thick notebook for this work, you shall need a lot of pages.

Let us go on.

Draw up all sorts of shapes of dining rooms, of kitchens, of bedrooms, each with its necessary dependencies (215). This done, try to reduce the dimensions to a minimum while assuring their perfect functioning. A kitchen? You will see that it is a question of city planning—circulation and workplace. Do not forget that the kitchen is a sanctuary in the home.

Now you will design the office of a businessman, that of his secretary, that of the typists, that of the engineers. Remember

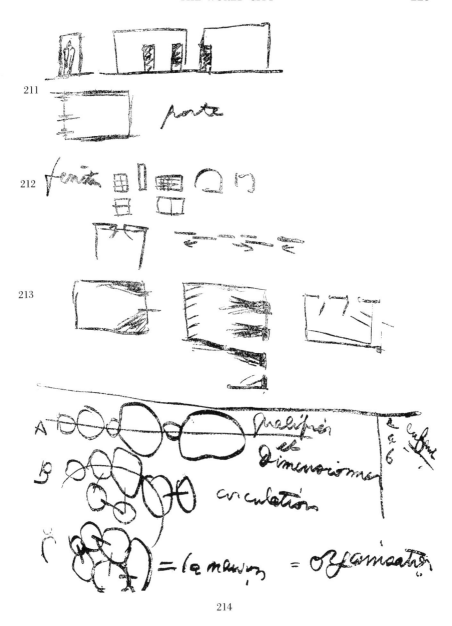

214

211 porte/door // **212** fenêtre/window // **214** qualifier et dimensionner/to detail and dimension // enfant/child // circulation/circulation // la maison/the dwelling // organisation/ organization

that a house is a *machine for living* and that a "building" is a machine for working.

You don't know what the *orders* are. Nor the "1925 style." If I catch you designing in the 1925 *style*, I shall twist your ears. You must draw nothing just for the sake of drawing. You install, nothing more, you equip.

Now you will try to solve one of the most delicate problems of today: the smallest possible dwelling.

First of all for a man or a woman alone. Then for two newlyweds. Don't think of children there. Then your household will move; there are two children.

Design a house for a household with four children.

As all this is very difficult, you will start by drawing a straight line along which you attach the series of necessary rooms, in the order in which each function succeeds another. And you give each space a minimum surface (214).

Then on a curve, or better on a sort of genealogical tree, you establish the circulations, the indispensable contiguities of the rooms of this little house. Finally, you will try to assemble these spaces to make up a house. Don't worry about "construction"; that is another problem. If, by chance, you like playing chess, you will be well served here; no need to go to a cafe to find partners!

You will visit construction sites to see how reinforced concrete is made, how roof terraces are made, floors, how a window is set in. I shall give you a card to get yourself admitted. You will make sketches. If you see idiocies on a site, do not forget to note them. Back here, you will ask me questions. Do not imagine that one learns to build by studying mathematics. That's a worn gimmick of the Academies (who are making fun of you)!

Nevertheless you will have to study a certain number of problems in statics. It is easy. Useless to feel obligated to understand exactly *how* the formulas for the resistance of materials were calculated by the mathematicians. With a little practice, you will understand how they work, but you will retain above all the way in which different parts of a building work. Try to understand what "moment of inertia" means. Once you've understood, you will have wings. These things are not mathematics: leave that to mathematicians. Your task is not yet finished.

You will keep busy studying questions of noise, of insulation, of expansion. Those of heating, of cooling. If you can enrich your knowledge here a great deal, you will congratulate yourself on it later.

Now draw this line of piers; then the buoys marking the channel (216). You will draw how a steamer of 200 meters comes to dock, how it leaves again; you need only cut a piece of colored paper in the rough shape of the boat, and you will show all its different positions on your drawing. Perhaps you will acquire some ideas on the way to design landing docks in a harbor.

Let us draw an office "building"; in front, a parking space: two hundred offices in the building (217). Try to find out how many parking spaces will be needed. As with the steamer, express all the maneuvers clearly. You will perhaps get ideas on the form to give the islands, on the size and shapes of the parking spaces, on their connection to the streets.

Consider this advice like gold: use colored pencils. With color you characterize, you classify, you read, you see clearly, you manage. With a black pencil only, you are stuck, you are lost. Every minute, say to yourself: *it must be legible.* Color will save you.

Here is a city intersection with the streets that open on it (218). Practice trying to understand how autos cross each other here. Try to imagine all sorts of crossings. Decide which are the most favorable to circulation.

Choose the plan of a living room—the doors, the windows. Lay out the indispensable furniture, in a usable way; this is circulation, it is common sense and much else still. You should say to yourself: Is this useful, this way (219)?

Now I shall ask you to do some writing. You will prepare a comparative analysis of the reasons for the existence of cities such as Buenos Aires, La Plata, Mare del Plata, Avejanella. Tasks rather difficult for a student. But you will understand thus that before drawing, one must always know "what it is about," "what it is for," "to do what." Excellent practice for fashioning one's judgment.

One day, you will go to the railway station where you will measure exactly, meter stick in hand, the restaurant car, from the dining room to the kitchen, its entrances. The same for the Pullman car.

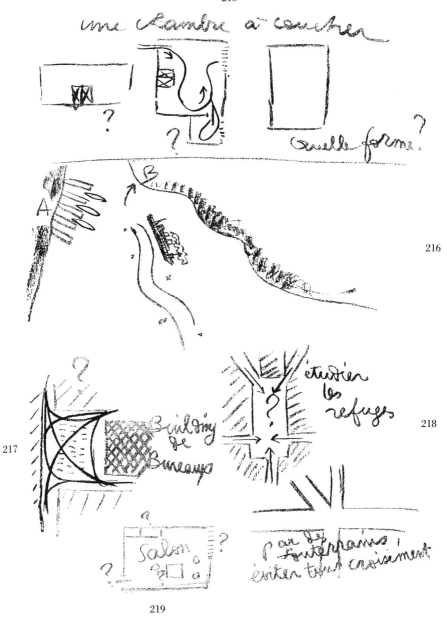

215

216

217

218

219

215 une chambre à coucher/a bedroom // Quelle forme?/what shape // **217** Building de Bureaux/office building // **218** étudier les refuges/study the street islands // par des souterrains éviter tous croisements/by underpasses, avoid all crossings // **219** salon/living room

Then you will go down to the harbor where you will visit a steamer. You will draw up the plans and sections, in color, showing "how it works." In fact, do you have an exact idea of what happens on a steamer? Do you know that it is a palace sheltering two thousand persons of whom one-third demand a *life* of luxury? Do you know that here there are, totally independent of each other, a hotel system in three waterproof classes; a terrific system of mechanical propulsion, with its headquarters staff and its teams of mechanics; finally a system of navigation with its officers and sailors? When you have been able to explain clearly, in plans and colored sections, the organization of an ocean liner, you could compete in the next project for the League of Nations Headquarters. You could make the plans of a palace. And now, student my good friend, I urge you to *open your eyes*.

Do you open your eyes? Are you trained to open your eyes? Do you know how to open your eyes, do you open them often, always, well? What do you look at when you walk in a town? Here you all say, "We have nothing here, our city is all new." The architects have magazines and albums on architecture sent to them from Europe. We are then shown with pride little villages of English cottages in the immense sea of Buenos Aires. Why then are we inclined to protest? Why do these cottages give us the impression of an insult?

Look, I draw a property wall; a door opens in it, the wall continues with the gable end of a lean-to, with a little window in the middle; to the left I draw a loggia, quite square, very neat. On the roof terrace, I draw this nice cylinder: a water reservoir (220). You think, "Well, here he is designing a modern house!" Not at all, I am drawing the houses of Buenos Aires. There are at least fifty thousand such. They were built—they are built every day—by Italian contractors. They are a very logical expression of the life of Buenos Aires. Their dimensions are right, their forms harmonious; their relationship to their sites well thought out. It is your folklore; it is fifty years old, it still exists today. You say to me, "We have nothing"; I answer, "You have this, a standard plan, and a play of forms in the Argentine light, a play of very beautiful, very pure forms. Look! Realize the scandal of these English cottages with their steep tile roofs, unusable, creating attic bedrooms, requiring annual expenses of maintenance. You have given birth naturally to roof terraces in Argentina. But the albums of European architecture bring you stupidly back three hundred years, in your model garden cities and resort villas at Mare del Plata!"

The other day, at twilight, we took a long walk in the streets of La Plata with Gonzalès Garraño. Property walls like this one, for instance (221). Just realize the *architectural fact* of this little door set into the wall. The other architectural fact of the door cutting the wall in two. The third architectural fact of the big garage door. The fourth architectural fact of this narrow passage between the two properties: on the one hand, the property wall on the right; on the other, the mass of a building with a sloping roof against it. The fifth architectural fact of the oblique line of the roof and its overhang!

Oh, you burst out laughing because I draw the steel windmill,[1] this windmill that turns everywhere in Argentina next to the houses. You think I shall denounce it, this windmill, because it is neither Doric nor Ionic nor Corinthian, nor Tuscan, but simply in steel? I say this to you: When you design a house, start first by drawing the windmill. And your house will be right, if it goes with the windmill which is an honest object!

Please, fill yourselves with the *spirit of truth*.

Attention! I shall suddenly blacken that praise made of the Italian contractors. What I have just drawn was the rear of the houses. Nothing more than needed to make them work. But in front, on the street, where one puts the house number and one's name, where one says "this is my house," the Italian contractor called in Mr. Vignola and his orders. The beautiful horror! The beautiful little South American pastry (222)! And, as finally the house was small and didn't climb up high enough, the Italian contractor often surmounted it with an attic of balusters and a big escutcheon. I write on it: *lies*.

Open your eyes, but for delight go *behind* the houses. And close your eyes in the street!

This said, I should give my student a problem to solve: go measure the houses, which, behind the facade, are decent. You

1. The windmill raises water from an underground sheet of water.

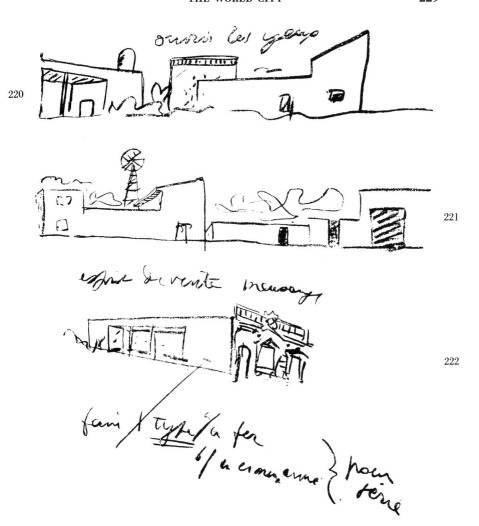

220 ouvrir les yeux/open one's eyes // **221, 222** esprit de vérité/spirit of truth // mensonge/lies // faire type en fer, en ciment armé pour série/make model in steel, in concrete for mass production

will study this sort of folklore for mass production, in steel for instance (dry-mounted) or in concrete (standardized and combinable elements).

Now that I have appealed to your *sense of truth*, I should like to give you, you the student of architecture, the *hatred of rendering*. For to render is only to cover a sheet of paper with seductive things; these are the "styles" or the "orders"; these are *fashions*. Architecture is in space, in extent, in depth, in height: it is volumes and circulation. Architecture is made *inside one's head*. The sheet of paper is useful only to fix the design, to transmit it to one's client and one's contractor. Everything is in the plan and section. When you have created a pure functional organism with the plan and section, *your facade will result from it*; and if you have within you some power of harmony, your facade could become moving. Say to yourself that houses are for living in, all right; but you will be a good architect if your facades are beautiful. Proportions are enough. A lot of imagination is needed to succeed in them and even more when the problem is small.

Architecture is organization. *You are an organizer*, not a draftsman.

*
* *

Ladies and gentlemen, let me conclude; it is time.

Architecture is the function by which useful vases are built to contain different human undertakings; suddenly it shows us, at this moment of crisis, that the traditional vases are unfit to contain the new functions of the modern world. That statement of fact, to which I have tried to bring palpable proofs, is a sign that a new time has taken hold of us, that a page of human history has been turned, and that we are here facing the free expanses of our modern tasks. So, our initiatives become indispensable and must no longer be paralyzed by the criminal maneuvers of laziness or by false emotions. Architecture materializes eloquently the trajectory of the evolution of the machine age.

*
* *

In this series of lectures, I showed you the cause: *mechanization*. The effect: disturbance. Our task: to adjust. The means: to free oneself of all academic thinking and to create. I affirmed: to create—anything, anyhow, to feel free, to judge—that is happiness itself.

I evoked man in his dimensions, in his reason, in his passion—fixed elements in the midst of the mobility of contingencies.

I showed the individual with needs that it is essential to satisfy.

Then, man in community, in the city, with another series of needs: architecture in everything, urbanism in everything.

I sought the *unity of architecture*: it goes from the house to the palace.

Informed by the realities of the present evolution or revolution in architecture, I didn't try to evade the tragic truth of eternal movement: we have felt, for human beings, for cities, for peoples, "time passing."

Starting from the "city without hope," we have desired the city happy and lively. On this point we have certitudes, but we need strength and courage.

At each moment I called for light, literally as well as metaphorically. Literally: one needs to see clearly in order to understand. To understand, to judge, is to intervene individually. Here we are in the spiritual: to intervene is joy.

And I appealed for wisdom: to attain the most with the least, the key to economy in general and the profound reason of the work of art. To economy, in its lofty sense. Thus one attains to dignity.

Estuary of the Gironde
December 21, 1929

Lecture at Rio de Janeiro
December 8, 1929
Architects Association

BRAZILIAN

COROLLARY

... WHICH IS ALSO URUGUAYAN

When everything is a festival,

when, after two and a half months of constraint and inhibition, everything breaks out in a festival,

when the tropical summer brings foliage out along the shores of blue waters, all around pink rocks;

when one is at Rio de Janeiro—

blue bays, sky and water, succeed each other far off in arcs, edged by white quays or pink beaches; where the ocean beats directly, the waves roll in white billows; where the gulf enters into the land, water splashes. Alleys of vertical palm trees, with smooth, mathematically curved trunks, run along straight streets; some claim they are 80 meters high; I am satisfied with 35. Luxurious shiny American automobiles are driven from one bay to another, from one big hotel to another, and turn around successive promontories falling into the sea. A big steamer enters solemnly and joyously into the harbor; a steamer has a solemn bearing and pace and its pure architecture is beautiful. The Brazilian navy

takes out to sea, passes in front of the hotels, makes its way
between pink and green islands. The palaces are in good modern
Louis XVI; they are big, new, comfortable, with the personnel
dressed in white and rooms overlooking the sea; this sea, seen
from the room of a palace, is a geography map of the time of the
Conquest, with its gulfs, its mountains, its boats; the inscriptions
are the lights at night, on the cliffs. A steamer, all lights on, sails
away; the lights of a steamer are intensely joyful, a solemn joyful-
ness always: there are so many different thoughts on board a
steamer leaving, in the heads of the thousand or two thousand
inhabitants of a steamer coming or going. The streets of the city
continue toward the interior, in the estuaries of the lowlands between the mountains falling from the high plateaus; the high plateaus are like the back of a hand fully opened crashing onto the
seashore; the mountains coming down are the fingers of the hand;
they touch the sea, between the fingers of the mountains there are
estuaries of land, and the city is in these; a gay, charming, right-
angled Portuguese city; on the seashore the homes of the rich are
Italian with many balusters and in imitation stone, frightful and
smiling, with palm trees, magnificent quays, the sea, the opening
toward the ocean full of islands and promontories; the promontories rise in the sky outlining innumerable mobile aspects with a
sharp nervousness—a sort of disorderly green flame above the
city, always, everywhere, and which changes appearance at one's
every step. The tourist is tireless in his praise, his enthusiasm is
reborn at every corner; the city seems to be made for his pleasure.
People wear light-colored clothes, they are hospitable; I am
greeted with open arms; I am happy; I am in an auto, a motorboat,
in a plane. I swim in front of my hotel; I go back to my room by
elevator in a bathrobe, at 30 meters above the sea; I stroll about
on foot at night; I have friends at every minute of the day, almost
till sunrise; at seven in the morning, I am in the water; the night
was a spectacle watching crowds in the streets meant for sailors,
stupefying, containing innumerable different passions and polite
complaisances, scowling or dramatic; there is not, for the tourist,
as in continental cities an hour of the night when everything stops,
when one goes to bed because there is really nothing more to see;
the sea and the sky are always there, and it isn't dark; the beaches
spread out bordered with quays and paved avenues; the harbor is
full of all sorts of lights: when the steamer left the other night,

more than two months ago, for Santos and Buenos Aires, Rio was no more than dark silhouettes against the night sky, sparkling, and at the edge of the phosphorescence of the water a golden line lay stretched, that of the innumerable candlesticks lit on the edge of succeeding bays. When one has climbed the *favellas* of the blacks, the very high and steep hills on which they have hung up their wood and wattle houses painted in bright colors, as mussels are attached to the rocks of the harbor—the blacks are clean and magnificently built, the women are dressed in white calico always freshly washed; there are neither streets nor alleys, it is too steep, but paths that are torrents as well as sewers; scenes of street life take place there of such great dignity that a school of genre painting would be very successful in Rio; the black has his house almost always on the edge of the cliff, raised on pilotis in front, the door is at the back, toward the hillside; from up in the *favellas* one always has a view of the sea, the harbors, the ports, the islands, the ocean, the mountains, the estuaries; the black sees all that; the wind reigns, useful in the tropics, there is pride in the eye of the black who sees all that; the eye of the man who sees wide horizons is prouder, wide horizons confer dignity; that is the thought of a planner—

when one has gone up in a plane for observation and glided like a bird over all the bays, has turned around all the peaks, when one has entered the intimacy of a city, when one has torn away in a single glance of the gliding bird all the secrets that it hid so easily from the poor terrestrial on his two feet, one has seen everything, understood everything; one has turned and returned many times; from time to time the pilot—an Englishman—punched my head from behind: to the right there were steep rocks 50 meters under the plane, and I, just then, was looking left toward the sea;

when, by plane, everything has become clear, and you have learned this topography, this body so hilly and so complicated; when, having conquered difficulties, you have been seized with enthusiasm, you have felt ideas being born, you have entered into the body and the heart of the city, you have understood part of its destiny;

when, then, everything is festival and spectacle, all is joy in you, everything contracts itself to retain the newborn idea, everything leads to the joy of creation;

when you are planner and architect, with a heart sensitive to natural splendors, and a mind avid to learn the future of a city, and a man of action by temperament and by the habits of a whole life;

then, at Rio de Janeiro, a city radiant in its universally proclaimed beauty that seems to defy all human participation, a violent desire comes to you, crazy perhaps, to try a human enterprise here too, the desire to play a match for two, a match of the "affirmation of mankind" against or with the "presence of nature."

Oh, enthusiasm, you will always finally tear away the quietude and rest of those who suffer your burns!

I swore not to open my mouth at Rio. And now I feel an invincible need to speak. I had excluded Rio from my architectural mission in South America, because my colleague Agache of Paris is at the moment working on plans for the development of the city and one should never come disturb anyone in his work.

But the architects of Rio came to dislodge me from Buenos Aires. And, when I arrived at Sao Paulo, disinterested managers obliged me to come to talk in Rio. So I agreed to talk about my ideas on architecture and the master plan of Paris.

But when everything is on holiday in Rio, when everything is so sublime and so magnificent, when one has taken a long flight over the city like a bird gliding, ideas attack you.

Ideas attack you when, for three months, one has been under pressure, when one has descended into the depths of architecture and planning, when one is on the way to deductions, when everywhere one envisages, one feels, one sees consequences.

In the plane I had my sketchbook, as everything became clear to me I sketched. I expressed the ideas of modern planning. And as I was too bursting with enthusiasm, I mentioned them to friends, I explained my sketches made on the plane, and here I am; I am going to talk to you about Rio.

I shall talk to you about Rio as a dilettante, from a taste for invention, by an epicurism of theory.

*
* *

On landing here I went with the Prefect to greet my colleague Agache at his office.

Agache says to the Prefect: "Corbusier is a man who breaks windows, a man who creates drafts, and we, we go through them afterward."

In 1923 at the Salon d'Automne, at a date when a few began to express with a certain lucidity the forms of architecture in reinforced concrete and the younger generation already brought their models and drawings before the public, Mallet-Stevens said to me: "We should patent our ideas, at least to protect them, under a recognizable brand."

But no, events showed the dilemma: an idea is fluid, a wave that seeks its antennas. Antennas are everywhere. The essence of an idea is to belong to everybody. One must choose between two solutions: give ideas or take ideas. In fact, we do one and the other; we give our ideas willingly, we use, we recuperate, we exploit for more special uses ideas that are common in every field and that one day, wholly or partially, come to our help. Ideas are in the public domain. *To give one's idea*, well, it is simple; there is no other solution than that!

Besides, to give an idea is not only pain or loss. One can find deep satisfaction, which need not be vanity, in seeing one's idea adopted by others. In fact, there is no other purpose to ideas.

It is the very basis of solidarity.

If I insist, at this particular moment, on giving an idea on Rio, it is because my colleague is in the room, and around him there is your numerous audience. Thinking of Rio, which I have begun to love, and grateful to this city for the magnificent hours it has given me, I shall try to make you understand, with illustrations of analyses from architecture and planning drawn in front of you, how I come to the conclusion of a coherent system. It is this systematic unity that I shall have the pleasure of explaining to you.

I shall draw similar conclusions for Buenos Aires, Montevideo, Sao Paulo, and Rio. The same principles, but profound diversity in their application.

You have seen the scheme for the creation of a business center for Buenos Aires: everything is concentrated in the precise site reserved for its function: on the river, at the back of a deep estuary, a city could rise on its enormous platform of concrete spread above the waves, carried on pilotis; magnificent skyscrapers, in rhythm and order, would constitute a grandiose architectural sight; a purely human creation.

At Montevideo, I arrived the first time by sea. The second from inland, but by plane. I left by plane over the sea, and returned the last time on the *Giulio Cesare*, a big Italian liner. The city is small and charming; the country is small too. The heart of the city is on a promontory with rather steep slopes up to the smooth plateaus of the interior. The harbor is below, curving around the promontory; the homes spread far out to the country in the midst of gardens and curving streets.

At the high point of the promontory, a sort of young skyscraper wrapped in ribbons has been planted. Yet the offices, the merchants, are very close to the harbor, on the slopes of the promontory. Spanish-style streets and traffic jams promise, very soon, the inevitable adventure of present-day Buenos Aires. The urgent question at Montevideo, as everywhere else: to create a business district! *where to create it?*

Remember that by valorization and state decrees . . . etc. (things already said).

I proposed the following: the skyscraper up there doesn't convince me; it is too far.

But suppose we start by raising the problem of future circulation? From above on the plateau (at 80 meters above sea level, I believe), I continue toward the sea, to the south, at the *same level* (80 meters), the main street of the city coming from the north, coming from the country. Let us continue it on this *level* opening it into two, three, four, or five arms (or fingers) that will go straight on as far as . . .

Where? Until *above* the harbor. The streets will be raised 80 meters above the harbor and will stop abruptly in space, on a sheer perpendicular (223).

Automobiles will go up to above the harbor, above the water's edge. From the autos, *one will go down to the offices.* For the offices will be the big backbones of the buildings carrying the streets, up on top. Under the streets, floors and floors will be built all the way to the ground of the hill, or till they dive into the sea, in the harbor.

We have thus gained a gigantic volume of building space, an enormous number of well-lit offices. We have put the business center at the harbor and we have led the autos not to the foot of the skyscrapers, as in our projects for Paris or Buenos Aires, but *onto the roofs* of the "seascrapers." For we have no longer built skyscrapers. We have built "seascrapers." Forgive me the pun!

And if, with so simple a gesture, having created at the right place the specific organs of a business district, we think a moment of the beauty of the city, of the pride its inhabitants will have in it, we shall see, rising at the level of the water, in the extension of the promontory, one of those magnificent architectural sights that, very young, we have already known at Marseilles (the Vieux Fort), at Antibes (the fort); at the "villa Adriana" of Tivoli (the big platform above the plain of Rome), etc. But how much more majestic this time!

*
* *

In the office of the Prefect of Sao Paulo, I examine the wall plan of the town with curiosity, the significant meanders. Here is what is relevant: curving streets going under others built on viaducts. "Do you," I say to the Prefect, "have a traffic problem?"

Sao Paulo is built on the high plateau of Brazil at an altitude of 800 meters, hills against hills; valleys and valleys between the hills; houses on the hills and in the valleys.

Suddenly, in a few years, Sao Paulo develops dizzily, and almost in one day the diameter of the city extends to 45 kilometers.

At its geographical center—as usual—one can no longer circulate. Why? Because—as usual—offices have invaded the dwellings, because houses have been demolished to raise buildings, even a skyscraper.

But, as far as one can see, Sao Paulo extends onto hillocks. The surveyor, as he has to attack hillocks, draws curving streets, viaducts, and a more and more complicated network of wormlike viscera.

Landing fresh in Sao Paulo and seeing on the Prefect's wall this image of confusing streets, passing sometimes one over the other, understanding the enormous diameter of the city, I couldn't help saying: "You have a crisis of circulation, you can't service a diameter of 45 kilometers by making spaghetti in this labyrinth."

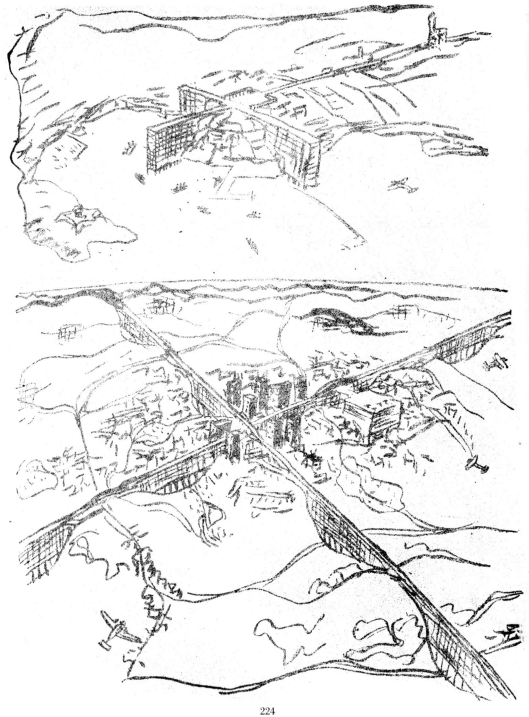

223

224

I had asked the pilot: "Fly in the direction of the center of Sao Paulo, first low on the ground; I want to see the outline of the city, where it rises, where it stacks up its floors as the result of the irresistible push of business." Toward the center of the region, we saw the city rise gently, then in the exact center, violently.

The beginning of growth. A characteristic criterion; an indisputable diagnostic of the disease of city centers.

Then, by auto, we made experiments: for instance that of the considerable time needed to go from one point to another: valleys, contours, slopes, etc. Then, from the countryside, we were well able to understand this general topography of hillocks and hollows, and the inadequacy of a network of streets that try uselessly to go straight.

Here is what I proposed to my friends of Sao Paulo:

There are distant origins for these roads that join in knots in the city: Santos, Rio de Janeiro, etc. The urban diameter is extraordinarily extended: 45 kilometers. You build expressways; at the moment, as they stay glued to the ground, they suffer its constraints.

If one did this: draw a horizontal of 45 kilometers from hill to hill, from summit to summit, then a second similar one at approximately right angles, to service the other directions of the compass (224). These straight horizontals are the expressways coming into the city, in reality crossing it. You won't fly over the city with your autos, but you will drive over it. Do not build expensive arches to hold up your viaducts, but carry your viaducts on reinforced concrete structures that will make up offices in the center of the city and homes in the outskirts. The volume of these offices and dwellings will be enormous, *acquired freely*; it is therefore a magnificent valorization. A precise project, an edict. An operation already described.

Like lines, automobiles will cross the too-spread-out city. From the upper level of the expressways, they will go down to the streets. The valley bottoms will not be built on, but left free for sports and for local parking. You will plant palm trees in them sheltered from the wind. Besides, you have already created the beginning of parks for trees and for autos in the center of town.

To overcome the curves of the hilly plateau of Sao Paulo, one can build *horizontal* expressways carried on "earthscrapers."

What a magnificent aspect the site would take on! Bigger than the aqueduct of Segovia, some gigantic Pont du Gard! Poetry would be possible there. Is there anything more elegant than the pure line of a viaduct in an undulating site and more varied than its substructures sinking into the valleys to meet the ground?

*
* *

From a plane, I draw an immense expressway for Rio (225) joining at mid-height the fingers of the promontories opening onto the sea, so as to connect the city rapidly with the high hinterlands of the healthy plateaus.

One branch of this expressway can reach the Pao de Açucar; then it unrolls in an elegant, ample, majestic curve above the bay of Vermelha, the bay of Botafogo; it touches the hill where the Gloria Beach ends, dominates this enchanting site in the background, touches the promontory of Santa Thereza, and, there, in the heart of the city at work, it opens, sending a branch to the gulf and the freight harbor to end on the roofs of the skyscrapers of the business center. The other branch goes on above that part of the city that sinks into the estuaries of land, and could continue in the direction of the road rising to Sao Paulo. If it were thought useful, nothing would prevent its continuing from the roofs of the business district above the gulf, on a wide but light bridge, to end in the hills of Niteroi, facing Rio.

At its beginnings toward the bay of Vermelha, it would go, dominating a famous site, to serve the ocean beaches of Copacabana.

You hear me saying: "to unroll above the bay," "to dominate an enchanting site," "to end on the roofs of the skyscrapers," "to pass above the city." You think, what does all this mean?

Well, the majestic highway may be at 100 meters above the ground of the city, or more; thus it approaches directly the promontories it touches. It is carried so far up not on arches, but by volumes of constructions for men, for quantities of men. And if desired, this expressway with its enormous volumes of construction can avoid *disturbing anyone*.

For nothing is easier than to build, with little disturbance, supports of reinforced concrete rising well above the roofs of existing neighborhoods. Only then, when one has escaped above the

225

226

roofs, will the supports be joined together, united by massive constructions in the form of immense flat arches like bridges. Thus, for instance, the volumes of housing would start only at 30 meters above the ground, from 30 to 100 meters, that is, ten floors of the double-height *immeuble-villas* [townhouse buildings].

I say *immeuble-villas*. For think of the quality, of the value of this ground conquered from the air, inside the city: in front of us the sea, the gulf, the most beautiful bays in the world, the ocean, this magical sight that affects us so much, with its movement of ships, its fabulous light, its joy; behind, the slopes on which rise beautiful woods, the enchanting silhouettes of the peaks. The *immeubles-villas*? They are apartments with public services, with hanging gardens, with window walls; all this raised above the ground, very high. It is almost the nest of a gliding bird. The "elevated street" at each floor, the elevators; one goes up; one is in the garage, under the expressway; the exit ramp goes off on one side, you go up with your car to the edge of the highway. There, at 100 kilometers per hour, you tear off to the offices, toward the city, out to the countryside, the forests, the high plateaus.

You can readily understand that elevator towers placed conveniently, like those of big garages, take your car down into town, below, to the usual ground and the ordinary street, or, from there, raise them to the highway.

From out at sea, I saw in my mind the ample and magnificent line of buildings, crowned horizontally by the highway striking from hill to hill and stretching hands from one bay to the next. Planes are ready to be jealous; such liberties seemed reserved only for them. The belt of constructions is on the "colonnade" (load-bearing, this one!) diving down between the roofs of the city.

When I arrived in Rio two and a half months ago, I thought: "To plan here, as well waste my time! Everything would be absorbed by this violent and sublime landscape. Men can only give in and run tourist hotels. Rio? A tourist resort!" And at Buenos Aires, facing the total aridity, the absence of everything, this nothing making a void, an enormous space, able to stop, it would seem, only at the Cordillera of the Andes, "here," I thought, "is something to inspire a man to work, to sublimate conceptions, to exalt his courage, to provoke creative acts, to awake his pride, to give birth to a civic sense. On this void, to try to build the city of the twentieth century! And too bad for Rio!"

But at sea off Rio, I took my sketchbook up again; I drew the mountains, and between the mountains the future highway and the big architectural beltline carrying it; and your peaks, your Pao de Açucar, your Corcovado, your Gavea, your Gigante Tendido, were much improved by that faultless horizontal. The steamers that passed, magnificent and moving constructions of modern times, suspended in the space above the city, found a response, an echo, a rejoinder there. The whole site began to speak, on the water, on earth, in the air; it spoke of architecture. This discourse was a poem of human geometry and of immense natural fantasy. The eye saw something, two things: nature and the product of the work of men. The city announced itself by the only line that can harmonize with the vehement caprice of the mountains: the horizontal (226).

Ladies and gentlemen, this year my attentive wanderings in Moscow with its steppes, at the pampa and in Buenos Aires, in the rain forest and in Rio, have deeply rooted me in the soil of architecture. Architecture acts by intellectual construction. It is the mobility of the mind that leads to the far horizons of great solutions. When the solutions are great and when nature comes to join them happily, or better still, when nature integrates itself in them, it is then that one approaches *unity*. And I believe that unity is that stage to which the unceasing and penetrating work of mind leads.

In a few months, another voyage will take me to Manhattan and the USA. I am afraid to face that field of hard labor, the land of selection in the violence of business, the hallucinating sites of out-and-out production. At minus 30°C in Moscow, dramatically interesting things are being set up; the USA is a Hercules, whose heart, it seems to me, is still timid and hesitant. We in Paris are drawers of essence, the creators of racing motors, the fanatics of pure equilibrium. You in South America are in a country both old and young; you are young nations and your race is old. Your destiny is to act now. Will you act under the despotic dark sign of hard labor? No, I hope you will act as Latins who know how to order, to regulate, to rule, to estimate, to measure, to judge, and to smile.

Paris, January 27, 1930

APPENDIX

THE TEMPERATURE OF PARIS

AN INSTITUT DE FRANCE OF THE MACHINE AGE

(Letter to Mr. Lucien Romier, economist and sociologist, on the occasion of the publication of *Toward the Paris of the Machine Age* by the Redressement Français, 28 rue de Madrid, Paris.)

. . . To organize studies of such a nature, to preside over such works of analysis, is to play the role of a real Institut de France. Men fully engaged in industrial or economic activities, considered "captains of industry" because of their risk-taking functions, representing the *productive* elite of the nation, disposing of the funds and organizations needed to make their conclusions known, give such ideas an efficient consecration. Knowing the ordinariness of existence, the violent struggle for life, they *handle disinterested ideas here; they initiate the debate on how to run the country.* THEORY WILL PRECEDE ACTION; ACTION WILL BE CONCERTED. Whereas at present, theory is crushed by events, events decide, and thought submits.

Let us reverse the conditions; let us dominate events! That is a sufficient motive for men to meet who will give the country a law; illuminating the future, they assure the course of the country.

If not, the idea of the machine age, under the spell of the cupolas, is nothing more than an auto driven in a fog, lights out: one sees nothing in front.

It is precisely because their discussion is not "practical" that here these men of action work usefully. . . .

ANOTHER PLACE OF DEBATE:
A COMMISSION OF PLANNERS IN 1929–30 STUDIES
THE CASE OF PARIS

"From the shock of ideas comes the light."
Lucidity and unconsciousness.

Inevitable unfolding of events.
Panic;
Actions.

Change of scale.

Statistics.

Reentering Paris.

Analysis of the situation.

"FROM THE SHOCK OF IDEAS";
LUCIDITY AND UNCONSCIOUSNESS

— . . . then, the railway stations having been taken out of the city centers where they created traffic jams, the circle line becomes the main station. . . .
— . . . let the trains be made up along the circle line, all right. But no station is possible that doesn't bring its passengers to the very heart of the city; a belt line, yes, but reduced to a diameter of 500 meters on which all the radial lines touch in tangents, where the trains, stopping only a few minutes, let off and take on passengers, turn around this small circle, and go on to their destinations. The Zoo station in Berlin, which is only a *transit* station, has an enormous turnover.
. . . .

— Since business makes the riches of cities and since business has so congested the centers of cities and made them uninhabitable, the center of Paris could be extended to the periphery, to the circle line. . . .

— Here you have a contradictory postulate: business is in the center because it obeys the necessity of being together; to put the center in the periphery is to reverse the very meaning of words and things. If one goes up in a plane, one will see, in a striking image, that in the cities whose rules do not limit the height of buildings, the business districts rise in the center, the place where contacts must be rapid. In a different context, Berlin, which till now has had a limitation on building heights, publishes a graph based on recent statistics; this graph expresses in successive layers the density of offices in the city; it resembles exactly what exists in the USA: a great height in the center.

On the other hand, one sees cities that spread without limitation into suburbs, in search of fresh air. Examination shows that in town or outside, residential neighborhoods have low densities. One also sees that in town vegetation has disappeared and that the houses are built up to the sidewalks, the windows open onto the ravines of the streets. If, using modern techniques, the buildings were brought together in the middle of the blocks, and if a new organization of the volumes were made by the introduction of public services, the density of residential areas could be increased, trees in uninterrupted parks would cover the city, the noisy streets would be further from the dwellings; streets would only be rivers of traffic *independent* of building sites.

Then the *perimeter of the cities could be drawn closer*, the suburbs could reenter the city, and *distances could be shortened*. The city-dweller's day would be improved. Thus Buenos Aires, Rio, Sao Paulo, like Paris, cover too much ground. One must tend to restrain the spread of cities. Louis XIV had already raised a barrier to the extension of the area of Paris.

— . . . If the center of the city were pushed out to the periphery [*sic!*] the buildings around it would be higher than those of the center, and the ventilation of the city paralyzed. . . .

— . . . Mr. Bonnier drew up a graph showing that it is impossible to build higher than 20 meters in Paris; otherwise, one would no longer be able to circulate in the streets.

— But the streets involved date from Henry IV and Louis XIV, from the time of the horse or carriage. Automobiles have arrived and it is with the transformation of the street—its width, its design—that planning should begin. The city officials of the machine age have not yet understood that the streets are not a crust set on the ground, but *longitudinal buildings*, edifices—*containers* and not skins.

. . . .

— . . . Besides, the center of Paris is displaced; it was Place de la Republique, now it is at the Etoile; the center of Paris f . . . s off.

— Since the war, business has been moving west, because business leaders can no longer park their cars in the center, near their offices. The center of Paris was on the Cité, then Place des Vosges; then in the Faubourg Saint-Germain, then at the Stock Market. Big companies are recent; during the war, when all the space in the center was immobilized by a moratorium, space was sought toward the west, because wider streets were found there for autos, and better-arranged and better-lit apartments were available. Nevertheless, the center is spiked, day after day, with new office buildings; that is an indication.

The examination of the city of Buenos Aires confirms the ideas of the immobility of the geometrical center of big cities: Buenos Aires was built entirely on the Spanish square of 120 meters on each side, *its streets are all the same width* (10 or 11 meters), *in the center as well as the periphery.* No one then was attracted away from the center by streets more suitable for automobile traffic; as traffic is the same all over and no neighborhood is privileged, business has *stayed where it was, where it is, and where it will stay:* in the center; here the center is a semicircle on the seashore, the typical case of all maritime cities.

— . . . We shall take Paris out along the "Triumphal Highway," from the Etoile to St. Germain-en-Laye (24 kilometers); Paris will be emptied in order to develop along our avenue. Stop bothering us, once and for all, with the center of Paris! The center of Paris will be emptied; we shall make a park for nursemaids out of it and we shall go there just to have fun.

— If one looks at the map of France, the map of the region of Paris, and the plan of Paris, one realizes that Paris is a concentric phenomenon, radial.

— Different events have brought Paris toward the west; the fear of invasions, military disasters, which are not ancient, have turned eyes away from the east. But one mustn't forget that at the present time of the automobile and the railway, Paris extends, to tell the truth, to the seaports and to the big rivers of the east and southeast. But Paris is bottled up on the east; no highway leads out of it, and it is the result of a constraint whose reasons perhaps no longer exist that the Parisians have become accustomed to looking west.

— If we make the Triumphal Highway the axis of the future business district, we must design this way for all sorts of traffic. . . .

— We shall superpose the means of circulation: metros, tramways, buses, and an expressway for direct service to the airport.

— Watch out, watch out! We can't put everything into our Triumphal Highway: luxury housing, office buildings, streets for strolling, expressways. One must know what one wants to do: is it an aesthetic way, is it a shopping street, is it an expressway?

. . . .

— . . . If one applied the new laws of building in "pyramids" [setbacks], one could add floors to floors, indefinitely, depending on the dimensions of the block where it would be built. But what would happen to the spaces inside the pyramid; would they be entirely in the dark?

— Excuse me—we would open courtyards.

— Yes, but the regulation of the 45° angle applied on the street side would also apply to the courtyards.

— Then there would no longer be pyramids, but buildings with courtyards like today!

— How would we find big enough sites to build pyramids? Presently properties are too small, they are innumerable, lopsided. . . .

— They must be grouped together!

— And if the owners don't agree?

— They'll be expropriated!

— So it is a revolution!

— No, the expropriated owner always makes a profit, it is well known!

— The regulation on construction in pyramids brings another surprise: *it leaves the question of the street intact.* The street stays the same as in the past: the street of the horse; the traffic jam of automobiles will remain.

— The regulations on streets should not be determined by those on buildings. Buildings go up in space; their organization will be dictated by the rhythm of the different volumes offering the play of their proportions to the eye. The street is meant for traffic; streets are streams and rivers, their courses must be *regular*; parking a single car on the bank of these rivers disturbs its flow. Parking will be provided in harbors or ports, opening along the rivers; these harbors or ports will find the necessary surface when the buildings have been pushed away—for their good—from the edges of the streets, raised in a vertical mass in the middle of blocks; this vertical mass can be conceived according to a plan in a Greek cross, a U, a double T, or a cross of Lorraine, etc. And, in the space left free by the rivers and the harbors, trees will be planted that will cover all the city with foliage. And from the high buildings in the centers of blocks, a sea of trees and space will be seen, and the noise of cars on the pavements will no longer be heard; the city of modern times will be a green city.

*
* *

INEVITABLE ADVANCE OF EVENTS; PANIC; ACTIONS

— A Paris taxi driver who earns his living only from tips barely manages to do 110 kilometers in a day, working 10 or 11 hours. Average: 11 kilometers per hour. There are 200,000 autos in Paris that run thus at *one quarter of their normal speed*, at one tenth of their possible speed. Evaluate the waste. Calculate the value of the time lost in travel by businessmen whose minutes are dear.

— If we furnish the French provinces and the region of Paris with expressways, whose capacity will be 3,000 cars per hour per highway, what will happen to the streets of the city, what will happen to traffic in the city!

— That's it! that is the question!

· ·

— A committee has been formed in New York to study the demolition and the reconstruction of Manhattan. A fine proof of energy!

— [a general of military aviation] French aviation develops without a program, without an overall view.

In France, there is *no doctrine of aviation.*

— And what of planning!

*
* *

CHANGE OF SCALE

— We should no longer measure streets in meters, but determine a unit representing the needs of an automobile (width of an auto and space needed to cross or to pass); a street would have 4, 6, 8 "auto units," and not 9, 13, or 21 meters. Thus *inappropriate dimensions* would be avoided.

— The same for all the new organs of life in the machine age. Take decisions, get into scale!

*
* *

STATISTICS

— In tax collection, Paris furnishes 23 billion, the whole of France 62.

— Which shows the power of attraction of big cities and the concentration, for productive contacts, of the energies of a country.

— Statistics inform. But there are no statistics in Paris. The temperature of the city is unknown, nor whether it has a fever.

— Excuse me, the hospitals furnish admirable statistics annually.

— It is very good to know of what disease we are dying. But it would be more useful to know how we live: *where* the citizens live, *how* they live (surfaces of different dwellings, square meters per inhabitant, number of beds in a room, if sanitary or slums); where they work (at home, in shops, in offices, in factories); where the different workplaces are in the city; how one gets to them (metro, bus, tram, etc.); how much time the citizen spends every day to get to work; where the jams are, the points of congestion that slow them up; where on the contrary are the rapid means of transport; how the suburbs are being settled (density, location of towns, access); how in practice the day of the suburbanite is really organized; in town,which apartments are used for offices, for workshops, where and how many they are; show where businesses are located, the concentration of business areas, etc., etc.

It is said that statistics abound, that the top floor of City Hall is nothing but an immense library of statistics. Very good. Our life as architects does not allow us to become bookworms. What makes for an *understanding of statistics* is not the mass of documents, it is the *sense of the study undertaken*, the subject of the study (a subject related to architecture or to planning); it is the way in which the results of the study are presented; the "reports on," the "studies of" are excellent, but they should be paralleled with *graphics to be visualized*, giving an instantaneous understanding of the question, without texts or waste of time. At Brussels the museum of human history at the World Palace is a magnificent example of *visualization*. Visualization is the stenography of ideas.

In Paris, a city of four million inhabitants, there are no statistical elements capable of making a bridge between this colossal mass of individuals and needs, and the architects and planners who are responsible, *in a void*, for the creation of a work of public welfare that is sure to fail, or at least to be incoherent, *because there are no statistics* and we are floundering in a bog. Besides, the disconcerting contradiction of ideas presented here could be transformed into coherent propositions, if there were *useful statistics*. Then we would know *how to save Paris*. At the moment, *no one knows*. Some, perhaps, can *guess*.

— Gentlemen, two years ago, faced with the urgent necessity of finding a solution to the crisis of Paris, a subsidy of half a million francs was requested of the Ministry of Interior to make a reliable data base.

We obtained a credit of fifty thousand francs!!

Later, this credit was raised to two hundred thousand. It is useless to say that we could do nothing with that.

— The Ministry of the Interior should establish an undersecretaryship for statistics. One would not merely assemble mountains of information there. *Statistical extracts meant for local activities in the country* would be issued. *Short "visualized" communiqués would be distributed* as in the past the Army General Headquarters did for other motives.

*
* *

REENTERING PARIS

— Only the city of Berlin has an airport *inside town*, whereas the airports of other cities are at such a distance from the center that the time saved by plane is simply lost by the time needed to go from the airport to the center. At Berlin, at the Tempelhof airport, they were satisfied with a central core 300 meters in diameter; on the perimeter of this core, a regulation covers all the surrounding constructions; it generates a cone, rising from zero at the perimeter at an angle of 15°; it is forbidden to build higher than the conical surface thus produced; simple, absolute, but also flexible.

— Besides, in two years, planes, not the big international planes but taxi-planes, will be able to land vertically in city centers.

— The railway station could become the "aerostation."

. . . .

—A clever legislation coming as the *result of ideas, of planning conceptions* (and not an a priori legislation, arbitrary, dangerous, paralyzing) can very well take the place of the dictator—king or politician—whom one tends too easily to desire when speaking of planning.

— Better still, the strongest authority can be due purely and simply to *self-interest*. Thus, the Place Vendôme, which is a fine example of unity, a real manifestation of authority, is not the result of a law, of a royal decree, etc. . . . The Place Vendôme is *a real estate development*, the result of selling well-regulated lots.

. . . .

— Gentlemen, I shall talk to you about a theoretical project, whose object is to show you that the case of Paris can be solved by appealing to *self-interest itself*; for believe me, it is possible to valorize the ground of Paris, especially that of the actual center, which is inextricably built up of unspeakably foul houses along foul alleys. We have taken for our demonstration, Mr. B. and myself, an area included between the Boulevard Sébastopol, the Boulevard Bonne Nouvelle, Rue Montmartre, and Rue Reaumur. In place of the 41 little streets that crisscross this space, we shall have only 6; they will be 30 and 20 meters wide. Along them we shall build only offices, ten stories high with two setbacks; these modern buildings will also open on courtyards.

— And I hope that the number of basements will be *unlimited*; one can build places for work as deep down as one wants to! . . .

— Inside the blocks formed this way, we shall build towers of twenty to thirty floors of 1,000 to 1,500 square meters, 180 meters apart.

The undertaking will be financed by the *valorization of the ground only*, for this ground is in the *center of Paris*. It belongs at present to 550 small owners. By appealing to the high financial intelligence of a few first-class businessmen who have offices in that area, it will be easy to organize a landowner's syndicate.

And thus, gentlemen, this first stage of the reconstruction of Paris, at the very point where the center of Paris undoubtedly now exists, would be carried out. This first step taken, one would take a second, then a third, then a fourth . . . and thus, in ten to fifteen years—perhaps less—Paris could be rebuilt; the center of Paris could be renewed. The first operation would cost two billion, but nobody doubts that the expense would immediately be covered by the users of this new model business district.

— Perfect.

— Very good.

— Perfect.

— That's it. . . .

— We *need a law*, a law to change the building code and to force recalcitrant property owners . . .

— Gentlemen, I end with these words: *the basis of money is in this neighborhood!*

— And here we are, after having sought the periphery of Paris at 30 or 50 kilometers from its center, *back inside Paris*; returned to the city!

. . . .

[What follows, I said privately at the end of the session to Mr. A.R., the author of the project; I abstained from expressing it in public, by a modesty that one can understand when one knows that during these debates the studies of 1922 and the Voisin Plan were never mentioned: "You can well imagine, sir, that I heard you with great pleasure and that I was delighted by the general approval that saluted your communication. We have been wandering desperately for such a long time in the countryside of the Ile-de-France, as far as Rambouillet, as far as Fontainebleau, as far as Compiègne, seeking the furthest limits of Paris: a radius of 30 or 50 kilometers, 60 or 100 kilometers of urban development! You have reentered Paris. You have placed yourself at the geometric center of the city, at the edge of the boulevard Sébastopol. In 1922 and in 1925, I had designated this area for the creation of the central business district (Voisin Plan of Paris). You join up the lots; 550 small owners become a single syndicate with a single governing board. You base your whole conception on the principle of the valorization of land in the center of big cities, and our colleagues approve you. You break the height limit of 20 meters at the cornice; you build 'towers'—in other words, skyscrapers. Your colleagues ask for a law. You affirm that your operation is not a sacrilege, considering the history of the city; you say it corresponds to the historical spirit of the city. You affirm that the physical realization of your program is quite normal; that there is no impossibility there, no audacity, no utopia. Then you say that you would extend the operation to adjoining neighborhoods, and that thus, soon, Paris would have in its center a business district, brilliant and sparkling like the helmet of Minerva! All our colleagues agree with you, no one accused you of madness.

"Allow the director of *L'Esprit Nouveau*, who in 1922 had already published such propositions, and the author of *A contemporary plan for a city of 3 million* in 1922 and the Voisin Plan of Paris in 1925, to bring you in his turn the support of his convictions."

One of our colleagues who was present at this conversation: "It is fabulous! In 1922, every one took you for a madman, and now! . . ."

At one of the preceding meetings, the amiable Mr. B., one of the two authors of the above project, said to me: "I know your book *Urbanisme* very well. You took rather a literary point of view. . . ."]

*
* *

ANALYSIS OF THE SITUATION

— If one tries to establish a rational zoning for the region of Paris, one is led to define different elements that make up the urban phenomenon, to assign precise surfaces to precise urban functions, consequently to analyze the present plan of the Paris region, recognize what it consists of and what goes on there; then to make permutations—to transport certain functions to certain places, to localize other functions, to displace, to create easements, in a word to regulate, to *intervene* where everything till now was left to free will. To enforce easements is to devalorize entire regions. To *devalorize* implies to *indemnify*. Where would we find the money?

— First of all it is impossible to *study* the plan of the Paris region; it is *not kept up to date;* entire zones are now covered with houses whereas the plan shows them as fields. If we had the statistics we are asking for, we could know, but we know nothing! We don't know how the four million inhabitants of the region of Paris live! So that even before starting, we are struck by immobility; we cannot undertake our work!

— Whoever says "*develop*" must say "*make money*"! Zoning must bring money by valorizing land. One always thinks of *surface*, on the ground, and one doesn't dream that construction is *overwhelmed* by modern techniques. One always calculates in terms of the 20-meter limit above the ground. This ceiling was the reasonable limit set by Louis XIV for masonry buildings. Modern techniques bring us steel and reinforced concrete. One must break through the 20-meter ceiling; it can be raised to 200 meters.

If we bring it to 200 meters, certain areas intelligently chosen in Paris will be enormously valorized. With the profits, the indemnities of easements will be paid. A limited zone must be indemnified by a zone developed in accordance with modern technological progress. A foresighted development, containing the common points of view of an industrial region where the creation of Parisian workplaces will furnish the profits. With the profits one can afford the luxury of open space. Zoning proceeds by profitable circles that will pay for unprofitable ones.

Who will decide all that, who will collect the profits and pay the indemnities? The value of private property is sacred. All right! But if a community initiative *valorizes an inert or unprofitable region*, who will advance the expenses leading to the valorization?

Community initiative; but who will collect the profits? The inert property owner who lets things be done? Only he? Never! He shall have his part, and the community initiative its part, in fair proportions.

But what is *community initiative*? It is authority. Who is the authority in this field? It needs to be defined, to be established. If one created an undersecretaryship of statistics, a ministry of planning could also be created. The whole country needs to be planned. The cities of France are the only ones in the world whose mortality rate is higher than their birth rate, as a result of their state of obsolescence and the absence of modern planning. It is a major problem.

Real estate ownership is too divided: it prevents any planning initiative; properties should be regrouped. And to avoid blackmail and speculation, to be able to follow national planning studies calmly, it is necessary, for public welfare, *to mobilize real property*. To mobilize? It will be for the purpose of valorization. There will be profits to share as a result of carrying out important works of public utility. Someone has said it here: the expropriated always profit.

Authority, mobilization of the ground; a decision on major projects is still necessary; the major projects of the Paris region, those of the whole country. The state guarantees them, that is enough; naturally, it doesn't undertake them itself.

There is no doctrine in French aviation. There isn't any in planning. Will the city spread out on 60 or 100 kilometers or on the contrary will it be drawn in on itself? Paris lives under its 20-meter height limit. Everything is compressed, without air, without vegetation, and density is too low. Consequently distances are too great. To work in town and live in a suburb is perhaps a deceitful dream. The enthusiasm for garden cities, which isolate men and deprive them of the advantages of organization—public services particularly—is perhaps the romantic error of recent times.

To spread the business district to the periphery is also a contradictory dream. Here we claim the right, in the name of technical progress, to dig underground as much as one likes; would it not be better to break through the 20-meter ceiling?

To escape from Paris, to transfer the city to a well-developed straight line is to annul, by a single gesture, the biggest real estate values, those of the geometric center of the urban region. It is risking a dangerous state of accounts to start by putting such high values in the loss column.

If we had statistics established for planners, we would no longer discuss, we would act and our theses would no longer be contradictory.

It has been asked: what are other cities in other countries doing? Many have their eyes fixed on Paris, from whom they expect a gesture showing that modern techniques themselves will bring the solution to the disturbances due to mechanization. This solution would write a new page of architectural greatness in the history of the city.

Moscow, March 1930

THE ATMOSPHERE OF MOSCOW

I am not trying to learn Russian, that would be a wager. But I hear people saying *krasni* and *krassivo*. I question. *Krasni* means red, *krassivo* means beautiful. Before, they say, the terms meant the same: red and beautiful. Red was beautiful.

If I base myself on my own perceptions, I affirm: red is what is a living being, life, intensity, activeness; there is no doubt.

So naturally I feel I have the right to admit that life is beautiful, or that the beautiful is life.

That little linguistic mathematics is not so ridiculous when one is preoccupied by architecture and planning.

*
* *

The USSR has decided on a general program of equipment for the country: the five-year plan. It is being carried out. It was even decided to consecrate the greater part of the product of present work to carrying out this program: that is why there is no longer any butter on the spinach[1] here, nor any more caviar in Moscow; the savings are used to make foreign exchange.

The equipment of the country, factories, dams, canals, mills, etc. So much for work. For the population—their dwellings—360 new towns will be built. They have already been started.

---

1. Translator's note: a French expression meaning to have the superfluous with the essential.

At the foot of the Ural Mountains, a tractor factory is being equipped, the biggest in the world: 40,000 tractors a year—one tractor every six minutes.

For the workers of the factory, a city of 50,000 inhabitants is being built. Cost: 120 million rubles for housing, roads, and landscaping; the first advance of 60 million rubles has been paid.

The architect was given the commission in January. The plans were made in one and a half months. The beginning of construction has been set for the end of April.

The data for the establishment of the plans are the following:

the factory will have 20,000 workers, men and women;

in addition, 30% for the technicians and the administration.

In addition, 25% represent persons not yet employed at the factory.

Then 37% children.

Finally, 7% invalids (old people).

Daily life in the new industrial cities of the USSR is determined by the organization of public services:

Till the age of seven, children are raised in pavilions connected to the big housing blocks, parents go to see them there at will.

From 7 to 16 children are in schools attached to the housing blocks.

For the present period (following the war and the Revolution), the following proportions are applied: for 5,000 adults, 800 children of 7 to 16 and 2,100 under 7.

The city is thus made up of groups each containing: five housing blocks for 1,000 persons each, with a pavilion for babies and a school for 800 children. Each housing block includes: four dwelling units for adults, an administrative and community services unit, a sports service, a home for children (210 children); a garage (the cars belong to the community, everyone can use one on his day off; see further on: *the fifth day of rest*).

There are no kitchens in the dwellings; food is prepared for the community in a central kitchen serving a number of restaurants.

There are no shops, but a big depot of consumer products delivers to a retailer in the entrance hall of each building.

Density is fixed at 300 persons to a hectare, other new industrial cities have lowered it to 150.

*
* *

Moscow is a *factory for making plans*, the Promised Land of technicians (without the Klondike). The country is being equipped!

A striking flood of plans: plans of factories, of dams, of mills, of dwellings, of entire cities. All of them under one sign: whatever brings progress. Architecture swells, moves, bestirs itself, and gives birth, breathed on and fertilized by those who know something, and those who make believe they do.

An architect gets a commission; 3, 4, 5, 7 are paid to compete against each other. In addition, for the big Ford automobile factory, an American architect specializing in industrial towns was called in; what he designed looks like a prison; it is nevertheless the model American company town. But the spirit of the times is not there; it seems anachronistic. Moscow laughs at it; it doesn't suit this new environment. This little incident is a touchstone; it gives the measure of the intellectual quality of Moscow planning.

Moscow is full of ideas in birth pangs, of ideas being elaborated, of juries who examine. The five-year plan is a battery firing modern technology.

*
* *

The entries rendered, the plans are exhibited in one place today, in another tomorrow. An attentive crowd bends over the graphics—young people, men and women (there are a lot of women architects in Moscow). They look, they discuss silently, avid, concentrated, intensely curious.

An architecture is being prepared here to which new objectives are assigned.

*
* *

Youthfulness everywhere, in these plans. That astonishes us a little, we Parisians crushed by an omnipotent academism. Let's not get excited: the academicians are around the Kremlin as they are around the Quirinal or the Quay d'Orsay, but they are camouflaged.

Among the young, a competition in invention. Blame them? What a misunderstanding! Sometimes one sees the axes in the form of stars of the Ecole des Beaux-Arts of Paris, like Mephistopheles, wearing a deceitful costume. Beware in Moscow (oh, exactly as everywhere else) of the apparition of an academism of the new times!

*
* *

The *Green Town.*

Here is what it means:

In the USSR Sunday has been suppressed, the *rest period of the fifth day* has been introduced.

This rest period comes by turns; every day of the year, one fifth of the population of the USSR is at rest; tomorrow, it is another fifth, and so on. Work never stops.

Committees of doctors have drawn the curve of the intensity of productivity in work. This curve goes down sharply at the end of the fourth day. The economists said: it is useless to be satisfied by a mediocre output during two days. Conclusion: the rhythm of machine age production is five days; four of work, one of rest.

But the doctors recognize that modern man overworks, is worn out nervously. Restore him during annual vacations? It is not enough and it is too late because he is used up. To keep him in shape, to maintain, to check the machine, yes. Besides, isn't modern medicine oriented by this new postulate:

> the sick are not healed,
> healthy men are made.

Vacations, once a year (fifteen days, a month), it is too late; defects have weakened the machine for good, incurably: wear, the modern world wears out.

It was therefore decided to create Green Towns devoted to the rest period of the fifth day.

To determine the data bases, committees of doctors, committees of women, committees of athletes went to work.

Great enthusiasm followed the decision to create Green Towns.

The *Green Town* of Moscow, 30 kilometers away, was begun at once: its territory defined, its program established. The first competition of architecture and urbanism has brought the bases for the discussion of the plans of green towns.

Here is the program of the Green Town of Moscow:

The site measures 15 kilometers by 12, its altitude varies from 160 to 240 meters. It is covered by big forests of pines with fields and pastures between them, there are little rivers, which a dam will turn into a lake in the part used for sports.

The "Green Town" of Moscow will be developed like an enormous hotel where the inhabitants of Moscow will come to rest every fifth day in turn, in accordance with precise schedules. The architectural problem is thus to create a rest unit for a man or a household, to group these units in a building, and to distribute these buildings ingeniously on the site. Here we shall have the *country*, nature, and nothing of the urban character of a big city.Nevertheless, as public services must function normally, the problem is to create from scratch a completely new architectural and urban organism.

The first year, they will build lodgings for 20,000 to 25,000 visitors per day, which represents $25,000 \times 5 = 125,000$ persons coming to rest, if one counts a rotation of once every fifth day; or $25,000 \times 5 \times 2 = 250,000$ if the rate is only every ten days; finally 375,000 if it is every fifteen days.

In three and a half years, at the end of the five-year plan of the USSR (this gigantic program that now galvanizes the country), 100,000 will be lodged, or 500,000 in a period of five days; one million in ten days; one million and a half in a period of fifteen. Enough to "relax" all of the population of Moscow.

In addition to the *rest period of the fifth day*, the Green Towns will be inhabited two weeks or a month at a time by officials or workers who will take their annual vacations there.

Finally the ill, not those with diseases requiring hospital care but those needing rest, will find sanatoria in the Green Towns.

Transportation must be developed; the existing railway station, Bratova-China, will become the main station (the line is already electrified). Still to be created: an expressway, radial roads, and a ring road; in addition, a farm and service network (for the food factory).

This spring the first two big hotels of 500 dwellings and four small ones of 100 will be built. Spread out on the site, ten tourist centers (hostels).

More than 3,000 peasants at present are dispersed in isbas in villages on the site of the Green Town. The isbas will be torn down and the villages destroyed; the 3,000 peasants will be regrouped in one place called an "agro-city" (a term honoring the current campaign for the industrial organization of agriculture all over the USSR).

One part of the Green Town will be organized in a big collective farm where 3,000 peasants will be housed around model installations equipped with machines made in the new industrial cities. The model farm will provide the food for the Green Town.

The rest of the site will be developed in vacation hotels whose form is still to be determined. The food center with a kitchen factory is connected by automobile service to the hotel restaurants. A sports city with an artificial lake, different playing fields, and a central stadium for big matches. A question to be solved is whether to develop sports facilities all over the site, also at the very feet of the hotels, physical culture being one of the decisive motives for the Green Town.

The hotel program extends from camping to caravansarais whose form is still to be designed and whose purpose is to give everyone a feeling of the greatest liberty at the same time as the benefit of common rooms and an organized hotel service.

Facilities are planned for the hospitalization of children, of adolescents, and of adults.

Very small children (preschool) will be with their parents; the others, up to 14 or 15, can come to take their rest period of the fifth day with their parents, but preferably will come in groups with their classmates, to draw all of the invigoration possible from their stay in the midst of fields and forests under the control of competent instructors.

The young will camp or be free in their lodgings; it is considered that at a certain age independence is needed.

Finally, adults, men and women, will dispose together or separately of these dwelling units whose shape and size are yet to be found and which raise a highly immediate architectural problem.

Such is, roughly, the texture of the Green Town on which preliminary work has begun in Moscow.

*
* *

A wave of urbanism is raising the country, which has remained till now without any other plans than those, with a few exceptions, that we may qualify as Asiatic and that undoubtedly have no relationship to the economic and social realities now facing the USSR. It is intended to bring to these problems the most "contemporary" solutions.

Perhaps in the general call to arms precipitating this country of peasants into a gigantic enterprise of mechanization, it is not completely clear as to what may constitute an urban phenomenon and in particular what characterizes the city of the machine age. The hideousness and the confusion of existing cities all over the world are arbitrarily considered the result and the expression of the capitalist system. I cry "attention!" The cities that we are inheriting from our fathers are simply the cities of the pre–machine age. And I quite agree *that we have not yet even dreamed of preparing the program of the cities of the machine age.* There is a gigantic sociological program there. We haven't done anything. In the USSR they are facing the problem and proposing systems. I believe that in planning, these phenomena are and should remain *human* phenomena. It is men who are involved, the needs of men who are grouped to work together, to produce and to consume, men who come together, as men always have, for cooperation, *material and spiritual.* I attach a value, a meaning to the spiritual fruit of this instinctive grouping that plainly is related to human happiness. I think therefore that in placing mankind ahead of doctrines, city planning will be better and more surely accomplished.

But the wave of urban development in the USSR has led from the first (in certain limited circles of course but intelligent and avid for new things) to a concept expressed strangely and typically by a word that flatters, tickles, and sounds good: *deurbanization.* (It is pronounced this way in Russian). There are words that carry their death in themselves; this one is really too contradictory, too paradoxical, it annihilates what it indicates. I had to examine some projects of deurbanization. I answered firmly: let's not play with words, not play with false *sentimental* feelings. Let us not avoid facts to escape to new Trianon sheepfolds. I affirmed: the daily life cycle of the sun conditions human life. It is in its 24-hour cycle that our activities must find their framework. Facing this cosmic event, which we cannot change, where we can change nothing, I wrote that other inevitable rule of the world, of nature, of physical and spiritual human work, the *law of economy.* Thus constrained by the law of economy and within the framework of the twenty-four hours of the sun's day, I think we must *urbanize* and not *deurbanize.*

Here is the letter I wrote to one of the most talented of the Moscow architects who, with three colleagues, drew up the preliminary plans of the *Green Town:*

Moscow, March 17, 1930

My dear Ginzburg,

    I am leaving Moscow this evening. I have been asked to write a report on the recent competition for the Green Town of Moscow. I haven't done so, not wanting to present a judgment on the work of colleagues. On the other hand, I answered the request that was made to me indirectly, by giving the Committee for a Green Town "some commentaries on the development of Moscow and the Green Town." My conclusions cannot agree with the enthusiasm that the simple word "deurbanization" seems to raise at the moment.

    There is a contradiction in the term itself; this word is a fundamental misunderstanding *that has deceived many western theoreticians and wasted a lot of the time of governing boards of industries—a fundamental misunderstanding that everything opposes and refutes. Society is complex; it is not simple. Whoever tries to bring hurried and tendentious solutions to its problems will meet opposition: it revenges itself, it falls into a state of crisis, and despite changes and regulations, it doesn't let itself be manipulated: it is life that decides!*

Last evening, in the Kremlin, in the office of Mr. Lejawa, the vice-president of the USSR, Mr. Miliutin, one of the commissars of the people, had a thought of Lenin translated for me that, far from supporting the thesis of deurbanization, on the contrary confirms the necessity of urban reform. Lenin said this: "If one wants to save the peasant, one must take industry to the country." Lenin did not say "If one wants to save the town-dweller"; one mustn't confound, there is all the difference! To take industry to the country, that is to say industrialize the country, that is to say create places of human concentration with machines at their disposal. The machine will make the muzhik think; nature did not make the muzhik think. Nature is good for the city-dweller whose mind has been galvanized by the city, who puts to work, in the city, the diligent mechanism of his mind. One must put to work the diligent mechanism of the mind. It is in the group, in shock and cooperation, struggle and mutual help, in activity, that the mind ripens and brings forth fruits. One should like to think so, but reality is there; it is not the peasant who looks at the trees in bloom and listens to the song of the lark. It is the town-dweller who does that. You understand what I mean, if, frankly, we are not fooling ourselves with words.

Men feel the need to get together—always, in all countries and climates. The group brings them security and defense, the pleasure of company. But as soon as climates become difficult, grouping encourages industrial activity, production *by means of which men live (are dressed, make themselves comfortable). And intellectual production is the daughter of united men. Intelligence develops, is sharpened, multiplies its play, acquires its subtlety and innumerable aspects, in the mass of groups. It is the very fruit of concentration. Dispersion frightens, makes poorer, and loosens all the ties of physical and spiritual discipline, lacking which men return to their primitive state.*

International statistics show us that death rates are lowest in the densest agglomerations; *they diminish as populations* concentrate. *These are statistical facts; they must be accepted.*

History shows the great movements of human thought at the mathematical points of greatest concentration. Under Pericles, Athens was closely peopled like one of our modern cities, and that is why Socrates and Plato were able to discuss pure ideas there.

Consider more exactly that ten centuries of premachine civilization have made these cities for us which at the moment of mechanical expansion are a frightful and dangerous grimace. Admit then that the evil is there, in that heritage, and that its salvation is here: to adapt the cities, which will continue to concentrate *themselves more and more (statistics and concomitant elements of modern progress: transports, intellectual attractions, industrial organization); to adapt our cities to contemporary needs, that is to say to* rebuild *them (as, besides, from their birth they have continually rebuilt themselves).*

My dear Ginzburg, modern architecture has precisely the magnificent mission of organizing the life of collectivities. I was the first to proclaim that the modern city should be an immense park, a green city. But to allow this seeming luxury, I increased the density by four and—instead of extending them—shortened distances.

I can nevertheless imagine very well, as a satellite to any urban agglomeration for working and living, a Green Town for resting, eventually organized as with you by turns every fifth day. I even pointed out in my comments that the compulsory attendance for rest, at least once in three periods, every fifteen days, could be applied like time-clocking for work: and would include the practice of an adequate sport by individual prescription of the doctors of the Green Town. The Green Town becomes the garage where the car is checked (oil, lubrication, verification of organs, revision, maintenance of the car). Besides, the intimacy with nature (radiant springs, winter tempests) incites to meditation, to introspection.

Please then do not see a hostile attitude in my serene and firm affirmation: "Mankind tends to urbanize."

Appreciate this characteristic detail yourself: one of the projects of deurbanization proposes, among other things, to build straw huts in the forest of the Green Town. Bravo, magnificent! as long as they are only for weekends! But do not say that having built huts in straw, you can then tear down Moscow.

Very cordially yours,

L.C.

En route from Moscow to Paris, March 20, 1930

"AN ASIDE"

I think that these ten lectures at Buenos Aires will be, for me, the last on the subject of "the architectural revolution fomented by modern techniques."

The world—Buenos Aires, Sao Paulo, Rio, New York, Paris, the USSR—is drawn toward the realization of urgent tasks, is trembling on the verge of "great works." The hour of *Great Works:* such is, it seems to me, the theme now offered to our reflections. "The Passing Hour, or the Equipment of Mechanized Civilization," that is the book one will want to write soon.